Regulation of the London Stock Exchange

In 1914, the notion of statutory regulation of trading in shares was anathema to both the Government and the London Stock Exchange. By 1945, a statutory scheme of regulation had been introduced. This book:

- Tracks the steps by which this outcome came about,
- Explains why the Exchange felt obliged in the process to abandon long-cherished policies,
- Analyses the forces which led to it and
- Accounts for the form in which it was implemented.

Throughout the period, the attitudes of both the Stock Exchange and Government were affected by widening interest in share ownership, the increasing tendency for business interests to look to the Exchange for long-term finance, and the increasing challenge of financing the Government's expenditure. At a disaggregated level, the market was able to respond to changing circumstances, taking advantages of opportunities and weaknesses. At an aggregated level, the Exchange was not able to foresee the implications of change or to forestall unfortunate consequences. This exposed the weakness of the criminal justice system and its failure to serve as a deterrent for abuse.

This study, the only book to take full account of the documents held by the National Archives in relation to the Bodkin Committee, examines the stages by which share trading in the United Kingdom came to be a statutorily regulated activity and by which the London Stock Exchange moved from being antagonistic towards public regulation in 1914 to lobbying in 1944 for the new scheme to be implemented.

Chris Swinson has been investigating failures to identify and report frauds for more than three decades; acting as an expert witness in litigation concerning audit negligence.

Financial History
Series Editors:
Farley Grubb and Anne L. Murphy

For a full list of titles in this series, please visit www.routledge.com/series/FINHIS

Regulation of the London Stock Exchange

Share Trading, Fraud and Reform 1914–1945

Chris Swinson

Routledge
Taylor & Francis Group

LONDON AND NEW YORK

First published 2018 by Routledge

2 Park Square, Milton Park, Abingdon, Oxfordshire OX14 4RN
52 Vanderbilt Avenue, New York, NY 10017

Routledge is an imprint of the Taylor & Francis Group, an informa business

First issued in paperback 2019

British Library Cataloguing-in-Publication Data
A catalogue record for this book is available from the British Library

Library of Congress Cataloging-in-Publication Data
A catalog record for this book has been requested

ISBN: 978-1-138-04021-2 (hbk)
ISBN: 978-0-367-88756-8 (pbk)

Typeset in Times New Roman
by Apex CoVantage, LLC

For Christine

Contents

Tables

Charts

Abbreviations

ADUR	American and Dominions Unbreakable Records Limited
AFT	Austin Friars Trust Limited
AIL	Agricultural Industries Limited
AIT	Association of Investment Trusts
AJSM	Association of Jute Spinners and Manufacturers
BPP	British Parliamentary Papers
BST	BST Limited (subsequently renamed British Shareholders Trust Limited)
CBL	Commercial Bank of London Limited
C&GS	Corporation & General Securities Limited
CCH	Clarence Hatry
CEFI	City Equitable Fire Insurance Limited
DBB	Dictionary of Business Biography
DI	Detective Inspector
DNB	Dictionary of National Biography
DORA	Defence of the Realm Act, 1914
DPP	Director of Public Prosecutions
F&B	Foster & Braithwaite
GDP	Gross Domestic Product
IMTA	Institute of Municipal Treasurers and Accountants
IPO	Initial Public Offering
JIL	Jute Industries Limited
LMA	London Metropolitan Archive
LML	Leyland Motors Limited
NP&RRA	Newspapers, Printers and Reading Rooms Repeal Act 1869
NSC	Northumberland Shipbuilding Company Limited
NYAG	New York Attorney General
NYSE	New York Stock Exchange
OTC	Over the Counter
PF(I) Act	Prevention of Fraud (Investments) Act 1939
SEC	Securities and Exchange Commission

SI	Statutory Instrument
S&RO	Statutory Rules and Orders
SSL	Secretarial Services Limited
VMH	Violet Hatry (Clarence Hatry's wife)

Acknowledgements

This book sprang from a chance encounter with Clarence Hatry at the end of the secondary banking crisis. I spent the whole of 1974 working in Pinners Hall in Austin Friars and discovered that it had also been the scene of events which led to the London Stock exchange crash in September 1929. For a decade after the end of the 1914–1918 war, a part of the building was occupied by Clarence Hatry, whose companies collapsed in 1929. Since then, his life and activities have proved an endlessly fascinating and rewarding study.

I have stood on the shoulders of the many librarians and archivists who have preserved and indexed the records mentioned in the text. It has been a delight to find public and private institutions that work quietly, without public display, but above all well. I am especially grateful to the teams at:

Bank of England Archive
Barings Archive
Bill Bryson Library, Durham University
Bodleian Library, Oxford University
British Library (including the erstwhile newspaper depository at Colindale)
Dundee University Archives
Guildhall Library, London
HSBC Archives
Institute of Advanced Legal Studies, London

Lloyds Bank Archive
London Library
London Metropolitan Archive
London School of Economics Library
National Archives
National Library of Australia
Royal Bank of Scotland Archives
St Andrews Special Collections
University of Lincoln

All of these teams have handled my many requests with care and sensitivity.

I also owe much to the many who have helped by providing information, answering queries or offering encouragement, including Rob Bryer, Shona Butterfield, Roy Chandler, Toby Dennis, Sarah Ferguson, Susan Gompels, Terry Gourvish, Richard Macve, Chris Napier, Robert Maas, Josephine Maltby, Michael Oliver, David Prince, Janette Rutterford, (the late) Bill Tiplady, (the late) Eddie Weiss and Martin Vander Weyer.

That I was able to embark on this project, I owe to Durham University Business School which, through the good offices of David McCollum-Oldroyd, offered a home.

That the project proved so stimulating I owe to the complementary insights of my supervisors, Ranald Michie and David McCollum-Oldroyd, who repeatedly challenged my thinking and assumptions. I will long recall the experience with gratitude and pleasure.

That I was able to persevere I owe to the support and unfailing encouragement of my wife, Christine, not least for accompanying me on my walks around London to locate the offices, houses and watering holes of the many people I have studied.

To all of them, I am more grateful than I can say.

CS
30 April 2017

1   Introduction

On 22 May 1946, a block of shares in St Helena Gold Mines Limited was placed on the London Stock Exchange. The price approved by the Exchange's New Issues Sub-Committee was 52s 6d. Interest was so great that by 1000 hours, the shares were trading at prices over £5 and ended the day at 4⅛ to 4½, falling subsequently to 3½.[1]

It was immediately rumoured that the shares had been 'rigged':[2] a rumour that became the subject of a disciplinary inquiry by the Exchange. The outcome was that the senior partner of the brokers responsible, Keith, Bayley & Rigg, was suspended for two years and six jobbers who had made substantial profits received lesser punishments. For some members, these punishments were not sufficient. J&A Scrimgeour wrote to the Stock Exchange Council suggesting that action should have been taken against the broking firm as a whole and not simply its senior partner:

> The times are difficult and the difficulties will not be alleviated by timid measures, neither can we expect the prestige of the Stock Exchange to be enhanced until full measures for the protection of the public, and members generally, are adopted.[3]

Scrimgeours' interest in the public's protection was shared by the council, which had asked the brokers' senior partner whether:

> the public, in order to obtain an interest in the shares, had to pay a premium to Keith, Bayley & Rigg and their friends of £2 a share.[4]

The senior partner agreed and went on to express his regret for the 'grave discredit' this had brought to the Stock Exchange.

For a member whose memory extended to trading on the Exchange before the 1914–1918 war, such an interest in the protection of the public would have seemed remarkable. Market rigs had been mounted before, and had been punished,[5] but on the grounds that rigs disadvantaged fellow members of the Exchange, not that they abused members of the public. In effect, between 1914 and 1946 there had been a sea change in the Exchange's thinking and in its practice. Whereas in 1914, the Exchange was solely concerned with overseeing the integrity of relationships between its members, by 1946, with government encouragement, the Exchange had accepted responsibility for protecting the interests of the wider investing public.

At the time, some commentators recognised the scale of the change that had occurred, for in June 1945, *The Economist* observed that:

> All these changes add up to an altered mentality among brokers . . . which prefers reasonable, but secure, profits to long risks with the alternative of brilliant success or equally striking failure.[6]

Subsequent commentators have referred to the same changes, although describing them in different ways. Michie (1999, pages 326–327) refers to a state of uncertainty after the end of the war and to the Exchange's need to secure a rapid return to peacetime trading conditions. Kynaston (2001, pages 30–31), dealing with a broader canvas, refers to concern among members that the Exchange had become a public institution rather than a private club that existed to facilitate its members' trading. Both largely attribute the changed circumstances to the economic effects of the 1939–1945 war and to the effect of controls implemented during the war. Doubtless the effect of the war was extensive, but it cannot account for the fact that the key legislation underpinning the regulation of share trading was passed in 1939 before the commencement of the war and manifestly not in contemplation of the onset of war.[7] Further, the legislation was brought into force in 1944, before the end of the war, as the Board of Trade acquiesced to lobbying by the Stock Exchange which had traditionally opposed such legislation.

This study examines the nature of the change in the regulatory arrangements for share trading that occurred between 1914 and 1945.

The study suggests that the Stock Exchange and the government faced five challenges posed by a change in the character of the demand for and supply of securities that had begun to be apparent before 1914. The investing community expanded to include many first-time holders whose holdings tended to be small: too small for the traditional relationship between stockbroker and client to be economically viable. Such holders either sought security through institutional intermediaries, partly encouraged by tax considerations, or traded without professional advice becoming prey to unscrupulous traders.

At the same time, vendors of shares increasingly saw the market not as a means by which to dispose of ownership but as a source of finance because of a decline in corporate profitability together with higher tax rates restricted businesses' ability to finance investment by retention of profit. This trend was reinforced by tax reforms which tended to favour companies whose shares were traded on a recognised stock exchange.[8]

As this was happening, the political environment also changed. During the 1914–1918 war, the role of government had become more important and its demands for financial support more insistent. At the end of the war, the political system had become more pluralist, with a greatly enlarged electorate, for the first time including the working class, bringing forward a Labour Party suspicious of business privilege with a burgeoning range of pressure groups representing workers and manufacturers.

The main question posed by these changes was whether it would be possible for the Exchange to preserve its independence of state control.

The outcome would depend upon four other challenges, the first of which was whether investors alone should be responsible for managing their own risks: *caveat emptor*. This principle was the foundation of the Exchange's relationship with members. Implicit in this approach was the assumption that clients had both the experience and, where necessary, the access to advice to enable them to manage their risks. As the market welcomed a larger number of smaller investors who had savings to invest but neither the experience to assess and mitigate their own risks nor the access to necessary advice, at what point would *caveat emptor* become an impractical and untenable principle?

The second challenge was to self-regulation as an organising principle for bodies such as the Exchange. To deal with changing circumstances, any organisation must be able to identify challenges and to face them successfully. In the case of the Exchange, self-regulation had been viewed as essential for the well-being of members, to the extent that the grant of a royal charter had been resisted because it would have involved oversight by the Privy Council. As the underlying assumptions were challenged, how successfully would the Exchange manage its responses?

The third challenge was to the criminal justice system. Beyond the London Stock Exchange and the provincial stock exchanges, share trading could take place free from regulation other than the constraint of criminal law and prosecutions. Would the criminal justice system provide an adequate response to abuse of unsuspecting investors in off-market transactions?

The fourth challenge was to the government's management of the financial system and the financing of its expenditure. Between 1914 and 1918, rather than relying solely on taxation, the government chose to meet a large part of the cost of prosecuting the war by raising loan issues that were traded through the Exchange, a studiously independent organisation. What measure of influence or control did the government need to achieve its own policy objectives?

By 1945, the answers to these questions had become clear. The London Stock Exchange had largely been able to preserve the appearance of independence, but after the twin crashes of 1929, it had been necessary to abrogate the principle of *caveat emptor*. The Stock Exchange had eventually been able to act with determination to defend the principle of self-regulation. The criminal justice system had failed to meet the challenge of abusive share pushers. The government had concluded that it could achieve its objectives through influencing rather than controlling the Exchange.

At no point in the period with which this study is concerned was the regulation of share trading a prime concern of the politicians involved in considering these issues. It waxed and waned in importance in their eyes in proportion to its perceived relevance to the achievement of other objectives. Politicians were prepared to compromise in implementing proposals for regulation of share trading once the objectives of prime concern to them appeared within grasp. In November 1914, the government responded to the imperative need to finance the war by agreeing that its interest in controlling new issues and share trading should be achieved by means of the Exchange's own regulations. In February 1919, the government was forced into an ignominious abandonment of proposals for extended capital controls. In 1938, this led to acceptance of the Stock Exchange's conditions for acceptance of the statutory scheme. These compromises were accepted even though they were known to embed weaknesses in regulatory arrangements which in due course led to calls for further reform.

The study also shows how, in the 1920s and 1930s, reliance solely upon the criminal justice system as a means of regulating abusive share trading, especially abusive trading outside recognised exchanges, became untenable. It may have been thought credible in the previous century, but by the 1930s such narrow reliance coupled with the widening public interest in share ownership was exposing to abuse a section of the public that was ill-fitted to protect itself. Regulation that depended upon post facto punishment and in many cases upon private prosecution did not serve to deter, eliminate or avoid the social damage caused by the abuse.

In other respects, prosecution proved more effective. The prosecution of Clarence Hatry in 1930 distracted attention from the causes of the collapse of many companies floated in the 1928 boom and enabled the Exchange to engage in a discreet reform of its new issue practices. The Royal Mail trial in 1931 initially appalled the City which sympathised with the plight of the defendants; but served as a warning. If in regulating itself, the City's rules became too far removed from the requirements of public law and public expectation its independence would be curtailed. By 1940, reform of the rules of disclosure in accounts had become inevitable.

That the Exchange could deal successfully with the weaknesses in systems and behaviour demonstrated so powerfully in 1929 can be attributed to two factors: the leadership of the Governor of the Bank of England and the blindingly obvious risk that the Exchange's independence would be lost. Confident in wider City support and the support of members, the self-regulatory Exchange was able to move boldly in a manner it did not demonstrate at any other point in the period covered by this study.

Chapters 2 to 5 describe the development of the share trading environment between 1914 and 1945, beginning in Chapter 2 with a brief outline of the economic environment. In Chapter 3, the developing changes in the demand for securities are charted, followed in Chapter 4 by an analysis of the supply of securities for trading in the Exchange's market. These developments were to affect demand for the services of the Exchange's members and the market's vitality: trends which are examined in Chapter 5.

Against this background, the development of a regulatory framework for the Exchange and for share trading more generally is analysed in Chapters 6 to 12.

Chapter 6 describes the developments that occurred during the 1914–1918 war from the initial imposition of new issue controls in January 1915 to their removal in 1919. Created by an agreement between the Stock Exchange and the Treasury which was enforced solely through the Stock Exchange's own rules, the controls proved dysfunctional because they did not apply to off-market transactions. The incentive to enter into transactions off-market which were not permitted on-market ultimately undermined the controls' purpose and frustrated the Exchange's members who had been happy to see controls introduced in January 1915 as a means of restoring their livelihood. In 1919, members saw the abolition of controls as vital to restoring the economic rents of membership. Others suggested that some continuing control would be desirable to avoid the abuse of the new class of inexperienced investors. In the event, the Treasury's attempt in January 1919 to impose permanent controls was to prove a humiliating failure. In returning to 'business as usual', *caveat emptor* remained a guiding principle.

The end of hostilities in November 1918 was accompanied by hope that commercial life would return to normality and prosperity. For a while, trade and the stock markets boomed. But there was also uncertainty about how the transition to a peacetime economy would be managed and whether markets which had been lost during the war could be recovered. In the event, the transition proved troublesome and markets were not recovered so that the post-war boom was followed by a crash in 1920. Slowly, business recovered, leading to a further boom in 1928.

As years passed, deeper uncertainties emerged. War had exposed the inefficiency of many old industries and had given fresh impetus to new technologies. The character of the investing public had been changed as had the risk appetite of many investors. Government expenditure, even when reduced in 1920, was at a higher level than before 1914 and required a higher level of taxation. Thus, attitudes towards investment were changing, with a search for higher returns within acceptable levels of risk and volatility. Sustained returns based on continuing relationships came to be more valued than short-term, speculative gains.

These circumstances challenged the incomes of Stock Exchange members which did not quickly return to pre-1914 levels.

The combination of uncertainty about the future of old and new industries and the emergence of many inexperienced small investors looking for higher returns was an opportunity for the unscrupulous, which tested arrangements for deterring and controlling abuse. Within the Stock Exchange, these arrangements depended upon the committee's vigour in refreshing and applying the rules. Beyond the Exchange, reliance was placed on prosecutions. Chapter 7 assesses the performance and failure of the Exchange and the criminal justice system between 1919 and 1929 in deterring abuse.

Matters were brought to a head by the two crashes of 1929: the first in the spring which saw the failure of many companies floated in 1928 and the second in September, precipitated by the collapse of Clarence Hatry's companies. The crashes became an existential threat to the Exchange, as they coincided with the election of a minority Labour government on a manifesto envisaging nationalisation of the Bank of England and the creation of a National Investment Bank to direct investment. Members were galvanised to support reforms of the new issue rules. Yet as the crisis gradually subsided, the members' support for reform also subsided with the result that certain of the proposals were not implemented. In this process, radical reforms were implemented, demonstrating that when certain conditions are satisfied self-regulating organisations could act decisively and successfully. These crashes of 1929 are reviewed in Chapter 8, and the regulatory reforms enacted in response are analysed in Chapter 9.

The events of 1929 encouraged the market's growing risk aversion. As institutional investors became important, the London Stock Exchange's membership became ever more polarised between brokers dealing with corporate business and those dealing with personal clients. There continued to be battles between these two groups of members which were usually determined in favour of a conservative majority of members. These developments between 1930 and 1939 are described in Chapter 10.

Although the reforms implemented by the Exchange in 1930 were successful in eliminating weak underwriting within the Exchange, they did not eliminate abuse altogether. Their principal effect was to drive abusive activity off-market. A series of scandals ensued which the Exchange, government departments and prosecutors were powerless to control. Embroiled in campaigns to increase middle-class readership, newspapers such as the *Daily Mail* and the *Daily Express* saw in these scandals an opportunity to gain support, and began to lobby for government intervention. The high point of these campaigns was reached in January 1936 when the *Daily Mail's* allegations concerning Maurice Singer, a share pusher, were completely vindicated in a libel action. This emboldened the *Daily Mail* to campaign for regulation of share traders, bringing to the fore the political debate on institutional reform which had begun in the early 1920s. In the autumn of 1936, the Exchange acquiesced in the government's appointment of the Bodkin Committee, ostensibly to inquire into the case for regulating share trading, but in practice to consider how a system of regulation could be introduced.

The report of the Bodkin Committee recommended an approach to regulation which was designed to respect the sensitivities of the Stock Exchange by proposing that the London Stock Exchange should be recognised but not subjected to any form of oversight by government. From the Exchange's point of view, this outcome was desirable because it would remain free to set its own rules and especially the Conduct of Business Rules which protected members' commercial interests. Officials, Conservative ministers and the Labour opposition all resisted this lack of oversight, but when the Board of Trade proposed to implement the recommendations in a way that would have avoided this problem, the Exchange resisted. Eventually, the Board of Trade backed down.

The events leading to the appointment of the Bodkin Committee and the negotiations which led to the implementation of its recommendations are described in Chapter 11.

Although the Board of Trade strove to implement the new legislation quickly, its efforts were defeated by the declaration of war. On this occasion, the Treasury had planned for the introduction of wartime control of new issues and the dysfunctionality of the 1914–1918 controls was not repeated. Nonetheless, concern among the Exchange's members grew about business bypassing the Exchange. Pressured by members, the Exchange's committee came to see in regulation a way of ensuring that its members and the members of other exchanges could compete, unconcerned about the activities of off-market traders because the registration scheme would virtually eliminate them. For its part, the Board of Trade accepted implementation of the Bodkin Committee's recommendations and thus the Exchange's power to regulate the conduct of members without oversight in return for the acceptance by the Exchange that in regulating the market (as opposed to members' conduct), it would respect the wishes of government. In effect, the government had concluded that it did not need direct control of the Exchange to be able to achieve its policy objectives. The events during the war which led to this conclusion are described in Chapter 12.

Finally, the factors that drove developments during the period are reviewed in Chapter 13.

Notes

1 *The Times*, 16 October 1946, page 2.
2 i.e. the manipulation of trading to achieve artificially high or low share prices.
3 *The Times*, 18 July 1946, page 7; Stock Exchange Council Minutes, Guildhall Library; Kynaston (2001, page 16).
4 Stock Exchange Council Minutes, Guildhall Library.
5 For example, the following rigs were reported in *Money Market Review*: Anglo French Corporation, 26 May 1917; Sehampang Sumatra, 14 July 1917; and Chaffers Gold Company, 25 August 1917. All of these rigs involved brokers reporting artificial trades in the Supplementary List to create the illusion of a rising market in the shares concerned.
6 *The Economist*, 23 June 1945, page 858.
7 Prevention of Fraud (Investments) Act, 1939 (PF(I) Act).
8 Reform of death duties in 1894, introduction of rules on close companies in the early 1920s, changes to the valuation of securities for death duty purposes in the late 1920s.

References

Primary works: unpublished

Stock Exchange Archive, Guildhall Library.

Primary works: newspapers and periodicals

Daily Express.
Daily Mail.
The Economist.
Money Market Review.
The Times.

Secondary works

Kynaston, D (2001), *The City of London: A Club No More 1945–2000*, volume 4 (Chatto & Windus, London).
Michie, RC (1999), *The London Stock Exchange: A History* (Oxford University Press, Oxford).

2   Coming to terms with change 1914–1945

At the end of the 1914–1918 war, it was feared that a remarkable period of human development had been brought to an end in August 1914. Whilst many in the population worked hard and enjoyed a low standard of life, many seemed contented. Escape was possible. For many men with greater-than-average capacities or character, it seemed possible to join the middle and upper classes, for whom life offered conveniences, comforts and amenities which were beyond the dreams of previous eras. It was possible, by telephoning from the comfort of one's home, to order goods of all descriptions and in whatever quantity, confident that they would be delivered to one's door without significant delay. By another call, it was possible to risk one's wealth in the natural resources and new enterprises of the four corners of the earth, in the hope of sharing in any benefits and advantages that might accrue. For those who were more risk-averse, it was possible to associate one's fortune with the prospects of any substantial community. If one wanted to travel, one could arrange cheap and comfortable means of journeying to any country without passport, with a minimum of formality and without prior knowledge of local language, religion or customs. When equipped with appropriate supplies of currency, the traveller might well feel aggrieved if any difficulty or interference were to be experienced. Those so favoured, regarded such conditions to be normal and permanent, and any deviation to be scandalous and avoidable.

One may argue about the proportion of the population for whom such a description of life in 1914 was realistic. There can be no doubt, however, that this description matches the outlook of many in the world of 1914 (see Keynes, 1919, pages 9–10).

Equally, there can be no doubt that there were sources of instability in that world: the instability of an excessive population in Germany, Austria–Hungary and Russia; the dependence of that population on a 'complicated and artificial organisation' which permitted free trade and movement; the instability of Europe's dependence upon the food supplies of the New World; and the instability of relationships between the labouring and capitalist classes'. The labouring classes were expected to accept a situation in which they could call their own very little of what they were needed to produce. On the other hand, the rest was taken by the capitalist classes, who were theoretically free to consume it. In practice, they were expected to consume less as they were expected to observe the duty of 'saving'.

The stock exchanges of the world and their members, especially the London Stock Exchange, had not only been prime agents of this system, they had also been prime beneficiaries. They had provided the channel by which inhabitants of London could venture their wealth 'in the natural resources and new enterprises of any quarter of the world'. They had provided the channel by which those same inhabitants could couple their fortunes with 'the good faith of the townspeople of any municipality in any continent'. Above all, they had framed the ambition of escape 'for any man of capacity or character exceeding the average', and many had been taking advantage of the channel which appeared to offer that escape.

All of these verities were to be challenged by the 1914–1918 war, but to an extent and to an effect that was not immediately understood. The initial assumptions that war could be waged by professional forces without disrupting business as usual had been discarded following the realisation that victory would require an all-consuming effort. Achieving the required transformation had involved sacrificing the pre-war social acceptance of inequality of wealth and prosperity. From being a creditor nation before the war, by 1919, the United Kingdom had become a debtor nation, and Europe's centrality to the financing of enterprise around the world had been lost. The complicated organisation by which free trade and travel had been possible in Europe had been destroyed and with it the means by which the aspirations of burgeoning populations had been sustainable. In the years following the 1914–1918 war, the challenge for governments was that the sacrifice of the pre-war verities was not immediately understood or accepted so that the need for social and institutional adjustment and its shape were only slowly beginning to be appreciated (Boothby et al., 1927, page 35; Marwick, 2006, pages 70–82, 340–344, 332; Gregory, 2008, pages 73, 208–212).

It is precisely Keynes's acceptance that the pre-war context had come to an end which makes his view exceptional. Many did not share his view, preferring to believe that as the war had been fought to protect the pre-war order it was to that order that the country should return and that this was possible. Although in government circles there was some recognition that this might prove difficult, there was a greater concern that frustrating this ambition might foment uncontrollable social unrest. As a result, the necessary post-war adjustment of government expenditure and borrowing was delayed until 1920 and a boom in consumer spending and stock exchange activity occurred. When, as was inevitable, government's policy was adjusted, consumer spending fell, unemployment rose, and stock market prices crashed. During this turmoil, many who had invested in government gilts out of a patriotic commitment to financing the war found that with the increase in interest rates, the value of their gilts holdings fell sharply. There were many shocks for businesses. Companies which had enjoyed the fruits of excess military demand for their production during the war had to face the demoralising task of winning back markets which had been forsaken in the process. Many were then obliged to reorganise their products, their production processes

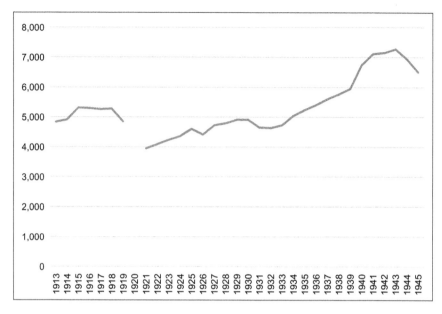

Graph 2.1 Gross National Product 1913–1945 (at 1938 prices) (£ million)
Source: Mitchell (1988, pages 843–844).

and their industries in the face of competition from industries overseas organised on modern lines and with newer plants. In this process, many organisations came to grief, having raised money in 1919 to take advantage of post-war expectations which proved unattainable. The economy had returned to a cycle of boom followed by depression, which was to persist.

Even this experience in the mid-1920s did not finally overcome the desire to return to the pre-war verities. Whilst there was among some a sense of impending disaster,[1] it was still possible to attribute company failures and difficulties to commercial misjudgements which did not imply systemic weakness. Consequently, throughout the 1920s, company and securities law were not reformed although official reviews were commissioned and undertaken leading to benign conclusions about the country's financial systems (Greene Committee report, 1926; Balfour Committee report, 1929). In parallel, there were many groups who saw a need for fundamental reform of industry and the financial system but no agreement on what shape that reform should take (Tawney, 1921; Laski, 1925; Independent Labour Party, 1926; Boothby et al., 1927; Liberal Party, 1928; Labour Party, 1928). Meanwhile, the attempt to return to pre-war conditions continued with the return to the gold standard in 1925. It was only with the London Stock Exchange crash of September 1929, the Wall Street crash of October 1929 and the 1931 politico-financial crises which led to the formation of the National Government that the impossibility of return to pre-war conditions came conclusively to be accepted, marked by dropping the gold standard.

From this point, there was a general acceptance that the country had been failed by the financial system. There was, however, no consensus on the nature and extent of the reforms that were in principle accepted as desirable; there was a nervousness that some of the prescriptions offered risked consequences which were difficult to assess and dangerous. Consensus only came with the depressing onset of another war during which a determination grew that the failure to reform which characterised the end of the 1914–1918 war should not be repeated. By the end of that war, the shape of the great reforms that followed had become clear and accepted.

In these developments, the London Stock Exchange was not a prime mover. The market's performance was shaped by the responses of investors and vendors to the pressures which they faced and their assessment of the direction of events.

The Exchange's task was to further the long-term interests of the members by providing a marketplace in which the transactions of potential investors and vendors of securities could be completed. It was hampered by the inherent difficulty of foreseeing how investors and vendors would react. It was constrained by its members' understanding of the direction of events and their willingness to respond.

The next three chapters will review in turn how each of these difficulties and constraints affected the Exchange.

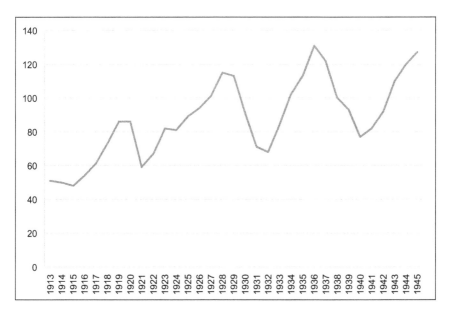

Graph 2.2 Share price index 1913–1945 (1938=100)

Source: Mitchell (1988, pages 688–689).

Note

1 'London Bridge is falling down, falling down, falling down' (TS Eliot, 1922).

References

Primary works: government and parliamentary reports

Board of Trade (1926), *Report of the Company Law Amendment Committee* (Cmd 2657). (HMSO, London). ('The Greene Committee Report').
Board of Trade (1929), *Final Report of the Committee on Industry and Trade* (Cmd 3282). (HMSO, London). ('The Balfour Committee Report').

Primary works: contemporary books and articles

Boothby, R, Macmillan, H, Loder, J and Stanley, O (1927), *Industry and the State: A Conservative View* (Macmillan, London).
Eliot, TS (1922), *The Waste Land*. Reprinted in Eliot, TS (1962), *Collected Poems 1909–1962* (Faber and Faber, London).
Independent Labour Party (1926), *Socialism in Our Time* (Privately Published, London).
Keynes, JM (1919), *The Economic Consequences of the Peace* (Macmillan, London).
Labour Party (1928), *Labour and the Nation* (Labour Party, London).
Laski, H (1925), *The Grammar of Politics* (George Allen & Unwin, London).
Liberal Party (1928), *Britain's Industrial Future: Being the Report of the Liberal Industrial Inquiry* (Ernest Benn, London).
Tawney, RH (1921), *The Acquisitive Society* (G Bell & Sons, London).

Secondary works

Gregory, A (2008), *The Last Great War: British Society and the First World War* (Cambridge University Press, Cambridge).
Marwick, A (2006), *The Deluge: British Society and the First World War* (Second edition, Palgrave Macmillan, London).
Mitchell, BR (1988), *British Historical Statistics* (Cambridge University Press, Cambridge).

3 The demand for securities 1914–1945

Introduction

Numbers of shareholders began to rise from the mid-nineteenth century. Government surveys found that whereas there had been about 170,000 shareholders in railway companies in 1855, by 1902, there were about 640,000. Similarly, the numbers of investors in banking companies had risen from about 82,000 in 1850 to about 260,000 in 1911. Clapham estimated that in 1914 about 1.3 million people were shareholders, about 2.8% of the population (Clapham,1946; Michie, 1987, page 118; Hannah, 2007, page 408). To match this, many British companies found that large numbers of people held small holdings of their shares.[1] A study of companies with a capital exceeding £1 million in the 1911 edition of *Four Shilling Investor Handbook* reported an average of 6,166 holders per company with a total number of shareholdings of 2,081,790. Extrapolating from these results, the study suggested that there may have been a total of five million shareholdings overall.[2] To estimate the number of shareholders implied by this total, Rutterford and Sotiropoulos (2017, page 12) divided the total number of holdings by the average number of holdings per person implied by an analysis of estates which suggested that there may have been about 1.1. million shareholders, about 2.4% of the population. In the years after the 1914–1918 war, the number of shareholders continued to grow.

Character of investors

Initially, equity investors had been wealthy individuals acquiring holdings in companies with which they had some connection either through business or through their locality (Jefferys, 1938, page 344; Cairncross, 1953, page 84; Cottrell, 1980, page 88.). Gradually, however, the development of stock exchanges in London and the provinces had tended to diminish the dependence on personal connections between investors and the companies in which they invested, Moreover, corporate practice in designing share capital structures changed. Shares in early registered companies were expensive, typically having a nominal value between £10 and £1,000, but nominal values had fallen substantially by the end of the nineteenth century in a ploy to increase their attractiveness to smaller investors. Growth in the number of small holdings by 1914 suggests that this ploy had been successful.

One result had been to introduce numbers of investors whose participation was not universally welcomed. Newspapers inveighed against premium hunters who were characterised as loafers and hangers on of the Stock Exchange, who were similar to the touts, blacklegs and welshers who infested racecourses.[3]

In 1897, F Faithful Begg MP identified another unwelcome group of investors: consisting of clergymen, widows and small investors prefer wild statements provided they are promised high dividends.[4]

Nevertheless, after the war, the numbers of shareholders were to grow even further. To a large extent, the government had financed the 1914–1918 war by borrowing, which entailed applying the skills of company promoters[5] and advertising agencies to the sale of government securities, with the result that large numbers of people were persuaded, for the first time, to become holders of tradeable securities and to think of holding their savings in this form. It became a patriotic duty.

After the war, interest in investment was maintained and broadened as holders became disillusioned by the post-war trend in market prices of government securities. The war had led to a growth in a middle class employed as supervisors, administrators and managers with incomes that enabled them to set aside money to provide for the long-term family obligations and other contingencies (Cole, 1935, pages 51, 89–90; Marwick, 2006, page 343). When interest rates rose at the end of 1919, so market prices of fixed interest securities fell, and there was a feeling among holders that they had suffered as a result of doing their patriotic duty during the war (Trebilcock, 1998, pages 492–494). In parallel, as it became evident that the wartime rates of taxation, especially Income Tax and Super Tax, were likely to be permanent, so the search for yield grew.[6]

This was not a new phenomenon, as yield had always been important for investors, whatever the scale of their investment, but with higher yields went higher investment risk. For most of the newer investors, whilst their holdings may have been small by comparison with the overall market, they are likely to have been material to their personal finances and annual income. They were therefore sensitive and vulnerable to the risk of loss. They were also likely to be ignorant of the market and the distinctions for example, between securities admitted to the Official List and securities admitted to dealing by way of Special Settlement which were less closely scrutinised by the Exchange. In short, they needed advice on how their investment risks should be mitigated.

There was no shortage of readily available advice. Although stockbrokers were not eager to form relationships with smaller investors, because their holdings were not large enough to generate viable levels of commission income, publishers had responded manfully to the challenge. Before the 1880s, investors and people interested in financial matters had relied upon reports in the general press. As early as 1825, *The Times* had begun publishing a column entitled *The Money Market* which had rapidly grown in scope until in the 1870s the newspaper regularly carried reports of companies' financial results before shareholders' meetings. The first daily newspaper devoted to financial news was the *Financial News* which was first published in January 1884 at a price of one penny. In February 1888, this was followed by the *Financial Times* which also had commenced publication in January 1888 but as a tri-weekly paper. By 1913, London-based publications included five daily newspapers which specialised in financial news, 44 weekly publications, three bi-monthly magazines, a quarterly and one subscription-only publication (Per table 6.1, Newman, 1984, pages 178–179. Vissink, 1985; Preda, 2001, pages 211–213).[7] By this stage, the *Financial News* and the *Financial Times* had both expanded and regularly published 12 pages and carried many advertisements. With the growth in the number of publications went a change in approach from the style of more established newspapers such as *The Times* which originally seldom indulged in 'any outspoken comment' or ventured any opinion on 'what may be called the new financial journalism' in which reviews of new issues were by no means 'colourless' and not necessarily trustworthy (Duguid, 1901, pages 99–102; Porter, 1986, page 2; Porter, 1988; Porter, 2000). In his book explaining to investors how newspapers' financial pages should be interpreted, Charles Duguid warned that interpreting financial articles correctly required more than an understanding of technical terms. Readers had to guard themselves against the risk of temptation, corruption, bribery and blackmail which were the unacceptable aspects of much financial journalism. (Duguid, 1901, page 103).

One of the weekly publications, the *Financial Review of Reviews*, was at the centre of an array of services designed to support the personal investor. The title was first published in 1905 following the formation of its publisher, the Investment Registry Limited, which was created to support private investors and was chaired by Sir John Rolleston. Through its weekly publication and books or pamphlets published in parallel, the Investment Registry offered advice on the risks that investors faced and how they might best be mitigated. An elementary guide written by Sir John Rolleston and entitled *Investment Risks and How to Avoid Them*, which was re-published many times, apologised that to many readers much of the book may seem simple, as it was not intended for investors with the time to study technical financial questions and analyse balance sheets or read prospectuses. The book had been written for casual investors who wanted to achieve the best return on their capital whilst avoiding pitfalls. (Rolleston, 1912, page 4).

It proposed three principles by which a mixed portfolio could be selected to mitigate the investor's risk. The first was that the securities selected should be subject to different influences, internal and external. The second was that there should be reasonable equality in the amounts of holdings in a portfolio. The third was that the stocks selected should, as far as possible, be similar in quality: speculative shares should not be mixed with high-class securities (Rolleston, 1912, page 10).

The text went on to show how by applying these principles, investors could select a portfolio of securities which would match their investment objectives, providing four different examples of portfolio distinguished by different assumptions about an investor's objectives. One was intended for investors wishing to provide a capital sum within a 'short number of years'. A second was intended for investors who did not want to draw income from the fund but might need capital sums at short notice. The next sample portfolio was intended for investors wishing to build up a capital fund for use on retirement. A final example was intended for investors wishing to maximise the income from the fund but not to draw down capital. In further support, the registry could provide valuation reports for members, circulars providing information on investors' stock holdings, an enquiry service and investment recommendations. The registry was also able to facilitate transactions. Other books gave more detailed advice on different sample portfolios (Lowenfeld, 1911; Crozier, 1911; Rutterford, 2006, page 13). The purpose of books and manuals such as these, which were matched by similar publications in other countries, was to clothe the practice of investment in the language and thought process of science (Preda, 2001, pages 357–360).

By this means, investors were encouraged to believe that provided a few rules were respected, investment could be not only lucrative but relatively sure, providing a legitimate source of income. The few rules principally concerned individual behaviour upon which financial success was deemed to depend. investors were encouraged to believe that, provided they eschewed an emotional approach, demonstrated self-control, studied the markets continuously and monitored joint-stock companies consistently, their investments would be (Preda, 2001, page 361).

There is evidence that advice of this sort could assist investors. Investors in Special Settlement issues could protect themselves by buying shares in those companies that disclosed information about historic profits and provided an asset valuation and avoiding issues of shares in companies which did not, for this appears to have been an effective signal of heightened risk of failure (Burhop et al., 2014, page 74).

For investors who either did not recognise the implications of such signals, or did not take heed of them, there was a risk that they would become prey to abusive operators and promoters, losing their money. Investors who heeded signals, followed advice and trusted their own judgement found themselves assessing the relative quality of securities and mitigating investment risk by diversifying their holdings.

Diversification

Large numbers of investors built diverse portfolios of small holdings, often by applying for shares directly in response to the prospectuses which were frequently advertised in the daily newspapers or information sent to them directly by specialist houses (Rutterford, 2004, page 120). The result was that many companies traded on the Exchange had large numbers of shareholders, as *The Economist* reported in 1926:

Table 3.1 Average shareholding December 1926

Company	Total paid-up capital £	Total shareholders	Average holding £	Percentage of shareholders with holdings less than £100
Imperial Tobacco	42,809,633	106,900	401	*36.7%*
Courtaulds	20,000,000	47,900	417	*47.6%*
Anglo-Persian Oil	19,450,000	57,500	338	*38.8%*
Brunner-Mond	13,749,303	37,200	370	*29.8%*
Vickers	12,468,968	70,400	182	*31.3%*
Dunlop Rubber	6,723,042	51,600	130	*28.8%*
Cunard Steamship	4,456,189	14,600	318	*25.0%*
TOTALS	119,657,135	385,500	310	*34.6%*

Source: The Economist, 18 December 1926, page 1054; 25 December 1926, page 1108.

The Economist also reported the results of a similar exercise in respect of ten 'concerns of moderate size in which the lowest average shareholdings were reported for Marconi Wireless Telegraphy (£132) and Rover Company (£127)'.[8] The results of a similar exercise were published by the Cohen Committee, which reviewed company law during the 1939–1945 war and suggested that the pattern of shareholding had not substantially changed between 1926 and 1944 (Wincott, 1946, page 42; Cohen Committee report, 1944).

The difficulty inherent in building a diverse portfolio by responding to prospectuses was that, unless investors had access to advice, it depended upon their own awareness of the different risks of investing in competing sectors and, if a portfolio were built by applying in response to published prospectuses, on the random complexion of securities that happened to be floated. Furthermore, investors would be left to supervise their own portfolios which, if they were to be successful, required them to have an informed view of the changing risks attached to their investments. Divorced from the informal advice networks of the City, most investors would have found this a challenging responsibility. Although company law prescribed that an annual report should be sent to shareholders, the financial information which the report was required to contain did not include a detailed profit and loss account so that the only information about a company's trading result might be a single line in the balance sheet showing the net balance of the profit and loss account at the end of the period. This information was more than ordinarily opaque when the company concerned was the holding company of a group, for its own profit and loss account might show the results not of trading but merely the receipt of such dividends as the subsidiaries had paid to it (Edwards, 1976, page 291; Edey, 1979, pages 226–277; Cottrell, 1980, page 41; Kennedy, 1987, page 126; Stewart, 1991, page 38; Arnold and Matthews, 2002, page 3).

As Le Maistre's investment manual warned, it was difficult for a shareholder when faced with poor corporate performance to distinguish between cases of bad management and cases of fraud. After all, shareholders were largely ignorant of the internal working of a concern and in most cases could not distinguish between bad management and fraud as causes of failure. Investors were encouraged to expect that incompetent directors would lay the blame of failure on economic causes to avoid admitting the effects of bad management and a lack of foresight. When profits dwindled and the price of shares fell, investors had to ask themselves whether it might be wise to face the loss, sell out and look for another investment whose prospects were more secure. In Le Maistre's view, although investors might naturally be reluctant to sell shares at a loss, they would be better advised to sell, even at a substantial loss, than to continue to hold shares which steadily fall in price (Le Maistre, 1925, pages 173–174).

In any event, bare historical accounting information was not helpful in a period of rapid technological change when historical dividend payments would provide no guide to the future earning potential of a business, and, in the case of a new company, there could be no historical information. As one eminent accountant wrote in 1928, the value of a balance sheet was widely exaggerated.

> 'in the case of some public companies, few documents serve their purpose better – they are intended to disclose nothing and succeed'
>
> (Jenkinson, 1928, page 1).

Most shareholders satisfied themselves regarding industrial stocks as though they were analogous to fixed interest securities, leading them to concentrate on two questions: do the expected dividends arrive as expected, as one would expect of a fixed interest security? Does the balance sheet demonstrate that the nominal capital is securely backed by tangible assets (Rutterford, 2004, page 116)? This approach had the merit that it appeared to be supported by the protections for fixed capital embedded in company law.[9] If both questions could be answered positively, most investors could be content. If the answers were not positive because, for example, a dividend payment were missed, investors would immediately consider whether they should sell (Hirschman, 1970, page 46; Hirschman, 1980, page 436).

Investors could, of course, compute the dividend per share as a return on the money they had invested and make some estimate of the earnings cover for the dividend. Both could then be compared with other securities individually and by sector (Rutterford, 2004, pages 121–122). Investors could also examine the balance sheet to determine the asset backing for the market value of the shares. Comparisons of this sort provided a basis on which to assess a company's relative success or failure and the extent to which share prices reflected the relative risk of investment in a company or sector and were assisted by the newspapers and periodicals which published summaries of accounts. Unfortunately, the reliability of these measures and thus their significance were severely constrained by the quality and extent of the accounting information on which they were based although the effect of these constraints was not always understood.

Reliance by investors on building and managing their own portfolios had other disadvantages. It did not take advantage of the greater security that was available from investing through an intermediary of some kind, nor did it take advantage of the favourable tax treatment attached to some collective investment schemes. Moreover, it assumed that investors had the time (and the inclination) to monitor their portfolios to mitigate the evident risk. In practice few investors may have had the time necessary to do this, and some authors suggested that private investors could not hope to watch their own holdings successfully even if they spent the whole of their time on the work. (Fisher, 1912, page 23)

Meanwhile, there was always a risk that investors would find themselves taken in by salesmen offering abusive share promotions. Many, heeding the risks attached to managing their own investments, and wishing to 'outsource' the research and judgements that this entailed, found themselves looking for intermediaries through whom to invest.

Investment intermediaries

Before the 1914–1918 war, investment trusts offered the most common form of collective investment arrangement, but after the war, encouraged by the tax reliefs that were made available, investment through life assurance policies and pension schemes became popular. After 1930, and the troubles experienced by some investment trusts during the 1929–1931 crisis, unit trusts attracted investors' funds.

By 1945, although the total funds of these various organisations were still dwarfed by funds held by other investment channels, their growth each year was significant in comparison with the amounts raised on the market by new issues and their importance grew in the eyes of issuing houses and the market generally.[10]

Table 3.2 Assets of financial institutions 1902–1933 (£ million)

Year	Investment Trusts	Banks	Insurance companies	Post Office Savings Bank	Trustee Savings Banks	Building societies
1903	70.0	934.0	352.6	146.1	57.2	65.0
1913	90.0	1,205.0	530.1	187.4	68.7	65.3
1920	112.0	2,604.1	712.1	267.1	91.3	87.0
1933	295.6	2,697.8	1,449.6	326.7	171.4	501.1
1948	392.7	7,663.5	2,904.0	1,948.0	799.2	1,037.8

Source: Table 7.1, Cassis (1990, page 144); Data for 1948 added: Burton and Corner (1968, page 79); Sheppard (1971)

Investment trusts

In 1919, investment trusts represented the most readily available form of collective investment. The trusts would invest the capital of their shareholders and pay a dividend based on the yield of their diversified investments together with the profits of their other operations. Their investments generally exceeded the amount of their ordinary share capital as trusts also issued debentures and other forms of security. Trusts would also borrow from banks against the security of their investments although prudence dictated that this source of finance should be used sparingly as it rendered a trust less stable against a falling stock market (Michie, 1983, pages 132–134). In a rising market, a trust's gearing would magnify the return to ordinary shareholders although in a falling market, losses would be magnified.

There is agreement that the first British investment trust was the Foreign and Colonial Investment Trust founded in 1868. Promoted by a solicitor, Philip Rose, the trust form was preferred to that of the limited liability company because the corporate form was unpopular and distrusted (McKendrick and Newlands, 1999, page 26). The prospectus proclaimed that the aim of the trust was to give investors of moderate means the same advantages as those with large portfolios spreading their investment over a number of different stocks enabled them to reduce the risk of investing in foreign and colonial government stocks.[11]

This was potentially attractive because it offered investors a way of profiting from the higher yields offered by overseas government stocks by comparison with domestic Consols without the private investor having to grapple with the challenge of becoming involved in individual transactions. Investors' possible concerns about the risks of overseas investment were countered by steps to emphasise integrity such as the choice of the trust form and the involvement as chairman of Lord Westbury, who, as Attorney General, had been responsible of the Fraudulent Trustees Act, 1857, and the careful selection of the trustees. The successful launch of this first trust was followed by imitators: 18 by 1875 and 70 by 1880. Although a number of these trusts were to offer opportunities for investment in domestic securities, many directed investment abroad, which continued to be attractive to investors (Michie, 1983, page 126).

It was, however, becoming clear that the trust form was imposing severe practical constraints, and after 1880 most new 'investment trusts' were formed as companies, a form which removed the fixed life of the trust, offered more freedom in the capital structures that could be employed and lessened the personal liability of those who acted as directors rather than trustees (Newlands, 1997, page 107 et seq). As companies, the investment trusts could offer preference shares and debentures as well as ordinary shares, thus offering a range of stock with different degrees of security and potential yield. In effect, the benefits of investing through investment trusts were being 'sliced and diced' to match the assumed differential preferences of potential investors. Thus, holders of ordinary investment trust shares would benefit from (and bear the risk of) any capital growth of a trust's investment funds whereas a debenture holder would not share either that benefit or the attached risk. After a hiatus in the early 1890s following the Barings crisis, in which the newer trusts with lower reserves had suffered more than the older trusts, investors had regained confidence in investment trusts which had led to another wave of flotations, 44 being offered between 1905 and 1914.[12]

Initially, investment trust boards had been dominated by bankers and merchants associated with prominent private bankers such as Sir John Lubbock of Robarts Lubbock and Company; Lord Hillingdon of Glyn Mills Currie and Company; Lindsay Eric Smith of Smith, Payne and Smith; and Richard B Martin of Martin and Company. With the disappearance of many private banks, leading to a decline in the number of such directors, there was a growth in the number of directors who were partners in merchant banks which formed investment trusts. In 1924, J Henry Schroder and Company founded the Continental and Industrial Trust, which was to be followed in 1928 by the Second Continental and Industrial Trust. In 1924, Hambros founded the Mid-European Corporation, and in 1926, Erlangers formed the City and International Trust. Practice in Scotland was somewhat different, as accountants and Writers to the Signet formed a larger proportion of boards of investment trusts registered there (Cassis, 1990, page 151).

In 1936, *The Economist* identified five London groups of investment trusts which were under the auspices of merchant banks[13] and six groups under the auspices of other leaders.[14] Eight Scotland-based groups were also identified.[15] Although the investment trusts in these groups were generally not linked by dominant shareholdings or cross-holdings, the boards of the individual trusts would be formed from relatively small groups of people who would sit on the boards of several of a group's trusts.

Although diversification of investments was one of the key attractions of investment trusts for the small investor, it is difficult to assess the range of distribution of trusts' assets as there was no requirement that they should publish details of their portfolios, and most did not do so (Cassis, 1990, page 145).

The preponderance of investment overseas before the war was affected by the government's wartime policies[16] so that by 1919, the proportion of overseas investments had fallen, a factor which Robinson demonstrated by reference to two investment trusts:

Table 3.3 Changes in the geographical distribution of investments in two investment trusts

	Merchants' Trust		*Industrial and General Trust*	
	1914%	1922%	1914%	1922%
Great Britain	14.85	29.59	29.26	40.09
British Empire	10.73	9.22	13.57	13.06
United States of America	50.74	30.97	23.69	6.45
South America	9.28	12.47	25.67	34.19
Europe	2.14	3.55	3.22	3.40
Others	12.26	14.20	4.59	2.81
	100.00	100.00	100.00	100.00

Source: Robinson (1923, pages 189–190).

Thus, although the extent of investment in overseas securities had fallen, it still represented for small investors an attraction by comparison with what they could achieve by direct investment. In the rising market which followed the 1914–1918 war, investment trusts' returns for investors rose, reaching a peak in 1930:

Table 3.4 Profits achieved by pre-war investment trusts 1924–1930

	56 English Trusts		36 Scottish Trusts	
	Total profits £,000	*Index 1929=100*	*Total profits £,000*	*Index 1929=100*
1924	4,230.0	66	1806.2	52
1925	4,669.7	73	2,109.3	61
1926	5,080.5	80	2,416.6	70
1927	5,509.6	86	2,6782.5	77
1928	6,032.0	94	3,454.9	87
1929	6,387.2	100	3,697.3	100
1930	6,425.8	101	3,371.9	107

Source: Table from *The Economist*, 1 December 1934, Investment Trust Supplement, page 3.

This growth in returns led to a demand for investment trust shares and to increases in the capital of existing trusts as well as the creation of new trusts. Between 1921 and 1930, 101 new trusts were created, raising various forms of capital amounting in total to £113,907,000, doubling the number of trusts and increasing the total capital by about one-half.[17]

The crash in 1929 and the period of depressed investment performance which followed was a challenge which not all investment trusts were able to surmount.

By the end of the 1920s, some had come to believe that the trust company, as an investment medium, would eventually supersede all individual investment in Great Britain. By 1934, investment trust stocks were the fourth lowest group in the Actuaries' Index.

In 1929, managed co-operative investment appeared to secure major advantages for investors: through risk-spreading, large-scale buying and continuous expert management. Why, *The Economist* asked in its 1934 review of investment trusts, had investment trust ordinary shares fallen more, instead of less, than those of the average British industrial company?[18]

In essence, the problems of 1929–1934 were not dissimilar to those experienced at the time of the Barings crisis in the 1890s. As the 1934 survey demonstrated, not all trusts had suffered equally: the extent of their problems had depended upon their ability to absorb the losses which followed the crash. Unsurprisingly, trusts which had been able to build up their reserves withstood the losses better than those which had not. Thus, older trusts proved more robust than younger trusts as did those which had been more conservative in declaring dividends. *The Economist* demonstrated this by comparting the performance of trusts created after the 1914–1918 war with those formed before the war. Trusts which had been more conservative in their investment policies fared better than those which had been more adventurous. Trusts which had been more highly geared fared worse than those which had borrowed less: a consequence which affected Scottish trusts disproportionately as they had tended to be more highly geared than English trusts.[19]

One small group of investment trusts demonstrates the problem that many post-war trusts suffered. The First General Investment Trust was established by A Emil Davies to attract the savings of small investors and subsequently was followed by the Second and Third General Investment Trusts. During the war, he had worked for Frederick Szarvasy (Scott and Goodall, 1986, pages 427–429), managing his shipping investments in Wales: an ill-starred venture which ended when it was alleged that information had been passed to the enemy leading to a number of sinkings. Davies had been obliged to leave Wales quickly. Davies had been elected to the London County Council, becoming an Alderman and eventually Deputy Chairman. In the 1920s, Davies had become financial editor of the *New Statesman* and had written pamphlets for the Fabian Society, including one on loan prospectuses issued by local authorities. He conceived the notion of an investment trust that would allow small investors to benefit from investment in quoted securities. These trusts suffered from two weaknesses. Virtually all their income was paid to shareholders so that their reserves were small. The second weakness was that to maximise returns, the trusts tended to invest in securities floated by Clarence Hatry. Thus, when the market fell in 1929, the trusts were quickly embarrassed by the decline in their portfolios' value and, as a result of their dividend policy, had no reserves on which to fall back. Thus, the trusts were obliged to announce an end to the dividend policy and to take powers to redeem investors' securities at a discount.[20] Although they hobbled on, investors were locked into funds that were disabled.

The result of these events was that the reputation of investment trusts was diminished and their growth was slowed. Even so, the damage to their reputation was much less dramatic than the destruction of the reputation of similar trust companies in the United States. Their downfall followed years of much more aggressive marketing as a way by which potential investors with small interests could participate in the stock market whilst diversifying their holdings. It was claimed that the spread of investment trusts would heighten the efficiency of investment by avoiding the waste of capital which resulted when individual investors were left to their own devices. When the 1929 crash happened in October 1929, it became clear that diversification had been a euphemism for risky investment strategies as brokerages and banks abused investment trusts linked to them by filling their portfolios with issues which the brokerage or bank was sponsoring. By 1932, the $7 billion that almost two million investors had placed in the shares of 675 investment trusts in 1929 was worth only $2 billion. As subsequent investigations uncovered the extent of the frauds that had been committed and investors recalled the assurances which had been given that investment trusts would provide a safe form of investment, the American trust movement's reputation was destroyed.[21]

The depression in stock market prices which followed the 1929 crash was deeper and longer-lived in New York than in London and thus would have been expected to have a greater effect on American trusts. Matters were made worse in New York, however, by the extensive evidence of fraud which had no counterpart in London where the trust movement survived and continued to grow, if more slowly.

Insurance companies

Although in 1914, investment trusts were the most readily available collaborative investment medium, their attractions were limited by two factors. There was no guarantee that the market price of an investment trust share would vary in direct proportion to the market value of the trust's investment fund. Usually by comparison with the underlying fund value, the market price of a trust's shares would incorporate a discount which would rise or fall to reflect market sentiment.[22] Thus, whether an investor proved able to take the full benefit implied by change in the value of the underlying fund would depend partly on the vagaries of the market and partly on the investor's freedom to choose the timing of a disposal. There was one other factor that affected the yield that could be expected from an investment trust holding by comparison with other investment media: the yields from insurance funds benefited from a favourable tax treatment whereas investment trust yields did not.

By the 1920s, the largest British insurance companies were composite businesses, writing all significant lines of insurance, whether fire, accident, marine or life, several of which produced poor returns in the inter-war years. Although accident premiums grew rapidly in the 1920s, so did costs so that accident profits did not grow, affected by workmen's compensation losses and poor motor underwriting results. Marine business also suffered. The decline in demand for shipping brought with it a decline in demand for marine insurance. By contrast, the growth in both life assurance premiums and life profits confounded expectations.

Increasing demand for life insurance reflected a sustained increase in the real income of large numbers of the population. Composite insurers had an advantage in selling life insurance to this developing audience: their networks of branches originally providing other lines of insurance provided opportunities to make new policies known quickly and cheaply to their target audience. Insurers also had the advantage that the yields they could offer were attractive. During the 1920s, the yield on Consols varied between 4.1% and 5.7% but by 1935 had fallen to 2.6%. Although this increased the challenge for insurance companies to achieve satisfactory returns, it attracted funds to them (Supple, 1970, pages 436–437).

Spurred by the opportunity to make good disappointing returns from other lines of business, the insurers set themselves to design policies that would appeal to their new target audience. In 1919, Standard Life introduced assurance plans at the same rates for women as for men.[23] Standard Life also introduced a new death duties policy which took advantage of the difference between the issue and the conversion price of Victory bonds. In 1921, Standard Life introduced the Acme policy with payments limited to 20 annual instalments, during which time no bonuses would accrue. At the end of the contract, the sum insured was increased by one-half and there were other benefits such as provision for disability and guaranteed surrender and paid-up values. In 1923, a new whole-life policy was introduced to appeal to the businessman under the age of 40. This policy included an option for the assured to convert the policy into an endowment or any other form of whole-life policy then available (Butt, 1984, pages 162–163; Moss, 2000, page 185).

Other companies responded with their own innovations. Short-term endowment policies called 'bachelor policies' were introduced by Royal Exchange providing the assured with the option of conversion into a whole-life contract (Butt, 1984, page 163).

This spate of innovation, spurred by the need to gain new business, continued into the 1930s, when the developing house-building boom provided more opportunities for innovation. Endowment policies were marketed as a way of saving to pay off a mortgage loan irrespective of whether the insurance company itself advanced a loan to the assured.[24] In 1934, for example, the Phoenix entered an agreement with the Woolwich Equitable Building Society by which the Phoenix would make 20-year endowment policies available against the building society's loans and pay a commission of 2½% of the premiums to the society. Similar arrangements existed between the Phoenix and the Cheltenham and Gloucester, Newbury, Newcastle and Gateshead and Portman building societies (Trebilcock, 1997, page 139).

All this innovation led to a rapid increase in the volume of life business:

Table 3.5 British offices' life business 1919–1940 (£m)

	Ordinary life			Industrial life	
	UK premiums		Sums assured	Premiums	Sums assured
	Total	New			
1919	37.8	6.1	n.a.	25.3	n.a.
1920	41.9	6.6	n.a.	29.3	n.a.
1921	44.1	4.6	n.a.	31.1	n.a.
1922	45.6	4.5	1,144	31.6	n.a.
1923	46.8	4.5	1,182	33.2	693
1924	51.5	4.9	1,209	34.1	716
1925	57.9	4.9	1,291	36.6	751
1926	58.5	4.9	1,353	36.8	832
1927	63.9	5.5	1,398	38.8	870
1928	68.2	5.8	1,439	40.9	903
1929	69.8	5.8	1,492	42.0	920
1930	66.8	6.0	1,591	43.8	953
1931	65.3	5.7	1,668	45.4	1,006
1932	67.9	5.5	1,706	46.4	1,035
1933	71.4	6.0	1,759	47.7	1,051
1934	71.5	6.7	1,809	50.1	1,089
1935	74.3	7.3	1,936	51.5	1,123
1936	77.3	7.7	2,061	53.6	1,176
1937	80.5	7.9	2,139	55.8	1,216
1938	83.9	7.6	n.a.	58.0	1,255
1939	84.1	5.7	n.a.	59.8	1,294
1940	82.8	4.3	n.a.	62.2	1,313

Source: Based on table in Supple (1970, page 427).

In achieving this growth, the insurers were assisted by the system for taxing personal income. Rates of Income Tax had been increased materially during the war, and after the end of hostilities it quickly became apparent that the rates of tax would remain at those levels. As a result, there was considerable interest in taking full advantage of the reliefs available, such as Life Assurance Relief. Although the relief had been reduced during the war (Hannah, 1986, page 33), the effect was that payment of a life assurance premium attracted a reduction in the policy-holder's income tax liability equal to one-half of the standard rate, which at the end of the war stood at four shillings in the pound.[25] On its own, this increased the real return of endowment policies compared with other forms of saving[26] but allowed the insurers to go further in designing schemes which would take full advantage of the relief. One such scheme featured single premium endowment policies which by 1925 came to represent just under 20% of the Phoenix's total life premiums. This scheme required a client to buy a single premium with profits endowment policy, using money lent by the Phoenix to pay the premium which would attract tax relief. Interest paid on the loan would also attract tax relief, reducing Super Tax liabilities. When the endowment matured, the amount due to the policy holder would be used to redeem the loan, and any surplus would be paid to the policy holder. The scheme proved too popular for it was ended by measures in the Finance Act 1930 which denied relief against Super Tax in respect of interest on loans to pay insurance premiums (Section 12, Finance Act 1930. Trebilcock, 1997, page 130; Trebilcock, 1998, page 536).

The changes brought about by the Finance Act 1930 provided a demonstration of the importance of Income Tax reliefs to the attractiveness of life insurance products as a form of saving. The life offices were so worried that all income tax privileges might be lost that they lobbied hard for the changes to be restricted and were successful, but at some expense. In March 1930, the Phoenix decided that it would not issue policies which were obviously being taken out to enable the assured to escape liability to Income Tax and Sur-tax. (Trebilcock, 1998, page 538)

Life Assurance Relief was also significant in its effect in reducing the cost of endowment policies linked to house purchase mortgage loans and thus increasing the returns to saving in this form.

The other major relief which was available was related to pension saving. There were two alternative ways by which an employer could establish a scheme. On the one hand, an employer could either set up an independent scheme with its own trustees and actuarial advice or buy an insurance policy or policies to cover employees. These two approaches were treated differently for tax purposes. Pension contributions paid to insurance companies were treated in the same way as life assurance premiums attracting relief equal to one-half of the standard rate provided that the scheme was approved by the Inland Revenue.[27] In 1921, employees who were members of an in-house pension scheme could claim their contributions as expenses and thus received tax relief at the full rate of tax.[28] Although this change in available tax reliefs made self-administered pension schemes more attractive, initially the possibility was only taken up by the largest employers as the organisational challenge proved a disincentive for smaller businesses. This disincentive was reduced when in 1927 an American insurer, Metropolitan Life, began to market to UK employers group policies which had proved successful in the USA. Initially, Metropolitan Life's schemes were bought by the UK subsidiaries of American companies but proved attractive to UK companies and led UK insurers to introduce new products in competition. In 1930, Legal and General sold its first big scheme, covering the 6,000 employees of the Gramophone Company. Three years later, when Metropolitan Life decided to withdraw from the UK market, its 150 UK schemes were 'acquired' by Legal and General which thus could secure its position as the leading UK provider of group life and pensions policies (Supple, 1970, page 435 et seq; Butt, 1984, page 166; Hannah, 1986, pages 35–37; Trebilcock, 1998, page 549).

Growth in funds managed by insurers was not merely fuelled by the vagaries of the tax system, clever policy design and marketing: achievement of satisfactory returns was critical. In general, life assurance offered returns which were attractive in comparison with other forms of saving, but it was also important for insurance companies to achieve returns that at least equalled those achieved by other companies. It was evident that individual customers compared bonus declarations, but companies with group life and pensions policies also had a strong interest in minimising their liabilities (Baker and Collins, 2003, pages 143–144).

In this respect, experience in the early years following the end of hostilities was not propitious. Life offices' traditional approach to investment favoured assets which would pay a regular income coupled with assured repayment of the capital even if the assets were not readily marketable. Assets such as debentures and mortgages were preferred to undated securities such as government perpetuities and corporate shares whose market value could fluctuate and which threatened a capital loss if the insurance company were ever required to sell (Baker and Collins, 2003, pages 143–144).

Insurers remembered their experience of falls in the market price for government securities in 1919 and 1920. Institutional investors believed that they had helped the government in its moment of need and were caned for it in the aftermath. Worse still, when prices were falling, the home and other governments were nonetheless also prepared to take from the insurers in taxation (Trebilcock, 1998, page 494).

These developments led insurers to reconsider their traditional approach to investment and to revisit suggestions that had first been voiced in 1912 when the Prudential's actuary had argued that a policy of diversification could increase yields by incorporating individual higher-risk, higher-yielding securities into a portfolio with low aggregate volatility (Scott, 2002, page 81). Whilst few had acted on these suggestions before the war, interest was re-kindled by the experience of investment returns in 1919 and 1920 and the publication in 1924 of an American study, 'Common stocks as long term investments' (Smith, 1924), which examined the relative performance of US equities (for a diversified portfolio of large companies) and high-grade bonds over different periods between 1866 and 1922. Smith demonstrated that equities had out-performed bonds in terms of both capital and income, and that stock prices implied a rate of return similar to compound interest of approximately 2.5% (Scott, 2002, page 81).

In 1927, the debates initiated by this study were reflected in two articles in *The Economist*, which bemoaned the lack of a UK study whilst encouraging UK insurers to espouse the new approach.[29] This led to a study based on UK experience which was undertaken by Harold Raynes (1928), the chief actuary of Legal and General, and was published in 1928 showing similar results to the earlier US study.

The impact of these new ideas took time to emerge, partly because insurers were cautious in changing their practices but also because insurance companies did not engage in active investment. As net annual additions represented on average only 4.7% of total life assurance assets between 1923 and 1937, asset distribution patterns were slow to change and determined by investment decisions taken many years before. Scott suggests that as a proportion of net annual life assurance company investment, investment in ordinary shares rose from 8.3% in 1923 to 27.4% in 1937 and in all corporate sector securities[30] rose from 42.4% to 57.9%. He also suggests that in the same period, investment in government securities (including domestic, foreign and colonial) fell from 56.7% to 16.6% (Scott, 2002, page 85).

The effect of this change in the pattern of annual investment was a slower change in the composition of the life assurance companies' portfolios.

Whilst these changes were significant for the life assurance industry, they remained small by comparison with the total value of securities quoted on the London Stock Exchange. On 24 March 1919, the total value of life assurance assets represented only 4.8% of the value of quoted securities which was of the order of £18.5 billion (Michie, 1999, page 277). However, this gives a misleading impression of the significance of life insurers to the market. In 1937, when the life offices' net investment in corporate sector securities amounted to £47.3 million,[31] all new industrial issues amounted to £113.8 million (Mitchell, 1988, page 685). For the insurer, new issues offered attractions for they offered a way in which substantial blocks of shares could be acquired without moving

Table 3.6 Composition of life assurance businesses' portfolios

| Year | Land, mortgages and loans % | Public sector % | Corporate sector investments | | | | Other % | Total assets £m |
			Debentures %	Preference shares %	Ordinary shares %	Total corporate sector %		
1913	35	23	25	6	3	34	8	395.8
1924	21	52	12	4	4	20	8	447.3
1929	23	43	16	6	6	28	7	551.0
1937	19	41	15	8	10	34	5	881.3

Source: Based on table in Baker and Collins (2003, page 149).

the price, and some insurers[32] invested in shares that were placed privately among investors prior to an application for a listing on the Exchange (Roberts, 1992, page 392). This practice appealed to issuers because the legal and administrative expenses were much lower and the cost of underwriting was avoided altogether which facilitated the access of smaller companies to the market.

In short, the life offices and pension funds became significant investors, a significance which was reinforced by their tendency to act together. When demand for group life and pensions schemes grew in 1928, the Standard, the Prudential and Legal and General agreed a tariff of premium rates and began to meet regularly. In 1931, they were joined by Eagle Star and some other companies (Butt, 1984, pages 166–167). Other institutional investors, such as the investment trusts, were forming investment protection committees to negotiate with issuers over securities restructurings (Avrahampour, 2015, page 5).

Unit trusts

One consequence of the 1929 Wall Street crash was a collapse among the United States equivalents of the investment trusts in England and Scotland. So great was the fall in value of investment trust schemes and so great the effect on small investors that a series of investigations followed. Even so, small investors still needed a way of investing relatively small amounts in diversified portfolios: a need that was met by the creation of a new type of investment fund. The fixed trust was essentially a trust that was formed to invest in a specified group of stocks and which had no investment discretion whatever. The motive was to make it easier for members of the public to place their confidence in a fund. Thus, each trust's portfolio was fully disclosed to investors. The portfolio was not to be actively managed: managers only being allowed to place on deposit funds becoming available from the sale of bonus issues, or rights. There was to be no leverage and the life of a fixed trust was pre-determined. Finally, fixed trusts were open-ended mutual funds which allowed investors to buy or sell at the market value of the underlying portfolio, thus avoiding the discounts to net asset value which had afflicted United States investment trust shares after the crash. These new funds proved successful.

There was some criticism of these new funds in the United Kingdom, where investment trusts had not been so damaged by the crashes in 1929. *The Economist* argued that, as investment trusts had not suffered so badly, investors would still trust investment managers to manage their portfolios actively and that there was little to be gained by the American combination of high commissions with passive management.[33]

Nonetheless, a first fixed trust was established in London in 1931, The First British Fixed Trust, which chose a portfolio of British equities. It offered a yield of 6.79% on its portfolio of shares in 24 British companies compared with the return of 4.34% which was available on 2½% Consols. A little more flexibility was allowed to the managers of the trust than would have been allowed of a trust in the United States so that the managers were required to sell a holding if the net average earnings or dividend fell below the previous five-year average. It did copy the high commissions that were usual in the United States: costs were estimated by *The Economist* to be around 9.4%.[34]

Although the first fixed trusts were successful in attracting investors' funds, the disadvantages of fixed trusts soon became apparent as they built up cash balances which they were not permitted to re-invest, leading to disappointing investment returns. By 1934, the first flexible trust had been created, and after 1936, no new fixed trusts were established. These new trusts published 'investment lists' of suitable equity investments which the managers could buy or sell as appropriate. Cash balances formed by cash subscribed by new investors or by realisation of existing holdings could be used to buy shares from the published list. These new trusts proved attractive to new investors. The Stock Exchange did not permit them to be traded on the floor of the Exchange, so that all transactions between the trusts and those who invested in them took place directly rather than through the Exchange. Although this may have seemed riskier, as the transactions were beyond the rules of the Exchange, it was also simpler, as brokers were not involved. Moreover, the trusts were prepared to deal in relatively small holdings, which were discouraged by the Exchange's standard rates of commission.

Notes

1 Hannah (2007, page 412) suggests that in 1900, four British banks and ten railway companies each had more than 10,000 shareholders.
2 The study examined 337 companies (Foreman-Peck and Hannah, 2012, page 1224).
3 *The Statist*, 14 July 1888, page 42.
4 *The Accountant*, 13 November 1897, page 1077.
5 Arthur Wheeler, a company promoter who went on to found one of the new issuing houses, Charterhouse Investment Trust, was knighted for his wartime service in selling government securities to finance the war (Keyworth, 1986, pages 759–762).
6 The standard rate of Income Tax had risen from 1s 2d in the pound in 1914 to 6s in 1919. Super-Tax had risen from 6d in the pound in 1914 on incomes over £5,000, to rates between 1s 6d and 6s for incomes over £2,000 (Board of Trade, 1921). Estate Duty was raised in 1919 to 40% on estates of £2 million and over (Daunton, 2002, page 47; Marwick, 2006, page 341; Cheffins and Blank, 2008, pages 702–703).
7 Per table 6.1, Newman (1984, pages 178–179); Vissink (1985); Preda (2001, pages 211–213).
8 *The Economist*, 18 December 1926, page 1054.
9 It was a cardinal principle of company law that companies could not dissipate fixed capital by payment of a dividend, although the law was uncertain on whether losses must be made good before a dividend could be paid (Stiebel, 1929, pages 71–75).
10 For a contemporary recognition that the investment funds held by insurance companies and investment trusts were regarded as influential, see Cole (1935, pages 146, 148, 154, 161).
11 Applications for Listing file (Stock Exchange Archive, Guildhall Library).
12 *The Economist*, Investment Trust Supplement, 1937, page 1.
13 De Stein, Robert Fleming, Hambros, Samuel (*The Economist*, 26 September 1936, page 507).
14 (Viscount) St Davids, Industrial and General, Robert Benson, Stockholders, Sir Miles Mallinson.

15 Brown Fleming and Murray, Grahams Ryland, Baillie Gifford, Layton-Bennet, Shepherd and Wedderburn, Moody Stuart and Robinson, Brander and Cruickshank, Paul and Williamson.

16 On 15 December 1915, a circular was sent to insurance and investment trust companies inviting them to sell or lend securities to the Treasury. The Government offered to buy at the current market price or borrow for two years paying the holder ½% above the interest actually earned. Both the owner and the Treasury could sell the securities during that time, the Treasury undertaking that it would pay the holders the price realised plus 2½%. Total purchases under this scheme amounted to £109 million and loans to £84 million, the scheme was later varied and the government took powers to requisition securities (Morgan, 1952, pages 326–331).

17 *The Economist*, 1 December 1934, Investment Trust Supplement, pages 2 and 5.

18 *The Economist*, 1 December 1934, page 1040.

19 The survey suggested that on average, Scottish trusts had £3176 of fixed interest capital for every £100 of equity capital. The English trusts' average was only £218 per £100.

20 *The Times*, 1 October 1929.

21 A subsequent enquiry by a Senate committee found evidence of abusive practices including self-dealing, deceptive reports to shareholders, exculpatory clauses exempting trustees and management from liability and conversion of trust assets for private use and profit (Bosland, 1941, pages 478–479; Ott, 2011, pages 169–181; Holt, 2008, Chapter 5).

22 Remarkably, in the late 1920s, investment trust shares consistently traded in New York at a premium to the underlying fund value presumably indicating that share prices could not fail to rise. 'Defenders of the trusts argued that this discrepancy was not "water" but the values generated by managerial strategies and expertise.' (Holt, 2008, page 375).

23 Until 1919, premiums for women of child-bearing age had been more expensive than for men because of the high mortality rate during pregnancy. Some offices declined to insure women of child-bearing age because the risk was too great.

24 Which many insurance companies were prepared to do at a rate of interest lower than the building societies.

25 This was subject to an overall limit: allowable premiums could not exceed one-sixth of total income.

26 At a time when other forms of investment were returning 3%, with profits endowment policies were achieving 10% (Hannah, 1986, page 33).

27 Income Tax Act 1918.

28 Finance Act 1921. Unlike insurance company schemes, the proceeds were taxable at a quarter of the standard rate of tax.

29 *The Economist*, 1 October 1927, pages 547–548; 8 October 1927, page 598–599.

30 Debentures, preference shares and ordinary shares.

31 Extrapolation from Scott (2002, page 85).

32 Scott (2002, page 95) mentions the Prudential, Pearl, Provident Mutual and National Provident Institution.

33 *The Economist*, 21 March 1931, pages 620–621.

34 *The Economist*, 2 May 1931, page 950.

References

Primary works: unpublished documents

Stock Exchange Archive, Guildhall Library.

Primary works: newspapers and periodicals

The Accountant.
The Economist.
Financial News.
Financial Review of Reviews.
Financial Times.
The Statist.
The Times.

Primary works: government and parliamentary reports

Board of Trade (1945), *Report of the Committee on Company Law Amendment* (Cmd 6659). (HMSO, London). ('The Cohen Committee Report').

Primary works: contemporary books and articles

Bosland, CC (1941), 'The Investment Company Act of 1940 and Its Background', *Journal of Political Economy*, volume 49, number 5, pages 687–721.

Cole, GDH (1935), *Studies in Capital & Investment: Being a Volume of New Fabian Research Bureau Studies in Socialist Problems* (Victor Gollancz, London).

Crozier, JB (1911), *The First Principles of Investment* (Financial Review of Reviews, London).

Duguid, C (1901), *The Story of the Stock Exchange: Its History and Position* (Grant Richards, London).

Fisher, WH (1912), *Investing at Its Best and Safe-Guarding Invested Capital* (s.n., London).

Jenkinson, MW (1928), *The Value of a Balance Sheet* (Gee & Company, London).

Le Maistre, GH (1925), *Investments for All: Their Importance, Selection, and Management* (John Murray, London).

Lowenfeld, H (1911), 'The Rudiments of Sound Investment', *Financial Review of Reviews*, volume 7, number 1, pages 77–91.

Raynes, HE (1928), 'The Place of Ordinary Stocks and Shares (As Distinct From Fixed Interest Bearing Securities) in the Investment of Life Assurance Funds', *Journal of the Institute of Actuaries*, volume 59, number 1, pages 21–50.

Robinson, LR (1923), *Investment Trust Organizatiuon and Management* (Ronald Press, New York).

Rolleston, JFL (1912), *Investment Risks and How to Avoid Them* (Privately Published, London).

Smith, EL (1924), *Common Stocks as Long Term Investments* (Macmillan, New York).

Stiebel, A (1929), *Company Law and Precedents*. (Third edition. Sweet & Maxwell, London).

Secondary works

Arnold, AJ and Matthews, DR (2002), 'Corporate Financial Disclosures in the UK 1920–1950: The Effects of Legislative Change and Managerial Discretion', *Accounting and Business Research*, volume 32, number 1, pages 3–16.

Avrahampour, Y (2015), '"Cult of Equity": Actuaries and the Transformation of Pension Fund Investing 1948–1960', *Business History Review*, volume 89, pages 281–304.

Baker, M and Collins, M (2003), 'The Asset Portfolio Composition of British Life Insurance Firms, 1900–1965', *Financial History Review*, volume 10, pages 137–164.

Burhop, C, Chambers, D and Cheffins, B (2014), 'Regulating IPOs: Evidence From Going Public in London, 1900–1913', *Explorations in Economic History*, volume 51, pages 60–76.

Burton, H and Corner, DC (1968), *Investment and Unit Trusts in Britain and America* (Elek Books, London).

Butt, J (1984), 'Life Assurance in War and Depression: The Standard Life Assurance Company and Its Environment 1914–1939', in Westall, OM (editor), *The Historian and the Business of Insurance* (Manchester University Press, Manchester).

Cairncross, A (1953), *Home and Foreign Investment 1870–1913: Studies in Capital Accumulation* (Cambridge University Press, Cambridge).

Cassis, Y (1990), 'The Emergence of a New Financial Institution: Investment Trusts in Britain 1870–1939', in van Helten, JJ and Cassis, Y (editors), *Capitalism in a Mature Economy: Financial Institutions, Capital Exports and British Industry, 1870–1939* (Edward Elgar, Aldershot).

Cheffins, BR and Blank, SA (2008), 'Corporate Ownership and Control in the UK: The Tax Dimension', *Modern Law Review*, volume 70(5), pages 778–811.

Clapham, Sir J (1946), 'Sir John Clapham's Account of the Financial Crisis in August 1914', Reprinted in RS Sayers (1976), *The Bank of England 1891–1944*, as Appendix 3 (Cambridge University Press, Cambridge).

Clayton, G and Osborn, WT (1965), *Insurance Company Investment: Principles and Policy* (Allen & Unwin, London).

Cottrell, PL (1980), *Industrial Finance 1830–1914: The Finance and Organisation of English Manufacturing Industry* (Methuen, London).

Daunton, MJ (2002), *Just Taxes, the politics of taxation in Britain 1914–1979.* (Cambridge University Press, Cambridge).

Edey, HC (1979), 'Company Accounting in the Nineteenth and Twentieth Centuries', in Lee, TA and Parker, RH (editors), *The Evolution of Corporate Financial Reporting* (Nelson, Sunbury-on-Thames).

Edwards, JR (1976), 'The Accounting Profession and Disclosure in Published Reports 1925–1935', *Accounting and Business Research*, volume 6, pages 289–303.

Foreman-Peck, J and Hannah, L (2012), 'Extreme Divorce: The Managerial Revolution in UK Companies Before 1914', *Economic History Review*, volume 65, number 4, pages 1217–1238.

Hannah, L (1986), *Inventing Retirement: The Development of Occupational Pensions in Britain* (Cambridge University Press, Cambridge).

Hannah, L (2007), 'The "Divorce" of Ownership From Control From 1900 Onwards: Re-calibrating Imagined Global Trends', *Business History*, volume 49, pages 404–438.

Hirschman, AO (1970), *Exit, Voice, and Loyalty: Response to Decline in Firms, Organizations, and States* (Harvard University Press, Cambridge, MA).

Hirschman, AO (1980), 'Exit, Voice and Loyalty: Further Reflections and a Survey of Recent Contributions', *Millbank Memorial Fund Quarterly/Health and Society*, volume 58, number 3, pages 430–452.

Holt, DS (2008), *Acceptable Risk, Law, Regulation and the Politics of American Financial Markets 1878–1930.* Unpublished PhD thesis, Department of History, University of Virginia.

Jefferys, JB (1938), *Trends in Business Organisation in Great Britain Since 1856.* Unpublished PhD thesis, University of London.

Kennedy, WP (1987), *Industrial Structure, Capital Markets and the Origins of British Economic Decline* (Cambridge University Press, Cambridge).

Keyworth, JM (1986), 'Sir Arthur Wheeler', in Jeremy, DJ (editor), *Dictionary of Business Biography*, volume 5, S-Z, pages 759–762 (Butterworths, London).

Marwick, A (2006), *The Deluge* (Second edition, Palgrave Macmillan, Basingstoke).

McKendrick, N and Newlands, J (1999), *'F&C': A History of Foreign & Colonial Investment Trust* (Foreign and Colonial Investment Trust Plc, London).

Michie, RC (1987), *The London and New York Stock Exchanges 1850–1914* (Allen & Unwin, London).

Michie, RC (1999), *The London Stock Exchange: A History* (Oxford University Press, Oxford).

Mitchell, BR (1988), *British Historical Statistics* (Cambridge University Press, Cambridge).

Morgan, EV (1952), *Studies in British Financial Policy, 1914–1925* (Macmillan, London).

Moss, M (2000), *The Building of Europe's Largest Mutual Life Company: Standard Life, 1825–2000* (Mainstream Publishing, Edinburgh).

Newlands, J (1997), *Put Not Your Trust in Money: A History of the Investment Trust Industry From 1868 to the Present Day* (Chappin Kavanagh, London).

Newman, K (1984), *Financial Marketing and Communications* (Holt, Rinehart & Winston, Eastbourne).

Ott, JC (2011), *When Wall Street Met Main Street: The Quest for an Investors' Democracy* (Harvard University Press, Cambridge, MA).

Porter, D (1986), 'A Trusted Guide of the Investing Public: Harry Marks and the Financial News 1884–1916', *Business History*, volume 28, number 1, pages 1–17.

Porter, D (1988), 'City Editors and the Modern Investing Public: Establishing the Integrity of the New Financial Journalism in Late Nineteenth Century London', *Media History*, volume 4, number 1, pages 49–60.

Porter, D (2000), '"Where There's a Tip There's a Tap": The Popular Press and the Investing Public, c1900–1960', in Catterall, P, Seymour-Ure, C and Smith, A (editors), *Northcliffe's Legacy: Aspects of the British Popular Press, 1896–1996* (Palgrave Macmillan, Basingstoke).

Porter, D (2006), 'Speciousness Is the Bucketeer's Watchword and Outrageous Effrontery His Capital: Financial Bucket Shops in the City of London c1880–1939', in Benson, J and Ugiolini, L (editors), *Cultures of Selling: Perspectives on Consumption and Society Since 1700*, pages 103–125 (Ashgate, Aldershot).

Preda, A (2001), 'The Rise of the Popular Investor: Financial Knowledge and Investing in England and France, 1840–1880', *Sociological Quarterly*, volume 42, number 2, pages 205–232.

Raynes, HE (1928), 'The Place of Ordinary Stocks and Shares (As Distinct From Fixed Interest Bearing Securities) in the Investment of Life Assurance Funds', *Journal of the Institute of Actuaries*, volume 59, number 1, pages 21–50.

Roberts, R (1992), *Schroders: Merchants and Bankers* (Macmillan, London).

Rutterford, J (2004), 'From Dividend Yield to Discounted Cash Flow: A History of UK and US Equity Valuation Techniques', *Accounting and Financial History*, volume 14, number 2, pages 115–149.

Rutterford, J (2006), 'The World Was their Oyster: International Diversification Pre-World War I', in Rutterford, J, Upton, M and Kodwani, D (editors), *Financial Strategy* (Second edition, John Wiley & Sons, Chichester).

Rutterford, J and Sotiropoulos, DP (2017), 'The Rise of the Small Investor in the US and the UK, 1895–1970', *Enterprise and Society*, volume 18, number 3, pages 485–535.

Scott, JW and Goodall, F (1986), 'Frederick Alexander Szarvasy', in Jeremy, DJ (editor) *Dictionary of Business Biography*, volume 5, S-Z, pages 427–429 (Butterworths, London).

Scott, P (2002), 'Towards the "Cult of the Equity"? Insurance Companies and the Interwar Capital Market', *Economic History Review*, volume 55, number 1, pages 78–104.

Sheppard, DK (1971, reprinted 2006), *The Growth and Role of UK Financial Institutions, 1880–1962* (Routledge, London).

Stewart, IC (1991), 'The Ethics of Disclosure in Company Financial Reporting in the United Kingdom 1925–1970', *Accounting Historians Journal*, volume 18, pages 35–54.

Supple, B (1970), *The Royal Exchange Assurance: A History of British Insurance 1720–1970* (Cambridge University Press, Cambridge).

Trebilcock, C (1997), 'Phoenix: Financial Services, Insurance, and Economic Revival Between the Wars', in Clarke, P and Trebilcock, C (editors), *Understanding Decline: Perceptions and Realities of British Economic Performance* (Cambridge University Press, Cambridge).

Trebilcock, C (1998), *Phoenix Assurance and the Development of British Insurance: Volume 2: The End of the Insurance Giants 1870–1984* (Cambridge University Press, Cambridge).

Vissink, HGA (1985), *Economic and Financial Reporting in England and the Netherlands* (Van Gorcum, Assen/Maastricht).

Wincott, H (1946), *The Stock Exchange* (Sampson Low Marston & Company, London).

4   The supply of securities 1914–1945

Introduction

To survive, the Exchange needed a constant supply of businesses which wanted their shares to be quoted and traded. Whereas in 1914, the Exchange's trading had been dominated by securities issues by overseas governments and by railway companies both domestic and overseas, by 1939, it was dominated by UK government securities and by domestic financial, industrial and commercial shares (Michie, 1999, pages 175 and 278). In a sea change, companies which previously would have been deterred by the drawbacks of seeking a quotation had overcome their distaste partly because there were strong incentives which drove companies towards the capital market and partly because the market changed its ways.

The end of hostilities

Like jockeys wheeling their horses before the start of the Grand National, many directors spent the summer of 1918 preparing their companies for the new issues boom that was expected to follow the end of the war. As a mark that it intended to join the race, on 17 August 1918, Leyland Motors (1914) Limited moved its registered office from Leyland in Lancashire to 6 Austin Friars in London, the office of Clarence Hatry, the well-known company promoter.[1] At the time, no-one knew precisely when the war would end or how.[2] Yet for some months, Leyland Motors, like many others, had been preparing. For the Spurrier family who controlled Leyland Motors, the key to exploiting a post-war future was capital. Moving the company's registered office was their first step towards a share issue to raise the funds they would need to realise their ambitions.

Throughout the war, the government's controls had virtually eliminated the flotation of shares and securities other than those intended to advance the war effort so that by the summer of 1918, there was a pent-up demand to make new capital issues. The motives behind the demand varied. Some companies wanted to re-finance development that had taken place during the war. Some companies needed capital to seize the opportunity to apply technologies proved during the war. Some family shareholders wanted to dispose of their holdings. Others wanted to use a flotation to realise accumulated profits without incurring Income Tax or Super-Tax.[3]

Many business owners knew that peacetime would bring challenges as well as opportunities (Dewey, 1997, pages 85–104). For the cotton and textile industries, meeting wartime demand had involved forsaking traditional markets overseas which would have to be won back in peacetime (Daniel and Jewkes, 1928, page 38; Sandberg, 1974, pages 185–187). For the jute industry, during the war, to meet the forces' insatiable need for canvas the government had met all the costs of production, however much they rose: a safety net that was bound to be removed in peacetime (Walker, 1979). Exporting industries, such as coal-mining (Supple, 1987, pages 174–175) and ship-building (Jones, 1957, pages 50, 64), depended upon a recovery in world trade but knew that this would depend on the ability of other countries to revert speedily from wartime conditions. Yet other industries were nervous of competition in the form of cheap products suddenly available for importation from former enemy countries.[4] The problems were many, but there was no assurance that the wisdom would be found to resolve them (Billings and Oats, 2014, page 98).

In such circumstances, asset valuations were problematic. Valuing the opportunities would be difficult enough, but their realisation would depend upon businesses overcoming their challenges. It would be difficult for 'insiders' to judge the relative prospects of different industries and businesses. For outsiders, the judgements would prove to be almost impossible.

There were of course warnings in the many reports of the Ministry of Reconstruction and the plethora of committees that it appointed.[5] For example, the Vassar-Smith Committee warned in 1918 that, to achieve the re-establishment of industry on sound lines would require the government to check any undue expansion of credit which would lead to a rise in prices and to take steps to reduce the war-time inflation of credit to normal proportions (*Vassar-Smith report, 1918b*, paragraph 36)

Not only did these warnings foresee the need for a potentially difficult economic adjustment, they suggested that, after the end of hostilities, it would still be necessary to control new share issues and the export of capital to ensure that available capital was directed to essential industries, and not to the support of enterprises of a speculative or unessential character (Vassar-Smith report, 1918b, paragraph 37).

Yet in February 1919, when the government attempted to follow this recommendation by prolonging the wartime control of new issues, the Treasury was obliged to withdraw the regulation ignominiously.[6] Neither the market nor potential investors were in a mood to listen to the warnings of experts. They wanted to return as quickly as possible to share trading as it had been known before the war, and this is what happened:

Table 4.1 Estimated value of dutiable Stock Exchange transactions £m

1913–1914	1914–1915	1915–1916	1916–1917	1917–1918	1918–1919	1919–1920	1920–1921	1921–1922	1922–1923	1923–1924	1924–1925
1,378	808	680	1,104	1,278	2,042	4,828	3,378	2,874	5,026	4,668	5,140

Source: Based on table in Baker and Collins (2003, page 149).

The rushed return to trading resulted from an optimistic desire to realise the commercial opportunities of peace accompanied by a careless disregard for the risk that some industries and businesses would not be able to surmount their challenges. As some recognised, the combination of optimism and careless disregard for risk created the danger of a speculative boom in which investors' inability to value prospects would be exploited (Toms, 2015, pages 3–4). Speaking of the large numbers of people who had been introduced to investment during the war, Arthur Comyns Carr wrote:

> After the war it may be expected that a large number of people who never were investors before will be willing to entrust their savings to commercial companies, but will not be very well equipped to select those which are worthy of their confidence. Simultaneously there will be a large crop of new schemes appealing for public support, mostly bona fide, but offering unique opportunity to the fraudulent and over-sanguine.[7]

The 1919–1920 boom

The speculative boom which Comyns Carr foresaw came to pass. Even the most careful companies were later shown to have raised money based on what proved to have been optimistic valuations.[8] Less scrupulous managements were able to re-finance their companies and create new combines on the basis of wildly exaggerated valuations.[9] They were joined by others such as Ernest Terah Hooley, who saw an opportunity to offer shares in meritless and fraudulent schemes for which he would later be prosecuted.[10]

Thus, in 1919, the Exchange began to return to business as usual, and the cycle of boom and bust which had been evident before the war.

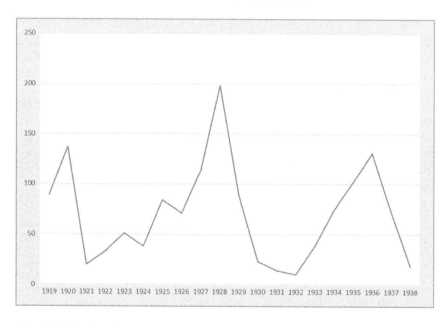

Graph 4.1 Total numbers of IPOs 1919–1938

Source: Based on table in Chambers (2010, page 57). Chambers based his statistics on the *Times Book on Prospectuses*. On many occasions, firms undertook further issues by making offers directly to shareholders without a prospectus. Such issues were therefore not in the source data used by Chambers who also notes that penny shares, or shares with an offer price of two shillings or less, were excluded (Chambers, 2010, page 56).

The total amount of funds raised by IPOs reflected this pattern:

Graph 4.2 Gross proceeds of IPOs 1919–1938 (£m)
Source: Based on table in Chambers (2010, page 57).

The result of this activity was a great increase in the number of domestic industrial and commercial shares dealt on the Exchange. In 1924, there were 726 companies in the manufacturing and distribution sectors of the Official List whereas by 1939 there were 1,712 in the Official and Supplementary Lists combined (Hannah, 1976, page 65; Cheffins, 2008, page 253). Even more strikingly, by 1951, shares quoted on the London Exchange originated from companies which accounted for the lion's share of UK corporate profits.

WH Coates, in evidence to the Colwyn Committee estimated that in the early 1920s about 57% of profits originated in public companies, and by 1951, quoted companies alone accounted for some 71% of profits generated by the corporate sector.[11]

For the faint-hearted private company director, the Exchange was a disturbing place as company directors operated in a laissez-faire environment with almost no formal rules to regulate their behaviour. Some have described the environment as similar to the Wild West (Braggion et al., 2013, page 577).

For shares to be admitted to the Official List, directors had to confirm that no less than two-thirds of any class of shares to be listed had been allotted to members of the public and so found themselves potentially ceding control. To secure a market for new shares, potential investors might be tempted by exaggerated promises which often could not be realised, which led to anger among shareholders and directors losing their position.

As described by Lavington in 1921, the work of selecting profitable new ventures, of capitalising their prospects in terms of securities and of selling those securities to the public, fell mainly on the company promoter. In practice, company promoters appeared in many forms. They might be parent companies engaged in the formation of a subsidiary or allied business enterprise. They might be the vendors of assets purchased by a new company, or financiers whose con-tract with the new company ceases when they have completed its flotation and sold any shares which may have been allotted to them. But whoever they may be, the interests of promoters were distinct from those of the companies they formed. When new companies were floated by promoters, their interest was bound up, not with the ultimate earning power of the venture, but with the difference between the price at which they had bought from the vendors and the price at which they sold to the public (Lavington, 1921, page 21).

Since owners were unlikely to sell their companies to a promoter for less than a reasonable valuation, the promoter's aim was necessarily to sell shares in the business either on the initial offering or in the after-market at a price that exceeded a reasonable valuation.[12] The greater the excess, the greater would be the profit for the promoter and his supporters. To maximise the excess, the promoter would aim to extol asset values, inflate a business's prospects and, if necessary, to engi-neer an active market in the shares (Lavington, 1921, page 214). Ideally, as far as the promoter was concerned, the outcome would be a quick profit.[13] In 1919, the opportunity to do this sprang from the eager enthusiasm of undiscriminating investors. Once the promoter's profit had been achieved, the company would find itself trying to meet the exaggerated expectations that investors had been encour-aged to hold and dealing with the disappointment caused among shareholders by any failure to realise those expectations. Attempts had been made to curb the abuse by augmenting the disclosure required in prospectuses and by extending the liability of directors, but with limited success.[14]

When the shares of Jute Industries Limited, a combine of six Dundee jute mills, were offered to the public in November 1920, the prospectus had warned that the company may not repeat the high levels of profit achieved during the war years.[15] However, this cautious note was not mentioned in the newspaper advertisements which accompanied the offer but for which the directors had not been directly responsible.[16]

At the first Annual General Meeting in March 1922, the directors reported that in the period ended 30 September 1921 trading had been disappointing. There had been a fall in demand from Brazil for yarn for coffee bags because the demand for Brazilian coffee had fallen. Moreover, the company had been surprised by a fall in the price of raw jute that had led to the need to write down stock values. The Chairman suggested, however, that had it not been for the stock write-downs, the year would have been one of the most profitable since 1916. The dismal financial news was repeated in following years as the company suffered from volatile raw jute prices and labour costs that proved beyond its control.

From their comments, shareholders were suspicious about the company's accounts. At the 1922 Annual General Meeting, they complained that there was insufficient information about the subsidiaries from which any trading profit was derived. At the 1924 meeting, shareholders again complained about the lack of trading information and asked whether the subsidiaries had made enough money to pay a dividend. At the 1925 meeting, shareholders alleged that the directors were holding back profits in the subsidiaries to depress the share price to enable family interests to buy back their shares at a heavily discounted price. Unfortunately, the shareholders' anger was aggravated by the chairman commenting that in view of the high coupon attached to the preference shares investors should have known that the issues had been somewhat speculative.[17] In 1926, the directors responded by publishing consolidated accounts, revealing that in the year 1925–1926, the group had lost £788,255 and that profits had not been held back in the subsidiaries' accounts.[18] At the 1926 Annual General Meeting, for the first time, the need for a capital reconstruction was discussed.[19]

When in 1928, the directors published proposals for a reconstruction it involved reduction of the preference share capital as well as the ordinary share capital for the losses exceeded the ordinary share capital.[20] When the capital reduction scheme was eventually submitted to the court for approval, the company's barrister acknowledged that the company's holdings in the formerly family-owned mill companies had been acquired at prices that in retrospect had proved to be excessive. The capital reduction had become inevitable because of depreciation in the value of investments.[21]

The values of the group's fixed assets reflected in the 1920 prospectus were all based on the notional cost of replacing the mills rather than their historical cost.[22] Despite the current trading difficulty, no consideration was given to whether it was realistic to assume that the existing mills would all be replaced.[23] In short, capital had been raised on the basis of inflated values which bore little relation to a cautious view of the jute industry's future prospects. It can be little wonder that shareholders distrusted the directors, most of whom had been owners of the mills that Jute Industries had acquired, and that to dispel misunderstanding, the company was forced to become one of the first in the country to publish group accounts, two decades before this became a legal obligation (Edwards and Webb, 1984, pages 49–54).

Other companies suffered a similar experience. After its re-flotation in 1919, Leyland Motors' performance failed to meet expectations because of unexpected problems and management mistakes. In the recession, which began in 1920, lorry sales were undermined by the government's sale of second-hand lorries in France. The company decided to buy the government's surplus lorries to avoid the reputation of its new vehicles being damaged by complaints about poorly maintained vehicles, but it took many years to recoup the cost of buying and refurbishing them (Turner, 1971, page 18 et seq).

As the arrears of dividends payable on the preference shares grew, shareholders became irritated and, when the company proposed to reduce the share capital, refused to approve the proposal even though this would have enabled the company to start paying dividends again. Some of the shareholders no longer had faith in the directors and suspected that the terms of the capital reduction scheme had been designed to favour members of the Spurrier family. As the shareholders withheld their approval, there was no choice for ordinary shareholders but to wait for their dividends until the company had earned sufficient profit to pay the preference share dividend arrears.

Shareholders in the Rover Company went further. In April 1928, an aggrieved shareholder, Herman Jennings, circularised Rover shareholders asking them for support in requisitioning an Extraordinary General Meeting to set up a committee with the power to appoint the managing director, directors and works manager. In response, the chairman of the board resigned and the remaining directors avoided the proposed meeting by inviting Jennings and the largest shareholder, Sudbury, to join the board, with Sudbury becoming chairman. Within a month, responsibility for management had been re-allocated. Poor results had provided a spur for activism as by 1928, shareholders had endured several years of disappointing returns.

Moreover, the poor returns for shareholders occurred in years when Rover achieved no growth in vehicle sales although rival companies were achieving substantial growth.

These three companies all suffered from creating expectations that could not be met. Whether the failure to satisfy expectations occurred because there had been flagrant exaggeration (in the case of Jute Industries) or misplaced optimism (in the case of Leyland Motors or Rover), the result was that shareholders had become suspicious of the directors. In extreme cases, directors had lost their position. Flotation had exposed companies and their directors to volatility and instability.

Table 4.2 Rover Company return on capital

1919	1920	1921	1922	1923	1924	1925	1926	1927
42.7%	14.6%	9.7%	214.0%	−3.5%	1.5%	−12.1%	−11.7%	−7.4%

Source: Foreman-Peck (1981, page 192). Profits are stated net of depreciation and taxes. Capital is paid up equity capital.

Table 4.3 Rover vehicle sales compared with vehicles produced by Austin and Morris

Year	Rover Vehicle sales	Austin Vehicles produced	Morris Vehicles produced
1920	1,389	–	1,932
1921	4,430	–	3,076
1922	6,291	1,787	6,956
1923	5,193	2,409	20,048
1924	6,792	4,800	32,918
1925	5,694	8,024	55,582
1926	5,433	13,174	48,330
1927	4,460	21,671	61,632

Source: Foreman-Peck (1981, page 194).

Why were the drawbacks ignored?

That the evident drawbacks of financing a business by means of selling shares through the Exchange did not prevent the rise of the domestic manufacturing and distribution sector of the market reflects the increasing attractiveness of Exchange financing relative to other sources of finance.

Traditionally, a considerable proportion of businesses financed development from retained profits (Thomas, 1978, page 6; Cottrell, 1980, page 248). Research carried out for the Colwyn Committee into a sample of businesses in 1912 found that out of trading profits amounting to approximately £312 million, companies put £96 million to reserve after tax and, of that amount, £48.4 million related to the manufacturing sector. Lavington agreed that a large amount of the capital required by British was provided internally or by private negotiation (Lavington, 1921, page 203).

Arnold quotes indices prepared by Feinstein (1972), Stamp (1932), Parkinson (1938) and Hart based on Inland Revenue data which suggest that after the war, on an inflation-adjusted basis, corporate profits fell to 80% of the level achieved in 1913 (Table 4.2 in Arnold, 1999, page 52). To confirm these indices, Arnold used a sample of 30 companies in several sectors, taking information from their published accounts and internal accounting records. Arnold calculated profitability in terms of the return on capital employed, and the returns to equity shareholders both before and after taxation, subjecting these calculated figures to adjustment on an overall basis to indicate the effect of inflation. These calculations also show a decline in the level of corporate profitability after the end of the war.

Arnold goes on to show that the effect of this decline in profitability on profit retentions was especially severe because of increases in the proportion of companies' value added taken by wages and equity shareholders.

Table 4.4 Profitability and gearing 1910–1924

Year	At current prices				Adjusted for inflation	
	Return on capital employed (%)	Gearing (%)	Pre-tax return (%)	Post-tax return on equity (%)	Return on capital employed (%)	Post-tax return on equity (%)
1910	8.44	47.33	9.89	8.76	10.43	9.88
1919	15.82	34.59	21.89	13.13	11.10	5.83
1920	13.80	33.02	17.81	10.71	9.14	3.96
1921	6.83	38.12	7.25	5.12	4.87	2.11
1922	5.46	37.11	5.93	5.15	3.91	2.53
1923	5.99	37.55	6.55	7.10	4.02	3.80
1924	6.90	37.10	7.93	7.29	4.87	3.95

Source: Based on Table 4.3 in Arnold (1999, page 58)

Table 4.5 Value added at constant prices

Year	Total value added (mean) £,000	Proportions of total value added taken up by:				
		Wages (mean) (%)	Profit taxes (mean) (%)	Fixed interest security holders (mean) (%)	Equity shareholders (mean) (%)	Company retentions (mean) (%)
1910	452.32	40.41	0.47	21.53	17.08	20.51
1919	876.59	48.05	18.41	12.35	17.36	3.83
1920	1,085.71	60.99	8.47	13.12	21.92	−4.50
1921	1,200.93	55.65	5.26	17.27	24.34	−2.52
1922	638.16	55.83	4.96	18.03	21.72	−0.54
1923	905.31	51.22	−2.14	21.38	26.24	3.30
1924	881.41	52.41	0.33	18.39	21.94	6.94

Source: Based on Table 4.5 in Arnold (1999, page 64).

Arnold's calculations suggest that once Excess Profit Duty had been reduced in 1919 and then repealed a year later (Daunton, 2002, page 90), companies would have struggled to maintain profit retentions. It is not surprising that companies sought to maintain distributions by way of dividend in view of the evidence that disappointing dividends encouraged shareholder activism and disputes with shareholders, but the consequence was that companies did not accumulate capital as they had done before the war (Hart, 1965, pages 118, 128; Thomas, 1978, pages 88, 94; Broadberry, 1988, page 26; Daunton, 2002, page 85; Cheffins, 2008, page 254 et seq.). Companies which proposed to continue investment for whatever reason were obliged to look elsewhere for finance.

There is no study of corporate profits for the period after 1924 to 1945, adopting Arnold's approach. However, a study based on a larger sample of companies but using published information rather than internal accounting records suggested that most companies were earning smaller profits in the early 1930s (Hope, 1949, page 164).

It goes on to suggest that profit retentions were also lower.[24]

Arnold's calculations also suggest that family shareholders in a company that they owned entirely would have found continued ownership more burdensome. To retain ownership of a business that continued to thrive, the family would have been obliged to sacrifice their dividends so that profits could be retained in the business to finance investment. In the following table, the figures in Arnold's tables are re-stated to show the profit that might have been available for distribution by dividend to sustain retentions at the pre-war level.

In short, the added value available to be distributed to the family shareholders would have been substantially reduced between 1919 and 1923 and, in 1920, if investment were to be maintained, the shareholders would have been obliged to contribute more capital unless the company itself borrowed more. This suggests

Table 4.6 Value added available for dividends

Year	Value added (mean) £,000	Value added net of wages, profit taxes, fixed interest holders (%)	Less: retention (%)	Value added available for dividend (%)	Value added available for dividend (£,000)
	(a)	(b)	(c)	(b)–(c)	(a)×((b)–(c))
1910	452.32	37.59	–20.51	17.08	77
1919	876.59	21.19	–20.51	0.68	6
1920	1,085.71	17.42	–20.51	–3.09	–34
1921	1,200.93	21.82	–20.51	1.31	16
1922	638.16	18.18	–20.51	0.67	4
1923	905.31	29.54	–20.51	9.03	82
1924	881.41	28.87	–20.51	8.36	74

Source: Assumes that the level of profit retention in 1910 would apply in each of the post-war years and that the proportion of value added paid to fixed interest security holders as shown in Arnold's table would have applied in the family-owned company, i.e. the gearing would have been the same.

that the family might have received a better return on its assets if they had been invested in other ways and would have justified asking whether the family company interest should be sold or diluted.[25] This would be particularly attractive if the family were prepared to invest the proceeds of a sale in an asset which did not attract a liability to United Kingdom Income or Super-Tax or left the jurisdiction.[26]

Faced with demands to finance corporate investment which were too great for a family to bear could lead either to divestment or dilution of the family's interest by means of share issues through the Exchange. GEC is an example of a company whose capital investment plans were beyond the scope of the family which originally owned the company, a constraint that was released by raising capital by capital issues. Planning had started well before the end of the 1914–1918 war and led to an ambitious peace programme. GEC's growth had been organic involving the gradual addition of new selling branches, factories and products. But GEC took the view that war had speeded up the development of the international electrical companies of all countries and the company embarked on a series of takeovers. Apart from Chamberlain and Hookham[27] and the outside shares in various associated companies, the main takeover was of Fraser and Chalmers of Erith for some £600,000 in 1918. (Jones and Marriott, 1970, page 83)

By 1918, GEC had issued ordinary shares, preference shares and debentures amounting to £1,500,000. Within four years, that total had risen to £8,900,000.

Families might also divest or dilute their interests where the business was too small to take advantage of economies of scale. Drapery Trust's creation in 1925 followed recognition of the economies of scale within retailing by RP Gaze, the managing director of Marshalls Limited, a group of department stores outside London which had been sold by Debenhams in 1917.[28] He realised that by copying Gordon Selfridge's initiatives to create larger groups of department stores, advantage could be taken of the economies of scale by improved selling, marketing, staff management and financial control. To realise this potential, in 1925 Clarence Hatry[29] created a new holding company, Drapery & General Investment Trust, of which Gaze became managing director. In the next two years, a group was formed by acquiring family-owned provincial stores, each purchase being financed by a public offer of shares. By 1928, the Drapery Trust group comprised 65 stores with 11,000 employees recording 18 million transactions each year. Eventually, Drapery Trust was itself acquired by Debenhams which brought together the London stores owned by Debenhams with the provincial stores owned by Drapery Trust (Corina, 1978, page 100). In this process, many formerly family-owned companies had been brought together to form a single combine to achieve higher profitability than could be achieved had they remained independent units. Simultaneously, many other family owned department stores were being acquired by competing groups: United Drapery Stores, formed by Sir Arthur Wheeler, and Selfridge's Provincial Stores, formed by Gordon Selfridge (Corina, 1978, pages 93–94).

Debenhams also provides an example of this process, although rather more abruptly. After Debenhams acquired Drapery Trust in November 1927, a new holding company, Debenham Securities Limited was created to acquire the former companies and to restructure their share capital. One of the consequences of this deal was that Ernest Debenham, the sole remaining representative of the Debenham family, ceased to be a director, somewhat to his surprise. He subsequently remarked that until a month before the transaction, he had hoped that the connection between his family and the business would be prolonged.[30]

Whatever Ernest Debenham's motives might have been, the effect of his withdrawal was to leave management in the hands of FH Richmond, who became Chairman, and GM Wright who exercised financial control and took responsibility for reorganising the newly enlarged group to realise the economies of scale were available.

Apart from business-related incentives to sell or dilute their interests in family companies, families also responded to incentives created by the tax system. By the end of the 1914–1918 war, rates of Income Tax and Super-Tax had been increased substantially and it became apparent that the rates would not fall. (Daunton, 2002, pages 98–102, 133)

At first, incorporation of previously unincorporated family businesses provided some measure of protection against the higher rates since the profits of a company would not be treated as income of shareholders unless and until the profits were distributed by way of dividend. Thus, shareholders could limit their liability to Income Tax and Super-Tax shareholders by agreeing that profits should not be distributed but retained within the company. In 1922, the government introduced rules to limit the tax effectiveness of profit retention by providing that, for the purposes of Super-Tax, a taxpayer's income could be increased from the amount of any dividends actually received from a family company to 'a reasonable part' of the company's 'actual income'.[31] This provision applied to any company which was under the control of not more than five persons and was not either a subsidiary company or a company in which the public was substantially interested (i.e. a company which was quoted in the official list of a United Kingdom stock exchange in whose shares dealings had taken place during the relevant period and in which the public held more than 25%).[32]

That this provision drove some shareholders to contemplate dilution of their interest in a family company is demonstrated by the example of William Morris (later Lord Nuffield). He had financed the development of Morris Motors by retaining substantially all of the profits. The Inland Revenue twice sought declarations that the company had not distributed a reasonable proportion of its profits. Whilst the Revenue's applications were not accepted by the Special Commissioners, William Morris came to believe that retaining substantially all the profits would not be possible if he continued to hold all of the ordinary shares and, as a result, he began in 1936 to reduce his holding.[33]

Similar encouragement towards seeking a listing for shares was provided in 1930 by a change in the law on estate duty which provided that if a company's shares were traded on a recognised exchange and there was regular dealing, the shares would be valued for estate duty purposes by reference to the stock market price during the year prior to death.[34] Otherwise, the shares would be valued by estimating the company's net assets and allocating to the deceased's estate a proportion of that value equal to the deceased's percentage shareholding at the time of death. In most circumstances, the stock market basis would be preferred because it was not subject to the vagaries of Inland Revenue officials' experience. But the stock market price would be advantageous as it would incorporate a minority discount especially if a company was under the control of a block as would often be the case with a company that was formerly family-owned.

Alternative sources of finance

Families deciding to dilute their interests in family companies were faced with a small number of choices. The clearing banks were not enthusiastic providers of long-term loans to industrial and commercial businesses which might prove difficult to recover and tended to price themselves out of this market (Lavington, 1921, page 145; Cottrell, 1980, pages 57–58). In any event, in the immediate aftermath of the 1914–1918 war, the clearing banks preferred to finance other entities to engineer changes in financing or ownership.[35]

Private sale of a substantial block of shares risked limiting the value to a family of control of a company by introducing a third party who might look askance at the benefits families gained through ownership. These benefits could be considerable as shown by the service agreements between Agricultural Industries Limited and the directors of its principal operating subsidiaries (the former owners) who, apart from being assured of their positions for at least ten years at pre-arranged remuneration, were to be provided with rent-free residences, free shooting rights and the free use of cars. The companies had to maintain the properties in good and substantial repair and were responsible for the payment of rates, taxes, insurance and outgoings.[36]

Moreover, there might be considerable social prestige attached to being directors of a substantial local enterprise such as Jute Industries Limited which, in the 1920s, was the largest employer in Dundee.[37]

Thus, if financing through the Exchange were to provide a means of prolonging these private advantages it could be attractive provided that the drawbacks could be managed.

How were the drawbacks reduced?

Even so, in spite of these incentives to dispose of or dilute an interest, it is unlikely that directors and shareholders in family-owned companies would have been attracted to raising finance by way of the Exchange unless the drawbacks had been reduced.

That the number of quoted domestic manufacturing and commercial shares increased so markedly between the wars suggests that the drawbacks to quotation were indeed reduced or at least that the fear of them was reduced.

In part, the fear of the drawbacks was based on ignorance of their practical effect. Whilst the rules for inclusion in the Official List included a requirement that at least two-thirds of a class of share to be listed should be allotted to the public, there was no requirement that all a company's share classes should be listed or that they should all have equivalent voting rights. It was therefore possible by judicious design of a company's share structure to preserve voting control in the hands of one group of shareholders whilst selling countless shares to others. Moreover, the rules governing applications for 'permission to deal' (i.e. admission to the Supplementary List) did not include a 'two-thirds' requirement.[38]

Some companies preferred to avoid complicating their capital structure because some commentators were suspicious and critical of 'management' and 'deferred' shares, in which case similar objectives could be achieved by interlocking or overlapping shareholdings. This was a device used by Clarence Hatry in obscuring interests in companies he created and, later, Florence identified six instances in which the largest shareholder was another company with a holding in excess of 20%.[39]

In any case, investors tended to be passive so that the owner of a block of shares would be confronted not by a united body of other shareholders capable of common action, but by a number of scattered individuals unlikely to attempt to interfere with the operation of the company. In practice, a 30% holding might be enough to ensure absolute control (Cole, 1935, pages 85–85; Hannah, 1976, pages 67–68).

In practice, directors were able to assume that shareholders would be quiescent unless a problem arose which excited their attention and galvanised them to oppose the directors, such as a failure to declare dividends at the levels shareholders had come to expect as occurred in Jute Industries, Leyland Motors, Rover and others (Samuel, 1933, page 6).

Concentration on dividend declarations had practical advantages for shareholders. It was a common practice for shareholders to manage their risks by holding numbers of relatively small holdings (Cole, 1935, page 92), so that it was unlikely that shareholders would be able to spend much time analysing the earnings of potential of each company in which they were interested, even if adequate information were available from prospectuses and annual accounts to permit such an analysis, which it was not:

> Paying attention to companies' dividend declarations, and to any reduction in dividends[40] provided shareholders with a convenient surrogate for detailed analysis of earnings potential. The result was that shareholders tended to be apathetic provided that dividends were paid. Conversely, when a company found itself unable to continue to maintain dividend payments, shareholders would become "panicky".
>
> (Jenkinson, 1928, page 27)

There was some practical wisdom in this. The incentives created by the tax system and the desire to avoid shareholder activism provided motives for directors to plan that their companies should be able to maintain dividends from year to year. Any proposal to reduce a dividend which could not readily be attributed to an external factor such as the inception of a war would indicate not only that the directors' plans had failed, but also that the failure was more serious than a temporary setback which could be managed within the company's resources. Moreover, a generous dividend policy that was not supported by the necessary cash flow would lead to an early appeal to the capital market and to serious difficulty if attempts to raise capital were to fail (Cheffins, 2006, page 1322).

From the shareholders' point of view, quite apart from the usefulness of dividend declarations as a signalling mechanism, a continuing commitment by directors to sustain dividend payments limited its ability to finance the business from retained earnings. In turn, this meant that the company was more likely to return to the capital market (Samuel, 1933, pages 145–146). Directors who expected to be subjected to the scrutiny involved when raising capital were more likely to be disciplined in managing the business.

For directors, it became an imperative that annual dividend declarations should be managed to achieve consistency from year to year and that annual accounts should be managed to allow that to happen (Baynes, 1966, page 84; pages 135–136; Arnold and Matthews, 2002, page 7; Edwards, 1989, pages 138–140; Napier, 1991).

Sir Mark Webster Jenkinson, a Chartered Accountant who spent most of his career working in engineering companies, explained why a smoothed annual profitability was desirable and how it was achieved. In his view, shareholders would always be asking for more, no matter how large the dividend already was. Consequently, the directors knew that if large profits were disclosed, a large dividend will be demanded. By creating a secret reserve the directors were, however, enabled to make the fat years pay for the lean years, in which they could draw upon the accumulated surplus without the shareholders being aware that the divisible profits had not all been earned in that particular year (Jenkinson, 1928, page 15).

Jenkinson was campaigning to improve the quality of annual accounts, yet, remarkably, he believed that the creation of secret reserves to smooth dividend declarations was acceptable, even though it necessarily involved inaccurate reporting of annual profits.[41] In this Jenkinson was supported by the leaders of the major practising firms but also by large numbers of public companies. Anecdotally, this is evident in cases such as the Royal Mail Steam Packet Company which 'smoothed' its profits for a number of years by releasing funds from secret reserves until there was no longer a secret reserve that could be used (Samuel, 1933, page 7).[42] Although the case ended in a trial, it was not the practice of smoothing which was impugned, or the existence of secret reserves, but the alleged failure to obscure from shareholders that any transfers were being made. (Brooks, 1933, page xxv)

As directors learned to use their control of annual accounts to eliminate fluctuations in dividend declarations, so they became intolerant of the traditional new issues process by which promoters and their syndicates sought to profit from flotations often without any thought for a business's long-term health. Gradually, this led some existing houses to develop a new issues business (Japhet, 1931, page 122) and to the creation of new houses with the financial support to provide assurance of stability and the sustained relationships that both investors and vendors increasingly sought.

In 1921, this led to the formation of Cull & Company by four ex-partners in a jobbing firm specialising in oil shares who had made a fortune shortly before the war when Burmah Oil was introduced to the Stock Exchange.[43] With a background in oil, this new house was quickly involved in sponsoring an issue of preference shares for Mexican Eagle[44] and in facilitating a £5.7 million sale by Royal Dutch of a portion of its holding in Shell Transport & Trading.[45] This was followed in 1922 by the creation of Power Securities Corporation which was formed by the utility engineering company, Balfour Beatty, with the support of British Thomson-Houston and which, like Cull & Company, became another client of Cazenove.[46] This company was to specialise in new issues for electricity supply undertakings such as Lancashire Electric Light & Power Company Limited.[47]

In succeeding years, a series of new creations followed: Gresham Trust in 1924, Charterhouse Investment Trust in 1925, Quadrant Trust in 1927[48] and Dawnay Day in 1928.[49]

Charterhouse's creation was a project conceived by Sir Arthur Wheeler, Harry Clifford-Turner, a solicitor, and Nutcombe Hume, who had together been involved in Gresham Trust, an issuing house founded by Wheeler in 1924 to sponsor small issues (Kinross, 1982, page 37). Hume had joined Wheeler in 1921 from Clare & Company,[50] having been introduced by Clifford-Turner who acted as legal adviser to both Clare & Company and Wheeler (Dennett, 1979, page 15).

The new trust's prospectus was published on 12 November 1925, and its first new issue was announced on 23 February 1926: a company called International Pulp and Chemical Company Limited which was formed to acquire the share capital of Koholyt, a company based in Koenigsberg which produced chemical pulp for use in paper manufacture. Charterhouse was to be responsible for four new issues in 1926, five in 1927 and a further five in 1928 (*Issuing Houses Yearbook*, 1929).

When the first edition of the *Issuing Houses Yearbook* was published in 1929, it listed 94 houses that had been responsible for new issues between 1926 and 1929:[51] a list that was remarkable for the fact that it was headed by Charterhouse Investment Trust, a house that had been formed as recently as 1925.

As the underlying source for the table excludes bond issues by home and overseas governments and public sector bodies, it understates the role of issuing houses such as Barings Brothers, NM Rothschild and Schroders which specialised in such issues.

For the new businesses, the quality of the issues sponsored was critical. Shareholders would not have welcomed losses any more than a promoter's supporters

Table 4.7 Top ten issuing houses ranked by total amount subscribed for issues in 1928

	Year of formation (per yearbook)	Number of issues	Total amount subscribed £	% age of total of all issues	Average amount subscribed £
Charterhouse Investment Trust	1925	6	7,867,500	6.7	1,311,250
British Foreign & Continental	1910	3	7,567,000	6.4	2,522,333
Barings Brothers	–	1	3,840,000	3.3	3,840,000
Scottish Finance	1926	13	2,912,775	2.5	224,060
Standard Industrial Trust	1920	6	2,755,000	2.4	459,167
Lothbury Investment Trust	1919	3	2,300,000	2.0	766,667
London & Yorkshire Trust	1919	5	2,233,500	1.9	446,700
French British & Foreign Trust	1924	13	2,232,500	1.9	173,269
Helbert Wagg	1919	3	2,165,000	1.8	721,667
Eastern Rubber Growers	1926	1	2,080,000	1.7	2,080,000
		54	35,973,275	30.6	666,172
Other issues		234	80,830,432	69.4	345,429
TOTALS		288	116,803,707	100.0	405,568

Source: The table is based on the list of issues included in Anonymous (1931). The list included only corporate issues and thus excludes bond issues for home and overseas governments and public sector bond issues. In respect of each issue, the list takes account of the first-named issuing house recorded in the *Issuing Houses Yearbook* (1929).

but were more likely to be long-term rather than short-term holders. They were also likely to be more risk-averse, having decided that investment through an intermediary was more attractive than investing directly through the Exchange. Moreover, it was more difficult to withdraw all profits instantly, protecting them by transfer to a wife. In short, investment trusts tended to be conservative in their choice of investments. In Charterhouse's early years, Nutcombe Hume's training in the City led them to turn down any proposal that was not totally sound. The background of a company for which Charterhouse made an issue or in which it intended to invest was always explored in detail. When the downward slide began, Charterhouse did not find itself committed to businesses that were likely to fail (Dennett, 1979, page 36).

This approach was attractive both to vendors discouraged by the disastrous experience of company promoters during the 1920–1921 stock market collapse, but also to prospective investors for in time it would lead to a reputation for prudent decision-making.

The development of these new houses was accompanied by the demise of the old-style company promoters. Although Clarence Hatry's business survived this collapse, his experience demonstrates why 1920 was so catastrophic for promoters. The problem lay in the share trading in which all promoters indulged to support the prices of the shares they sponsored and to provide some assurance to small investors that there would be a market in the stock offered for sale. As Sir Robert Kindersley, a director of Lazards, later told the Macmillan Committee:

> the average investor today does not like anything without a market, and you cannot possibly have a market with £50,000 of stock or £100,000 of stock for that matter, there is bound to be no market in stock and it is very difficult of negotiation in consequence.[52]

To ensure that there was an active market, promoters were prepared to support applications for shares and to buy shares in a falling market to sustain the price. They would in any event hold parcels of shares themselves so that they could benefit from any increase in the price of a share after issue.

In these endeavours, Hatry had for some years been assisted by Gerard Lee Bevan, the senior partner of Ellis & Company, Hatry's principal stockbroker, and Chairman of City Equitable Fire Insurance Limited (CEFI), which Hatry had sold to him in 1915. Bevan controlled personally the investment decisions of both of these concerns[53] and used his authority to support Hatry's new issues. Thus, when Jute Industries Limited was floated on Armistice Day 1920, Ellis & Company issued a guarantee to certain directors that within a short period after the flotation it would buy any equity shares for which they applied on flotation.[54] The effect of these applications was that the company was able to announce that the issue had been substantially subscribed, although underwriters were left to take up 30% of the shares offered for sale.[55]

The unfortunate consequence was that, as share prices fell in 1920, both Ellis & Company and CEFI were left with substantial holdings of shares that fell substantially in value, exposing the bank loans that had been raised to finance the holdings. As the loss in value threatened the stability of both firms (and thus a complete collapse in the market price of Hatry issues), Hatry involved himself in attempts to save both of them. In 1921, he contributed to a scheme by which CEFI floated a new company, City Equitable Associated Interests Limited, which acquired three smaller insurance companies whose investment funds were immediately amalgamated with those of CEFI.[56] This somewhat desperate ruse failed because the market continued to fall. As a result, both Ellis & Company and CEFI became insolvent and were liquidated. Hatry then sought to buy holdings from the liquidators to avoid open market disposals that would undermine further the value of holdings in the hands of his own company, Commercial Bank of London Limited (CBL).[57] This approach also failed and led to the liquidation of CBL although, on the basis of assurances given by Hatry about the prices at which shareholdings would be realised, the liquidation took the form of a Members' Voluntary Winding Up which assumed that the company was solvent. These assurances proved difficult to make good when the liquidator came to realise the remaining assets.[58]

Hatry was thus faced with a commercial disaster for he risked having to dishonour a promise to his supporters that they would not suffer a loss through the liquidation of CBL and the possibility that, having dishonoured his promise, he would be obliged to cease his business activities. He was saved from this prospect by good fortune: an introduction to Arthur Collins.[59]

Collins was an exceptional combination of entrepreneur and local government accountant. He had been a prize winner in the first competitive examinations of the Institute of Municipal Treasurers and Accountants (IMTA), a young Treasurer of the City of Birmingham and also a young President of his Institute. Before the war, Collins had travelled widely lecturing on local government financial management and had seen an opportunity to advise local authorities on long-term planning and the raising of loans. During his year as President, he resigned as City Treasurer of Birmingham, and at the end of his year established the Municipal Loans Bureau which by using the connections he had made through the Institute developed a business advising local authorities on how to raise money.[60] By 1925, his attempts to reduce the cost to local authorities of raising new loans through the money market had come to nothing, having been opposed by three firms of brokers[61] which dominated the market and were able to dictate the terms that local authorities were obliged to accept. Frustrated by his failure, Collins was still seeking a way of breaking this impasse.

For Hatry, the introduction to Collins must have seemed like an answer to a prayer. Hatry was able to combine Collins' expertise and connections with his own market skills to break the stranglehold of the three incumbent brokers. This opened the way to a new business that offered the prospect of considerable profits, not least because at this time, local authorities were more interested in raising new loans than private businesses were interested in new issues. Hatry incorporated a new company, Corporation & General Securities, to undertake this business and offered shares in the new company to the former shareholders in CBL, discharging his promise to them that they would not lose as a result of the collapse of CBL.

Hatry was able to survive the collapse of 1920, but the effort this required serves to explain why many promoters did not survive. The company promoters' business model had run its course and was not to survive the 1929 crash for its fundamental weakness had been exposed.

Company promoters had long depended upon the willingness of people and institutions to join syndicates to finance their promotions, in effect using short-term money to buy companies that were then immediately to be sold by some form of public offer. It was of the essence that syndicate members should be able to realise their interest in the promotion as quickly as possible, probably at a substantial profit, but at least without too great a risk of loss. For example, the agreement covering the formation of the Preliminary Steel Syndicate in April 1929 specified that the syndicate should be closed within six months. In practice, this meant that the syndicate should be closed within a relatively short time after the projected issue of shares.[62]

In return for acting as ringmasters for syndicates and vendors, the company promoters were able to take substantial profits for themselves. Both syndicate members and vendors must have realised that this was happening and must also have been prepared to tolerate it for so long as their own commercial ambitions were realised. Jute Industries Limited provides a transparent example of this. Having decided to realise their equity, the mill owners approached Hatry with a view to his floating their companies (Grimond, 1979, page 24; Pearson, 1961, page 112); presumably they expected to realise a price that reflected their view of their entity's value whilst allowing an appropriate fee for Hatry. He realised a substantial profit which was justified by valuing the mills at replacement cost: a value which the mill owners obviously thought could not be justified by their private expectations of future profit.

When market conditions militated against the realisation of a substantial profit by immediate sale, there was risk of substantial loss. Company promoters were certainly aware of that risk and protected themselves by extracting profits as they were made and giving them to their wives, where they could be protected under the Married Women's Property Acts.[63] Hatry's wife, Dolly, was certainly used in this way, as is attested by the memoirs of the family of his former insurance broking partner, Deighton Patmore (Patmore, 1968, page 2); her ownership of the Hatry stud at Alfriston;[64] and the fact that she made substantial profits from share trading during Hatry's imprisonment in the 1930s and in part financed his purchase of Hatchards after his release from prison.[65]

But however readily promoters could protect their own profits, to continue in business their financial supporters also had to be confident of profits.

This is the significance of Hatry's experience in 1921 and 1922. As the stock market fell in 1920, so it became more difficult to attract investors by public offers. Yet again, the flotation of Jute Industries Limited illustrates this. Hatry's initial supporters would have expected to realise their interest quickly and at a profit, which in Hatry's case was only possible with the support of Gerard Lee Bevan and Ellis & Company's guarantees. For Hatry to remain in business, it was necessary for him to honour promises to his supporters that they would not lose. There is a tendency in some biographical references to Hatry to characterise this honouring of promises as a demonstration of an ethical approach to business (Pearson, 1961, page 137). It was a matter of commercial necessity: a matter of life and death. Promoters could not afford to disappoint their supporters too often.

The result was that the old-style promoters gradually disappeared. Clare & Company withdrew from company promotion after the death of Oliver Clare in 1921. Sperling & Company became deeply involved in ultimately unsuccessful attempts to rescue its ship-building interests from the effects of the slump in demand for new ships. Hooley was obliged to withdraw from company promotion by prosecution arising from the fraudulent promotion of Jubilee Cotton Mills Limited. Hatry survived, partly because by offering shares in a new venture he could claim that syndicate investors had not lost, and partly because his business took a new direction. On the one hand, he managed loan issues for local authorities, and, on the other hand, he concentrated on the formation of combines rather than the speculative issues that had disfigured the 1919–1920 boom.[66]

Even those, such as Frederick Szarvasy, who had been successful and continued as promoters for some time, eventually withdrew to concentrate on other things: in Szarvasy's case, on company rescues.[67]

Conclusion

Notably, the evident changes in the market for new securities occurred largely without regulatory interventions. Although in 1930, the Exchange reformed the rules governing the introduction of new securities, those changes occurred after the rise of new issuing houses and the eclipse of the company promoter. The more aggressive techniques of company promoters were being frozen out by the market's choice and the effect of the reforms was to complete rather than initiate that process.

Notes

1 National Archives, file BT 31/22241/135481.
2 'No one knew how long the war would last. Some of the best-informed journalists were furthest out in their calculations' (Wrench, 1935, page 334).
3 This could be achieved by liquidating an existing company and selling its business to a new company whose shares would be offered for sale. The original company would then be liquidated and its remaining assets distributed by the liquidator to the shareholders. For tax purposes, these distributions would be regarded as capital payments which would not attract tax liabilities in the hands of the recipients. Originally named 'Super-Tax', the name of the tax was subsequently changed to Sur-Tax.
4 Representations from the glass bottle industry reported the threat of imports of cheap bottles from Germany (memoranda submitted to Lord Balfour's committee on Commercial and Industrial Policy, 1918, pages 64–65).
5 In its report published in 1919, the Ministry listed some of the committees which it had appointed and their reports, highlighting the concerns which had been expressed (report of the Ministry, 1919).

6 Regulation 30F.
7 Reservation by AS Comyns Carr to the Wrenbury Committee report, 1918, pages 13–14. Comyns Carr was a barrister who before the war had co-authored a book on National Insurance with Dr Addison, the Minister for Reconstruction. With an introduction from Addison, Carr became a member of the staff of the Ministry supporting several of its committees and becoming a member of the Wrenbury Committee on amendment of company law.
8 Leyland Motors offered shares for sale in 1919 but later proved to have over-estimated the demand for its heavy lorries and buses. Other automotive manufacturers such as Austin and Kommer were caught by similar problems.
9 There was a spate of issues to recapitalise cotton mills valued on the basis of notional replacement cost (Higgins et al., 2015).
10 Jubilee Cotton Mills Limited. Richardson and Richardson (1985, pages 329–332).
11 Colwyn Committee Minutes of Evidence, 1927, QQ 8550–12, NIESR, 1949–1953, pages 7–8. Hannah warns that not all public companies were quoted (Hannah, 1976, page 65).
12 This might, for example, be achieved by exaggerating the book value of the business's assets (e.g., Jute Industries Limited) or by extracting cash from the business before flotation by way of dividend (e.g., Agricultural Industries Limited in 1919, and Jute Industries Limited in November 1921) (Application for Listing files, Stock Exchange Archive, Guildhall Library).
13 For example, the syndicate agreement relating to Hatry's steel reorganisation scheme in 1929 provided that the syndicate would be terminated within six months of its formation (Winchester, 1934, pages 281–284).
14 Development of the law was reviewed in: Spafford (1921) and Hibbert (1898).
15 *The Times*, 11 November 1920, page 20.
16 *The Times*, 15 November 1920, page 20 (emphasis in original). The advertisements were placed by the issue's promoter, Clarence Hatry, in 93 newspapers (Application for Listing file, Stock Exchange Archive, Guildhall Library). At the time of this issue, the Issues Department in Hatry's organisation was headed by Charles Duguid who had been City Editor of the *Pall Mall Gazette* and the *Daily Mail*, and who, in the latter capacity, had before the war launched the *Daily Mail's* share transfer scheme as an alternative to the Stock Exchange for small investors. Before joining Hatry, he had established a new advertising agency, which was responsible for the advertising campaign which supported the flotation of Jute Industries.
17 *The Times*, 9 February 1925, page 21.
18 Stock Exchange Archive, Guildhall Library.
19 *The Times*, 1 February 1926, page 20.
20 *The Times*, 13 February 1928, page 20.
21 Court report: *The Times*, 7 May 1929, page 5.
22 The archived records of Jute Industries Limited do not include detailed schedules supporting the original valuations. However, they do include a paper which reconciles the valuations in 1929 to the original 1920 balance sheet which strongly suggests that a replacement cost basis was used (Jute Industries Limited papers, Dundee University Archives). Further, the accountants who assisted Hatry with the creation of Jute Industries Limited also assisted with negotiations in 1921 to form a similar combine of esparto paper mills which failed to agree prices at which the mills would be bought. Documents recording the negotiations claimed that in valuing the fixed assets at notional replacement cost, the accountants were following the precedent set by Jute Industries (Tullis Russell papers, Special Collections, St Andrews University).
23 The surviving accounting records of the largest mill acquired by Jute Industries, Cox Brothers Limited, suggest that, at the time of the flotation, the company was trading at a loss which the management was attempting to reduce by reducing the labour force (Jute Industries Limited papers, Dundee University Archives).

24 Hope (1949, page 177). Consistent with Arnold's findings, a number of other studies report that the proportion of companies' net profits distributed by way of dividends was higher (Hart, cited in Thomas, 1978, pages 94 and 96; *The Economist*; May, cited in Bank, 2004, pages 11–12).

25 In many instances, the family might receive other benefits from a family company which would justify retention. Such other benefits might include family members holding management positions, family ownership of properties occupied by the company etc.

26 Cheffins (2007, page 795). Until 1936, a proprietor of a UK family company who sold his interest 'could avoid tax on the income from the proceeds until the company was wound up so long as the foreign company invested in assets not subject to British income tax in the hands of non-residents'. Alternatively, the vendor might opt for exile in a country with a benign tax environment.

27 Manufacturers of electric meters, acquired in 1917.

28 In 1917, Debenhams had acquired Marshall & Snelgrove which consisted of a London store with a number of provincial stores. Following internal disputes, it was Debenhams' policy to limit its operations to London, so the provincial stores owned by Marshall and Snelgrove were then sold to a new company, Marshalls Limited, which was to be quoted on the Exchange (Corina, 1978, pages 77, 99).

29 Hatry was introduced to this opportunity by Stanley Passmore, a solicitor, who beside being the chairman of Marshalls, acted for Hatry in most of his flotations.

30 *The Times* had drawn attention to Ernest Debenham's withdrawal, to which Debenham responded with a letter with an explanation of what had happened (Corina, 1978, page 101).

31 Section 21(1), Finance Act 1922. That these provisions were a serious constraint on business practice is evident from the amendments that quickly became necessary to control tax avoidance. Initially, the determination of what was a reasonable level of distribution was left to the discretion of the Special Commissioners. With effect from 6 April 1928, the discretion was limited to exclude payments under post-war agreements for the redemption of debt or acquisition of businesses and any payments under 'fictitious or artificial transactions' (Section 31(1), Finance Act, 1927; Cheffins, 2006, page 1316).

32 Section 21(6), Finance Act 1922.

33 From 99.9% in 1936 to 18.8% in 1951 (Florence, 1961, page 211; Andrews and Brunner, 1955, page 174 et seq.).

34 Finance Act 1930, section 37.

35 SS Hammersley, *The Times*, 29 December 1928. Quoted by Cottrell, 1992 page 56. This competition is redolent of the competition between Lloyds Bank Limited and Westminster Bank Limited in the late 1920s over loan proposals from Clarence Hatry (Fanning, 1985, pages 110–114) (Lloyds Bank Archives).

36 Agricultural Industries Limited was formed in 1919 as a vehicle for floating the agricultural interests of the Dennis family which included extensive farm properties in Lincolnshire. None of the leading members of the Dennis family became directors of Agricultural Industries Limited, but remained directors and, in effect, controllers of the principal operating subsidiaries. Agricultural Industries Limited was floated on 1 November 1919 (Board of Trade Inspector's report dated 5 June 1950, pages 10–11, unpublished, private source).

37 The service agreements for the directors of Jute Industries Limited provided security of tenure for three years (rather than ten years in the case of Agricultural Industries) and the private benefits were more limited: free electricity was to be provided, as before flotation, to their private residences (Jute Industries papers, Dundee University Archives).

38 Cheffins et al., 2013, page 686. The limited practical effect of these requirements is demonstrated by a study suggesting that there is little evidence of diffusion of ownership during the 1920s and 1930s (Franks et al., 2009, page 4035).

39 Florence, 1961, pages 196–217. Samuel analysed the conflicts of interest created by interlocking directorates and shareholdings (Samuel, 1933, pages 171–194).

40 Courtaulds' announcement in 1926 of a reduction in its interim dividend provides an example of a reaction to a single dividend reduction (*The Times*, 9 July 1926). *The Economist* also commented on the reduction that it 'set in train a good deal of uneasiness among holders of shares of other industrial companies. People who had been running after the industrials, and buying the shares more on tips than on sound reasons become suddenly frightened.' (*The Economist*, 24 July 1926, page 151.)

41 'We should oppose hidden reserves put aside for purposes other than the equalisation of dividends or contingencies' (Jenkinson, 1928, page 16). Jenkinson was not alone in this view of secret reserves (Edwards, 1979, page 290; Kitchen, 1979, pages 112–113).

42 Samuel (1933, page 7).

43 *The Times*, 3 October 1921, page 17.

44 *The Times*, 3 May 1922, page 20.

45 *The Times*, 13 June 1922, page 15.

46 *The Times*, 20 October 1922, page 18; Kynaston (1991, pages 103–104).

47 *The Times*, 2 February 1923, page 16.

48 Formed by Phillip Hill, this was to lead to the formation of Phillip Hill & Partners a few years later. In 1928, the company sponsored issues by Madame Tussaud's, Timothy Whites (chemists) and Taylors (chemists).

49 Formed by Guy Dawnay and Julian Day. In 1928, the company sponsored an issue by Financial Newspapers Proprietors.

50 A company specialising in company promotions which had recommenced operations after its principals returned from service in France. The company withdrew from company promotions after the death of Oliver Clare in 1921.

51 Individual issuing houses listed in the yearbook were not necessarily independent of each other. In several cases, houses were related to each other, dividing business between them on, for example, grounds of size. Thus, Sir Arthur Wheeler was associated with three houses: Moorgate Issues Limited, which dealt with small issues and was a subsidiary of Gresham Trust, which dealt with larger issues, and Charterhouse Investment Trust which dealt with even larger issues.

52 Minutes of Evidence, Macmillan Committee, Question 1526.

53 The circumstances in which Bevan came to exercise this degree of control are set out in the judgment of Romer J in the litigation which followed: *Re City Equitable Fire Insurance Corporation*, (1925) 1 Ch 407.

54 Dundee University Archives; reference MS 66/II/10/50.

55 *The Times*, 18 November 1920.

56 The circumstances were described in Sir Richard Muir's opening speech for the prosecution at Bevan's trial, and in the statement of G Adair, a director of one of the three companies acquired by CEFI (National Archives; file HO 144/2745).

57 Correspondence in May 1922 between JD Langton & Passmore, solicitors acting for Hatry, and the Legal Department of London Joint City and Midland Bank (HSBC Archive, file UK 0273/0026).

58 For example, the liquidator disposed of CBL's remaining holding of shares in Agricultural Industries Limited by a sale at a nugatory sum to members of the Dennis family from whom Hatry had first acquired the business in 1919. This is one of the means by which the Dennis family retained control of the family farming estates which they had first sold in 1919 (Board of Trade Inspector's report, National Archives).

59 There is no record of the way in which this introduction was effected. It may have come about through Sir John Crisp, a partner in Ashurst Morris Crisp, who had taken over as Hatry's solicitor on the death of his father, Sir Frank Crisp, and who is recorded as having introduced Hatry to Foster & Braithwaite, the stockbrokers, who became involved in the new business and who proved instrumental in securing its acceptance by Stock Exchange members, notwithstanding fierce opposition by jobbers and the incumbent

brokers. It was Foster & Braithwaite who in turn introduced Hatry to the Marquess of Winchester, who chaired Hatry's new company.

60 Biographical note published in the IMTA Journal on Collins becoming President. An advertisement for the new Bureau appeared on page one of the first issue of the journal after Collins left office as President.

61 R Nivison & Company, Mullens Marshall & Company, J&A Scrimgeour & Company. Documents relating to attempts by these brokers to preserve their position are held in a Crown Agents file (National Archives; file CAOG 9/108).

62 Memorandum on Steel Industries of Great Britain Limited, M Samuel & Company Limited (Lloyds Bank Archive; file S/1/1/6/228). In the event, matters were delayed, and in June 1929, members of the preliminary syndicate were persuaded to become members of a successor syndicate: 'the A Share Syndicate'. The agreement for that syndicate envisaged that the A shares in question would be sold by 19 December 1929, within six months of the formation of the new syndicate.

63 Devices of this sort had long been a resort of fraudsters and promoters (Holcombe, 1983 page 160).

64 Examination of telephone directories.

65 Other promoters seem to have used a similar approach. For example, after his imprisonment and bankruptcy, Hooley continued living on his estate at Papworth Hall. Similarly, although he was obliged to sell his stud at Alfriston (to Hatry), Bottomley was able to retain his nearby country house.

66 The combines with which Hatry became involved included Drapery Trust (provincial department stores), London Public Omnibus Company (London bus operators), Associated Automatic Machine Corporation (coin-operated machines on stations and other public places), Allied Ironfounders (small foundries) and United Steel (steel manufacturers).

67 Such as Dunlop Rubber and, eventually, Royal Mail Steamship.

References

Primary works: unpublished documents

Dundee University Archive: Jute Industries Papers.
HSBC Archive: Midland Bank Papers.
Lloyds Bank Archive.
Lloyds Bank Archive: M Samuel Papers.
National Archives.
St Andrews University Special Collections: Tullis Russell Papers.
Stock Exchange Archive, Guildhall Library.

Primary works: newspapers and periodicals

Daily Mail.
The Economist.
Issuing Houses Yearbook.
The Times.

Primary works: government and parliamentary reports

Board of Trade (1918a), *Appendix to the Final Report of the Committee on Commercial and Industrial Policy After the War* (Cmd 9035). (HMSO, London). ('Appendix to the Lord Balfour Committee Report').

Board of Trade (1918b), *Report of the Committee on Financial Facilities* (Cmd 9227). (HMSO, London). ('The Vassar-Smith Committee Report').

Board of Trade (1918c), *Report of the Company Law Amendment Committee* (Cmd 9138). (HMSO, London). ('The Wrenbury Committee Report').

HM Treasury (1927), *Minutes of Evidence Taken Before the Committee on National Debt and Taxation* (HMSO, London). ('Colwyn Committee Minutes of Evidence').

HM Treasury (1931), *Minutes of Evidence Taken Before the Committee on Finance and Industry*. Two volumes (HMSO, London). ('Macmillan Committee Minutes of Evidence').

Ministry of Reconstruction (1919), *Report on the Work of the Ministry for the Period Ending 31st December 1918* (Cmd 9231). (HMSO, London).

Primary works: contemporary books and articles

Anonymous (December 1931), 'The Results of the 1928 New Issue Boom', *The Economic Journal*, volume 41, number 164, pages 577–583.

Baker, M and Collins, M (2003), 'The Asset Portfolio Composition of British Life Insurance Funds 1900–1965', *Financial History Review*, volume 10, number 2, pages 137–164.

Brooks, C (1933), *The Royal Mail Case: Rex v Lord Kylsant, and Another* (Wm Hodges & Company, Edinburgh).

Cole, GDH (1935), *Studies in Capital & Investment: Being a Volume of New Fabian Research Bureau Studies in Socialist Problems* (Victor Gollancz, London).

Daniel, G and Jewkes, J (1928), 'The Post-War Depression in the Lancashire Cotton Industry', *Journal of the Royal Statistical Society*, volume 91, pages 159–192.

Hibbert, WN (1898), *The Law Relating to Company Promoters* (Effingham Wilson, London).

Japhet, S (1931), *Recollections From My Business Life* (Privately Published, London).

Jenkinson, MW (1928), *The Value of a Balance Sheet* (Gee & Company, London).

Lavington, F (1921), *The English Capital Market* (Methuen, London).

Parkinson, H (1938), 'British Industrial Profits: A Survey of Three Decades', *The Economist*, volume 133, pages 597–603.

Samuel, HB (1933), *Shareholders' Money* (Heinemann, London).

Spafford, CH (1921), *The Law of Misrepresentation in Prospectus* (Butterworth, London).

Stamp, J (1932), 'Industrial Profits in the Past Twenty Years: A New Index Number', *Journal of the Royal Statistical Society*, volume 85, pages 658–683.

Wrench, JE (1935), *Struggle 1914–1920* (Nicholson & Watson, London).

Secondary works

Andrews, PWS and Brunner, E (1955), *The Life of Lord Nuffield: A Study in Enterprise and Benevolence* (Blackwell, Oxford).

Arnold, AJ (1999), 'Profitability and Capital Accumulation in British Industry During the Transwar Period 1913–1924', *Economic History Review*, volume 52, number 1, pages 55–68.

Arnold, AJ (2017), 'Industrial Profitability in the Trans-World War II Period 1938–1950', *Accounting History Review*, volume 27, number 1, pages 101–114.

Arnold, AJ and Matthews, D (2002), 'Corporate Financial Disclosures in the UK 1920–1950: The Effects of Legislative Change and Managerial Discretion', *Accounting and Business Research*, volume 32, number 1, pages 3–16.

Baynes, TH (1966), *Share Valuations* (Heineman, London).

Billings, M and Oats, L (2014), 'Innovation and Pragmatism in Tax Design: Excess Profits Duty in the UK During the First World War', *Accounting History Review*, volume 24, numbers 2–3, pages 83–101.

Braggion, F and Moore, L (2013), 'How Insiders Traded Before Rules', *Business History*, volume 55, number 4, pages 562–581.

Broadberry, S (1988), 'The Impact of the World Wars on the Long-Run Performance of the British Economy', *Oxford Review of Economic Policy*, volume 4, number 1, pages 25–37.

Chambers, D (2010), 'Going Public in Interwar Britain', *Financial History Review*, volume 17, number 1, pages 51–71.

Cheffins, BR and Blank, SA (2007), 'Corporate Ownership and Control in the UK: the tax dimension', *Modern Law Review*, volume 70, number 5, pages 778–811.

Cheffins, BR (2006), 'Dividends as a Substitute for Corporate Law: The Separation of Ownership and Control in the United Kingdom', *Washington and Lee Law Review*, volume 63, number 4, pages 1273–1338.

Cheffins, BR (2008), *Corporate Ownership and Control: British Business Transformed* (Oxford University Press, Oxford).

Cheffins, BR and Blank, SA (2007), 'Corporate Ownership and Control in the UK: The Tax Dimension', *Modern Law Review*, volume 70, number 5, pages 778–811.

Cheffins, BR, Koustas, DK and Chambers, D (2013), 'Ownership Dispersion and the London Stock Exchange's "Two-Thirds" Rule: An Empirical Test', *Business History*, volume 55, number 4, pages 667–690.

Corina, M (1978), *Fine Silks and Oak Counters: Debenhams 1778–1978* (Hutchinson Benham, London).

Cottrell, PL (1980), *Industrial Finance 1830–1914: The Finance and Organisation of English Manufacturing Industry* (Methuen, London).

Daunton, MJ (2002), *Just Taxes: The Politics of Taxation in Britain 1914–1979* (Cambridge University Press, Cambridge).

Dennett, L (1979), *The Charterhouse Group 1925–1979: A History* (Century Books, London).

Dewey, P (1997), *War and Progress: Britain 1914–1945* (Longman, London).

Edwards, JR (1979), *A History of Financial Accounting* (Routledge, London).

Edwards, JR and Webb, KM (1984), 'The Development of Group Accounting in the United Kingdom to 1833', *Accounting Historians Journal*, volume 24, pages 259–279.

Fanning, D (1985), 'Clarence Hatry', in Jeremy, DJ (editor), *Dictionary of Business Biography*, volume 3, H-L, pages 110–114 (Butterworths, London).

Feinstein, CH (1972), *National Income, Expenditure and Output of the UK 1855–1965* (Cambridge University Press, Cambridge).

Florence, PS (1961), *Ownership, Control and Success of Large Companies: An Analysis of English Industrial Structure and Policy 1936–1951* (Sweet & Maxwell, London).

Foreman-Peck, J (1981), 'The Effect of Market Failure on the British Motor Industry Before 1939', *Explorations in Economic History*, volume 18, number 3, pages 257–289.

Franks, J, Mayer, C and Rossi S (2009), 'Ownership: evolution and regulation', *The Review of Financial Studies*, volume 22, number 10, pages 4009–4056.

Grimond, J (1979), *Memoirs* (Heinemann, London).

Hannah, L (1976), *The Rise of the Corporate Economy* (Methuen, London).

Hart, PE (1965), *Studies in Profit, Business Saving and Investment in the United Kingdom 1920–1962* (George Allen & Unwin, London).

Higgins, D, Toms, S and Filatotchev, I (2015), 'Ownership, Financial Strategy and Performance: The Lancashire Cotton Industry 1918–1938', *Business History*, volume 57, number 1, pages 96–120.

Hope, R (1949), 'Profits in British Industry From 1924 to 1935', *Oxford Economic Papers*, volume 1, number 2, pages 159–181.

Jones, R and Marriott, O (1970), *Anatomy of a Merger: A History of GEC, AEI and English Electric* (Jonathan Cape, London).

Kinross, J (1982), *Fifty Years in the City: Financing Small Business* (John Murray, London).

Kitchen, J (1979), 'The Accounts of British Holding Company Groups', in Lee, TA and Parker, RH (editors), *The Evolution of Corporate Financial Reporting* (Nelson, Sunbury-on-Thames).

Kynaston, D (1991), *Cazenove & Co: A History* (Batsford, London).

Michie, RC (1999), *The London Stock Exchange: A History* (Oxford University Press, Oxford).

Napier, CJ (1991), 'Secret Accounting: The P&O Group in the Inter-War Years', *Accounting Business and Financial History*, volume 1, pages 303–333.

Pearson, M (1961), *The Millionaire Mentality* (Secker & Warburg, London).

Sandberg, L (1974), *Lancashire in Decline* (Columbus, Ohio).

Supple, B (1987), *The History of the British Coal Industry, Volume 4, 1913–1946: The Political Economy of Decline* (Oxford University Press, Oxford).

Thomas, WA (1978), *The Finance of British Industry 1918–1976* (Methuen, London).

Toms, S (2015), *Fraud and Financial Scandals: A Historical Analysius of Opportunity and Impediment*, MPRA Paper Number 68255. Downloaded 31 January 2016 from https://mpra.ub,uni-muenchen.de/687255

Turner, G (1971), *The Leyland Papers* (Eyre & Spottiswoode, London).

Walker, WM (1979), *Juteopolis: Dundee and Its Textile Workers 1885–1923* (Scottish Academic Press, Edinburgh).

5 The Exchange's marketplace 1914–1945

Introduction

On the brink of war in 1914, the London Stock Exchange was without question the dominant organisation of its kind in the world, whether measured in terms of activity, connections or sophistication. It was at the heart of a world-wide network that linked the most important personal and institutional investors with the largest corporate and state borrowers and was central to the world's money and capital markets. It had grown to this state by ferocious competition which had led to a series of crises which had brought pressure for regulation which had been countered by the development of internal rules and conventions (Moran, 2003, pages 54–55). The range and depth of the securities trading which it hosted reflected a willingness to contemplate dealing in the riskiest securities (Burhop et al., 2014, page 74) and made it a preferred source of finance for business and governments seeking to embark on capital intensive projects.[1] By the end of the war, these accomplishments were to be challenged and then damaged in ways that were not fully to be recovered by 1945.

Effect of the 1914–1918 war

The onset of a war for which there had been little planning led almost immediately to the closure of the Exchange through the unforeseen difficulty of settling bargains with overseas traders who had now to be regarded as enemy traders. Even though the Exchange was able to re-open after a few months, the volume of trading and, as a result, members' incomes were severely restricted.

Some reduction in the level of trading was foreseeable, but the Exchange had been obliged to accept restrictions as a condition of the government's facilitation of the reopening. The government's objective had been to eliminate trading which was not in the national interest of concentrating the nation's resources on the war effort. To discourage speculation, the fortnightly settlement arrangement was abandoned for the duration of the war together with contangoes: the procedure by which a bargain could be carried forward from one account to the next through the simple payment of the difference between the current and agreed prices at the end of each account. In other words, all bargains had to be settled immediately in cash.

Trading in options was not permitted. New issues were to be discouraged. Arbitrage trading was to cease. Although there was a hint that some domestic issues might be permitted, overseas issues were virtually prohibited. The membership of non-UK nationals was to be discontinued (Sonne, 1915, pages 45–51).

The effect on members' incomes was significant. There was bound to be a reduction in the volume of trading caused partly by the reduced attention of clients, but the official discouragement of speculation and new issues activity also reduced members' commission income. Before the war, members had augmented their incomes by indulging in speculation themselves and financing their clients' speculation either by lending money explicitly or through the fortnightly settlement procedure. These additional sources of revenue were denied to members.

Even though the government's initial intention to pay for the war by issuing transferable debt appeared to create a source of additional business for members, in practice this was not attractive, as it might have appeared as many of the bargains were comparatively small and incurred transaction costs which were not always easily covered by the fixed commission rates.

Matters became especially difficult as the squeeze on revenues was exacerbated by heightened costs. Before 1914, many brokers had looked to overseas banks for loans at rates of interest that were lower than British banks would offer. With the onset of war, this source of finance was closed. Although British banks were prepared to replace loans from overseas banks, higher rates of interest had to be borne. Moreover, the members' largest item of expenditure, the cost of staff, increased substantially even though, on many occasions, members found themselves employing people with less experience than those who had left to serve with the forces.

Nor was the Exchange as an organisation immune to these pressures. Active membership declined during the war, and with it the income that the Exchange could raise from members' subscriptions. During the war, it forgave subscriptions nominally due from members on active service. Combined with other factors such as the expulsion of German members, this produced a reduction of annual subscription income from about £232,000 in 1914 to £98,000 in 1918. The Exchange's costs also rose so that, for example, its annual salary costs rose by almost 90% during the war (Michie, 1999, page 197). In wartime, the Exchange had used short-term measures such as the sale of property to mitigate the financial embarrassment, but members knew that when the war ended the Exchange would have to increase its income and that this would entail increasing either the number of members or the rate of subscriptions. Neither approach was palatable. Increasing the number of members would intensify the competition for business and, unless there was a marked increase in activity, would reduce incomes by sharing the available business between more people. An increase in subscriptions would merely add to members' cost pressures.

These were not the only pressures that members faced. Firms knew that partners and staff returning from war service would have to be re-integrated and that profits would have to recover quickly to provide the incomes they would quite properly expect. To achieve this, markets and lines of business lost during the war would have to be recovered, and the sooner this could be done, the better.

Members hoped there would be new opportunities. They could look forward to a surge of new corporate issues, after the virtual suspension of new issues during the war. There would also be new demand from international borrowers as governments and corporations sought large loans to finance reconstruction projects. Yet the post-war Exchange was not as well placed to take advantage of these opportunities as the pre-war Exchange had been. New York had taken advantage of London's enforced withdrawal from international business during the war and had enhanced its status. High taxation and enforced asset disposals such as the repatriation of US railroad stocks had weakened the financial power of the British investor.

During the war, there had been differing appreciations of the difficulty of reinstating business as usual and recovering lost ground. Some had been hopeful, almost complacent:

> I do not suppose anybody thinks the centre of finance will ever go away from London and I believe the prosperity of the Stock Exchange will increase with a rush when peace comes. I most certainly believe in the future and look forward to the future of the Stock Exchange with a great deal of confidence.[2]

Others were more troubled. In February 1917, the Exchange's committee submitted a memorandum to the Chancellor of the Exchequer seeking a rapid release from government control:

> to maintain its position as the leading market for securities in the world . . . the freedom of markets should not be impaired and that London should remain as heretofore a clearing house for transactions in such securities.[3]

If the Exchange were to minimise the losses it had suffered and maximise its possible gains, it would have to be free from controls which had sacrificed its position as the clearing house for international transactions. Having achieved that, members would have to be vigorous in competing with strengthened international competitors and flexible in adjusting to meet the demands of new investors: especially those who had bought government debt to finance the war and found themselves for the first time holding transferable securities. Time would be critical as by January 1919, overseas markets had already been untroubled by London's competition for four years (Kynaston, 1999, pages 57–58).

Returning to business as usual

The early events of 1919 were not propitious. A return to normal trading conditions required the government's assent because of undertakings given by the Exchange in 1914 when negotiating the reopening of the Exchange. Although members were able to defeat the government's attempt to prolong its control of new issues beyond the end of the war,[4] they quickly found that the government would not permit the removal of other restrictions such as the requirement for immediate cash settlement of bargains, the ban on option trading and the ban on arbitrage trading. In spite of the Exchange repeatedly requesting the government to release the restrictions,[5] there was a delay until the government declared that 1 September 1921 should be the formal end to the war.[6]

At this point, the Exchange found that its membership was not united in desiring an immediate return to pre-war trading conditions. Some members had found that trading under the wartime restrictions was safer and less risky as immediate cash settlement removed the risk of finding that one had been trading with an insolvent member who could not honour his commitments:

> the one outstanding feature in dealings in the 'House' during the past four, inherently difficult, years has been the well-nigh perfect safety for all concerned. Not only did the cash basis of our transactions reduce to – practically – zero the risk involved in the ultimate completion of each bargain, but it tended to stabilise markets in a most salutary and hitherto unknown manner.[7]

Thus, when the Exchange was free to consider terminating the wartime Temporary Regulations,[8] it found that some members were reluctant to countenance the reversion to fortnightly settlement. In response, the Exchange proposed that whilst fortnightly settlement should be re-introduced for domestic corporate issues, it would not extend to government issues or to foreign issues. As a foretaste of the disagreements which were to come, in March 1922, this elicited complaints from 40 firms, led by Leon Brothers, who were largely involved in foreign business and feared that their business would be undermined. Fortnightly settlement had minimised the capital required to undertake arbitrage business as by the time transactions had to be settled most would have been balanced. This helped them to compete with better-capitalised outside houses, such as the overseas banking corporations.

At root, this was a dispute about the degree of risk that members generally would tolerate in the interest of sustaining the Exchange's international competitiveness. Members such as Leon Brothers, who before the war had a well-established arbitrage business, argued that that the risk was acceptable as the price of withstanding competition and securing the:

> enormous amount of business arbitrage firms bring to the Stock Exchange, which would otherwise never come to London at all. As an instance, Paris deals with London, and London distributes that business to New York, Japan or other centres. Paris and other countries would cut out London, if London could not give the quickest, and most efficient facilities.[9]

In opposing this case, brokers such as Kemp-Gee who had not enjoyed a substantial arbitrage business and did not share a concern for international competitiveness emphasised the threat implicit in relaxing settlement arrangements:

> forward dealings with the present fluctuations in Continental Exchanges might lead to disaster, as fluctuations in exchange such as had recently occurred in Germany might swamp the capital of either the London or Foreign House or the foreign speculator.[10]

The arguments were rehearsed again two months later, when the committee proposed the re-introduction of contangoes. On this occasion, the proposal was opposed by no fewer than 1,289 members who appeared unconcerned by the Exchange's international position:

> Since dealings have taken place for cash only, the prestige of the Stock Exchange has risen, and we doubt if it ever stood so high in the estimation of the public as it does at the present time . . . we consider that the contangoes system, in providing an uncontrollable measure of credit to the public, is inimical to the best interests of the Stock Exchange, a source of great danger in all times of political or financial stress, and weighs especially heavily on Brokers who have far the greater share of responsibility for the due fulfilment of obligations.[11]

Notwithstanding these objections, as in March 1922, the committee decided that the survival of a significant number of firms depended upon the facility to carry over bargains from one account to the next and that restricting the time for which a deal could remain open risked driving business into the hands of other markets: either the provincial exchanges or overseas exchanges. On this occasion, the committee was able to favour contangoes were re-introduced with effect from September 1922.

At the same meeting, trading in options was again permitted with effect from September 1922, although options contracts were limited to a period of three months.[12]

The significance of these debates was that even when the government's restraint had been removed, the Exchange was not able immediately to free members to begin recovering its international position. For example, the resumption in September 1922 of contangoes and options trading took place about four years after the cessation of hostilities: a delay almost equal to the length of the war itself and almost one year after government restraints had been removed. The preference of some members for risk-free trading had caused a significant delay. Throughout this time, overseas exchanges had been able to consolidate their position without troubling over competition from London.

Whilst these debates continued, members were attempting to control their costs and, in particular, the cost of membership of the Exchange. In April 1919, a group of members including Rowe & Pitman, W Greenwell & Company and de Zoete & Gorton proposed that the membership should buy out the proprietors arguing that:

> Under the present arrangement, the greater the exertions of the members to get more business, the higher became the entrance fees and subscriptions, and the bigger is the dividend paid to the proprietors.[13]

Although the objections were justified by reference to the returns paid to proprietors, it is likely that members were as much concerned to gain control of the Exchange and more particularly control of the number of members which had been capped since 1904 (Morgan and Thomas, 1961, page 158; Michie, 1999, pages 84–85).

Whilst the proposition was supported by a large majority of the membership, its weakness lay in the consideration which would have to be paid to buy out the proprietors. They would expect to receive the value of their interest which would at least be equal to the present value of the expected income stream. Payment could only have been commercially attractive if members believed that purchase would lead to a reduction in the cost of membership either through reductions in the Exchange's costs or realisation of other sources of income. When the interest was valued in November 1919 at £3.6 million,[14] there was no enthusiasm among members either to make an initial contribution or to accept the cost of servicing a loan which would have increased rather than reducing the annual subscription. An alternative scheme by which the Exchange would have been owned by a new company owned equally by the membership, which would have been limited to 4,000, was rejected by the proprietors in May 1921.[15] The matter was not pursued further.

Membership

On this occasion, the members failed to perfect their control of all elements of the Exchange's constitution, but knew that time was on their side. Under the terms of the agreement reached in 1904, new members were expected also to become proprietors by buying shares so that as the proportion of the proprietors who were also members was gradually growing, inexorably the day was drawing near when members would control a majority of the proprietors' votes (Morgan and Thomas, 1961, page 158; Michie, 1999, pages 84–85). In the meantime, although members had not achieved control, the proprietors had been reminded of members' hostility towards a general expansion of numbers and henceforth satisfied themselves by looking to entrance fees and annual subscriptions for their income rather than an increase in the number of members. In practice, when the post-war boom ended in 1920, so the debate over the number of members withered, only reviving towards the end of the 1920s when activity rose again.

By 1931, members no longer had to rely upon the proprietors being aware of the problem as they had by that time established control of the Exchange. By October 1931, 2,878 out of 2,987 proprietors (or 96%) were also members. At the beginning of 1931, the proprietors agreed that purchase of a nomination would be the only route to membership and that additional nominations would only be created if it were agreed that the total numbers were too low.

That limiting the number of members was only spasmodically a controversial issue for the Exchange indicates that only occasionally did the demand for membership become pressing. Whatever the merits of membership of the Exchange, between the wars the average income of members was not attractive, especially when compared with the experience of other professions. As professionals generally operated as individuals or as partnerships, and their income was not publicly disclosed, reliable data about the income of a particular profession is difficult to obtain. Such data as are available suggest that the average income of people involved in share trading would have been disappointing.

Table 5.1 Stock Exchange members 1918–1939

Year	Total number of members	Number of members acting as principals	Number of members acting as clerks
1918	3,884	3,188	696
1919	3,987	3,299	688
1920	4,035	3,221	814
1921	4,023	3,198	825
1922	3,928	3,123	805
1923	3,896	3,081	815
1924	3,874	3,162	702
1925	3,858	3,065	783
1926	3,883	3,092	791
1927	3,899	3,114	785
1928	3,913	3,116	797
1929	3,941	3,113	828
1930	3,925	3,140	785
1931	3,932	3,116	816
1932	3,911	3,055	856
1933	3,941	2,996	945
1934	3,961	3,021	940
1935	3,988	3,038	950
1936	3,995	3,078	917
1937	4,035	3,090	945
1938	4,076	3,014	962
1939	4,053	3,096	957

Source: Stock Exchange annual reports (Stock Exchange Archive, Guildhall Library).

Table 5.2 True Gross Income for stockbrokers and jobbers 1909–1938 (£'000)

Assumed basis period for assessments	1909	1927	1932	1936	1937	1938
Years of assessment	1911–2	1928–9	1933–4	1937–8	1938–9	1939–40
Stockbrokers and jobbers	9,450	15,540	12,370	15,870	3,550	180
Professions in general	30,750	74,650	69,880	88,920	89,310	84,750

Source: Worswick and Tipping (1967, pages 99–101). True Gross Income is defined as income reported in accordance with Income Tax rules but adjusted to remove permitted tax deductions. The rules for assessing professional income changed towards the end of the 1920s. Before the change, an assessment was raised on the basis of the average of the profit in three basis periods (essentially the previous three years). After the change, an assessment would be raised on profit earned in the accounting year which ended in the tax year before the year of assessment. The table shows both the basis period to which it was assumed that the assessed profit related and the years of assessment on which that assumption was based.

The group includes all assessments for people calling themselves stockbrokers or jobbers, whether as members of the London Stock Exchange or elsewhere.

Table 5.3 Stockbrokers and jobbers' average True Gross Income per assessment 1909–1938 (£)

Assumed basis period for assessments	1909	1927	1932	1936	1937	1938
Years of assessment	1911–2	1928–9	1933–4	1937–8	1038–9	1939–40
Stockbrokers and jobbers	2,750	5,500	4,800	6,200	1,850	100

Source: Worswick and Tipping (1967, pages 119–121).

The average income shown by tax returns submitted by stockbrokers and jobbers remained substantially higher than the average income of other professions, but was volatile and had not grown as quickly. Moreover, as the years 1927 and 1936 were boom years and represented high points in Stock Exchange incomes, the tables give a slightly flattering impression of the income of brokers and jobbers.

Nonetheless, some firms were modestly successful. Foster & Braithwaite's profit, for example, ranged between £70,000 and £160,000 in the 1920s.[16] In 1919–1920, James Capel & Company's five partners divided profits of £89,000 (Reed, 1975, page 74).

During the first post-war decade, Cazenove's business was steadily rather than exceptionally profitable (Kynaston, 1991, page 117).

However, Philips & Drew, with five or six partners at the time, might only achieve profit of £10,000 (Reader and Kynaston, 1998, page 11).

These few indications of the profitability achieved by some of the more prominent firms show how important were sources of income other than straightforward processing of transactions leading to commissions. Cazenove, for example, developed as a sponsor of new issues, either alone or in association with an issuing house. Building on its experience before the war, Cazenove supported Balfour Beatty in fostering the creation of Power Securities Limited to finance electricity supply companies, presumably to ensure that there was a demand for its own construction business (Kynaston, 1991, page 111). Foster & Braithwaite, which also had pre-war experience of flotations, acted for Clarence Hatry's local authority loan-issuing company, Corporation and General Securities Limited, which was established in 1925 (Swinson, 2016, pages 125–126).

Polarisation

This pattern was symptomatic of a growing polarisation of the Exchange's membership. Some firms, such as Cazenove, took advantage of changes in the demand for and supply of securities. In Cazenove's case, the firm became aligned with the new issuing houses that began to develop in the 1920s and with institutional investors. Attracting and sustaining such business became fiercely competitive. As institutional investors grew in scale and confidence, they became more demanding in the support expected from brokers and tended to concentrate their business in the hands of fewer firms. In April 1926, Cazenove had been included in a list of

55 London firms approved by the board of Standard Life. From these firms, Standard Life expected not only the capacity to complete deals, but advice on market conditions. As Standard Life's holdings became more significant, it was more frequently approached for its views on rationalisation schemes and found that it was convenient to use its brokers as a conduit by which its views could be made known. By 1950, Cazenove was handling about 25% of Standard Life's transactions (Moss, 2000, pages 194–195).

Brokers who essayed this type of business eventually found that they were obliged to develop their back offices to support a higher volume of activity. Kynaston charts this development within Cazenove by recording the recollections of Antony Hornby who in time became the leading partner of the firm. He recalled that Cazenove was the first Stock Exchange firm to begin mechanising its back office. After suggestions made during a conversation at WH Smith about new accounting processes, the firm installing a system which required that information about a bargain would be entered on a master sheet from which the contract was produced by impression and, in the same way, by a series of masks, relevant information would be posted to the various ledgers of the system to eliminate manual posting and error once the right information had been entered on the master sheet and checked. As a result, a greater volume of business could be transacted with no increase in back office staff (Kynaston, 1991, pages 130–131).

The demands of such a business were quite different from those other brokers, usually smaller, which continued to rely on the more traditional business model, serving individual clients on a personal basis. New clients would be gained by personal introductions or recommendations and connections would be sustained by personal contact. The limited volume of business transacted did not require large numbers of staff, mechanisation or, indeed, capital.

The gradual divergence of the interests of these two groups became evident in a series of struggles over the Exchange's rules, commissions being the area most frequently disputed.

Minimum commission rates had first been imposed in 1912, as a result of agitation largely from smaller, more traditional firms against the opposition of larger firms which would have preferred to continue reaching their own agreements with clients, agents and introducers (Morgan and Thomas, 1961, pages 153–154; Michie, 1999, pages 121–122). By the early 1920s, when removal of the wartime restrictions was being considered, the minimum commission rates had become generally accepted so that there was no serious opposition to the retention. The scale of rates remained contentious, however, as firms involved in institutional business faced pressure from institutions to relieve larger transactions from the official rates. When they raised this possibility with the committee, they were opposed by smaller firms who preferred that there should be no change. The disagreement rumbled on for some time but there was no change.

Thereafter, the question of commission rates returned periodically: usually when members' income came under pressure. Thus, the matter arose again in the form of a proposal that the rebates paid to business introducers should be reconsidered, recued and possibly eliminated. Under the existing rules, it was recognised that a broker might agree to pay a rebate of up to 50% to agents or introducers. The rebates were questioned partly because the payment of a rebate reduced the member's income so that members who wanted to avoid paying rebates wanted the possibility to be removed from the rules. But it was suspected that rebates were used by some firms as a way of reducing the official rates. That suggestion attracted strong opposition because there was a risk that denying rebates to some introducers would encourage them to bypass the Exchange altogether. By far the most significant introducers were the clearing banks which attracted business from customers through their branch networks. It was feared that eliminating rebates payable to the clearing banks would result in their establishing their own clearing house so that their customers' transactions would not pass through the Exchange at all.

Provincial brokers were another source of business that would have been affected by the elimination of rebates. The relationship with provincial brokers had already been damaged by the imposition of the 'dual capacity' rule before the 1914–1918 war. Before members had insisted that compliance with the rule should be closely monitored, several jobbers had been prepared to accept bargains directly from provincial brokers. When the rule had been enforced, it became necessary for provincial brokers to approach the London market through a London broker, which entailed paying the London broker's commission. The 50% rebate of the London broker's commission enabled the provincial broker to share in the benefit of dealing with the bargain. Its elimination would mean that the provincial broker might be left with no benefit from the bargain and would provide an incentive to find an alternative to dealing through London.

On this occasion, nothing came of the proposal. Doubtless the fear that the banks might make other arrangements was thought realistic, but the outcome was assisted by the increase in market activity (and thus members' incomes) in 1927 and 1928.

The heightened level of activity did not last long, however, and the question was raised again in 1931 and 1932 when the continued desirability of the rebate arrangements was raised again. On this occasion, it was agreed that the rules should be changed. The full one-half rebate was to be available only to serious, full-time introducers such as the clearing banks and provincial brokers. A reduced rate of one-third would be available to introducers who did not fall into this category but were accepted as introducers by the Exchange which created a register of introducers for the purpose. Whilst this irritated many solicitors and insurance companies who did not fall into the category of introducers entitled to receive 50% rebates, the distinction between categories proved shrewd because there is no evidence of these other groups of introducers attempting to bypass the Exchange.

Although this agreement satisfied many for a while, the question was raised again in 1938, another year in which members' incomes were disappointing, but discussions had not reached a conclusion before war was declared.

Whilst the occasional warnings from banks that they might make their own arrangements were noted, members did not take seriously the threat that provincial brokers might clear their own bargains, which is exactly what happened. By the 1930s, provincial jobbing firms had been established which handled a considerable volume of business that otherwise would have been expected to be referred to London and the Exchange was obliged to take note. It made various attempts to persuade the provincial exchanges to discourage the practice and to adopt policies that were similar to those followed in London, but on each occasion received the same response. The provincial exchanges would make the rule changes sought by the London Exchange but only if the Exchange agreed that provincial brokers could approach London jobbers directly, i.e. not indirectly through a London broker. As the London members were not prepared to make this concession, no agreement could be reached.

The London offices of American broking firms were in a similar position. Rather than introducing bargains to the London Exchange through a London broker, incurring an additional commission for clients, the American brokers in London increasingly referred business to New York, bypassing London.

All these debates were united by a common theme. Price competition was to be eliminated by maintaining official commission rates. Rebates were as far as possible to be limited and monitored to ensure that they were not used to soften the official commission rates. Members were prepared to uphold these policies even if they resulted in business bypassing the Exchange. The members' attitude implied that the Exchange enjoyed a monopoly of domestic share trading which it did not possess and yet again exhibited a preference for hiding behind the supposed protection of the Exchange's rules rather than the eagerness to compete for business which would have been necessary if recovery of the Exchange's pre-war position were ever to be possible (Thomas, 1978, pages 171, 180, 293, 316; Kinross, 1982, page 42; Michie, 1999, page 240).

In parallel with these struggles over commission rates, there were many other arguments about the conduct of business. Typically, these arguments were initiated by firms wanting the rules to be changed to permit firms to accommodate the demands of a changing market. They were generally opposed by smaller, more traditional firms seeking to preserve traditional approaches and protections.

In 1923, a group of larger firms proposed a change to the rule which limited the number of clerks that could be employed by a firm. The practical purpose of this rule was to increase the gearing between profit-sharing partners and clerks who would be paid salaries. The change was opposed and defeated on the ground that if a firm could employ any number of clerks the cap on the total number of members would be rendered ineffective. The same firms repeated the proposal in 1928 and 1930 with the same result.[17]

In 1925, an advertising agency proposed that advertising offered a channel by which the new army of investors could be informed and educated about investment. Some firms recognised that if the Exchange's members were to contact and win business from new investors, they would need to use new means of communication. Smaller firms feared that permitting advertising would encourage the development of large firms which would come to dominate business for personal clients. The proposal was defeated not only in 1925 but also in 1927, 1928, 1929 and 1934 when it was repeated.[18]

Another related proposal would have permitted members to open branch offices. Stockbrokers were allowed to have an office in the City but this was expected to be as close as possible to the Exchange itself and there was no provision for branch offices elsewhere so that brokers could not build networks of offices that could channel business to London. This proposal was defeated in 1929 and again in 1936 because, like the proposal to permit advertising, it threatened the creation of large groups dominating personal investment.[19]

In the same way, members would not tolerate any proposal to permit members to incorporate: they were obliged to trade either as sole practitioners or as partnerships. Whenever this issue arose, it was argued loftily that members of a profession should accept full personal responsibility for the consequences of their advice and that incorporation as a limited liability company was incompatible with that principle. It is however undeniable that the rule had a number of practical advantages. It disguised a limit to the size of firms, because the Partnership Act limited the size of partnerships. It excluded corporate entities such as banks from any possibility of membership. It emphasised the personal duty of members to meet liabilities to other members (Lindley, 1891, pages 1–4). In each of these three ways, the ban on incorporation protected the traditional business model from competition.

To many, prevention of incorporation was therefore almost an article of faith. In 1934, Foster & Braithwaite found itself under investigation when a report was received by the committee that the firm was holding shares through a company and was suspected of wanting to convert surreptitiously into a company. On enquiry, it was discovered that the firm had formed a nominee company in 1929 to hold shares while a bargain was arranged or payment was awaited. Use of a nominee company rendered share transfer and registration easier than registering shares in the names of partners which would have been the alternative: an explanation which the committee eventually accepted.

More problematic was the request in the same year by Frisby & Company, a jobber specialising in rubber stocks, to convert into an unlimited company to mitigate its liabilities to Income tax and Sur-tax. To provide liquidity, jobbers maintained holdings of the major stocks in which they traded. For tax purposes, at the end of each year, the holdings would be valued at current market prices and any unrealised gain or loss would be added to or deducted from the profit for the year. Jobbers thus could be obliged to pay Income Tax and Sur-tax on unrealised profits which might never be realised. Incorporation offered some relief because the partners would only have to pay Income Tax and Sur-tax to the extent the company's profits were distributed to them by way of dividend. This proposal was rejected on the ground that corporate practice was unacceptable in principle, but the committee accepted that a way should be found to mitigate the tax burden. When the brief 1936–1937 boom was ending, the matter arose again. Jobbers were calculating their boom-year tax liabilities and wondering how to finance them when the end of the boom had weakened their cash flow. On this occasion, a sub-committee was formed to enquire whether it would be possible to achieve a better tax treatment for jobbers: perhaps by reaching an agreement with the Inland Revenue that jobbers' books should not be valued at full market price. Agreeing an exceptional treatment for jobbers would have required an act of charity on the part of the Inland Revenue. Predictably, the approach to the Inland Revenue was refused so that the sub-committee was obliged to report that the only method under which members could be relieved from the inequitable burden of taxation involved their forming themselves into unlimited liability companies.

The report went on to recommend that the Exchange should remove any barrier to members carrying on business in corporate form. This recommendation was accepted by the committee in 1939 with an admission that:

> carrying on of business as a private unlimited liability company is for all practical purposes indistinguishable from the present practice of carrying on business in partnership.

This admission contrasted with the committee's view in 1934 that incorporation was incompatible in principle with the professional practice of members. The delay in reaching this conclusion demonstrates the difficulty of persuading a majority of members that a compromise was necessary to alleviate the financial problems of one section of the membership and the extent of the financial burden that the majority expected that group to tolerate so that a traditional protection, valued by the majority, could be preserved.[20]

It also implies that most members were seriously concerned that by compromising on incorporation they would expose themselves to competition which they would not be able to withstand and that they had come to rely upon their control of the rules, rather than their competitiveness, to safeguard their future. This defensiveness was hardly in keeping with the spirit of competition which was needed at the end of the 1914–1918 to win back lines of business that had been sacrificed during the war. It was symptomatic of a community that had become risk-averse.

The same aversion to innovation is evident in the early 1930s in the Exchange's response to the inception of the unit trust movement.

Mutual, open-ended investment funds were initially brought to London and developed by members of the Exchange: Messrs Burton-Baldry and Fairbairn who looked to the Exchange to provide a market for these new securities (Gleeson, 1981, pages 1–20). For Burton-Baldry and Fairbairn, it seemed natural to look to the Exchange for this facility, but for other members, it seemed yet another threat. The committee set up to examine this issue reported early in 1936:

> The introduction into this country of the Fixed Trust brought before the investing public a new commodity capable of being offered in a very attractive form as an alternative to the methods of investment which it had hitherto employed. The Public, not unnaturally, turned to those through whom it was accustomed to invest its resources, and it thus became necessary at an early stage that the Committee of the Stock Exchange should set itself to consider whether, and if so to what extent, and under what safeguards, the Stock Exchange should open its market to, and allow its members to take part in dealings in the new commodity.

Appropriate action was accordingly taken to investigate this aspect of the question, and the conclusion reached in the early part of the year 1934 was that, for the time being at any rate, it was not desirable to provide a market on the Stock Exchange for the Units and sub-units of Fixed Trusts, or to take any official cognisance of the movement, after this date, however, the Fixed Trust 'birth-rate' rose so steeply that the Stock Exchange felt itself constrained to make a further investigation of the position, mainly with a view to determining whether it lay in its power to guard the public from exploitation by affording a market restricted to the Units and sub-units of such Fixed Trusts as might conform to standards set up by the Stock Exchange for the protection of the investor.[21]

The Exchange seems to have feared that unit trust managements could create a false market by manipulating the price of units and that this would damage the reputation of the Exchange. The result was that the committee not only refused to approve dealing in units, but went further. In 1939, the Exchange banned partners of stock broking firms from being directors of unit trusts and from managing trusts from their own office. Crews & Company and another broker, Grieveson Grant & Company, were required to sell their holdings in unit trust management companies. Crews & Company had been a pioneer of the unit trust movement, launching trusts which specialised in investing in rubber plantations, tin and gold mines. These investments were acknowledged to be speculative and their regular valuations involved a high degree of judgement about prospects and were, thus, somewhat volatile. The Exchange's concern was that such investments might be inappropriate for the risk-averse small investor and risked bringing the Exchange's name into disrepute.

The Exchange's caution doubtless reflected its experience of the 1920s. 'Units' then had a bad name. In November 1919, on the first occasion on which the Exchange refused a listing for units, there was good reason to be nervous if only because of the reputation of the principal promoter.[22] In the mid-1920s, abusive share hawkers had taken advantage of unsophisticated investors by attempting to sell 'Ford units'.[23] The unit trusts of the 1930s bore little resemblance to these earlier abusive schemes, not least in their transparency. Moreover, they were to be successful in filling the gap which had been left by the failure in 1929–1930 of investment trusts which had been created specifically to meet the demands of small investors and in whose shares dealings had been permitted by the Exchange. Not only did these events demonstrate that the Exchange's members were capable of the competitive innovation which the Exchange required so badly, but they also demonstrate its decline into risk-averse resistance to change

Constitutional misfortune

In short, after the 1914–1918 war, the Exchange failed to minimise the losses it had suffered and to maximise its potential gains. The loss of international pre-eminence would have been difficult to reverse. For most of the war, New York had been able to trade on a peace time basis without opposition from London and had used this opportunity to establish itself as a major market. Connections had been made, relationships had been established, trust had been earned. This development was always likely to be difficult to disturb.

Admittedly, the Exchange was not assisted by the government. Slowing down the return to peacetime trading conditions reinforced New York's position by retarding London's ability to compete. But even when the government relented and allowed the Exchange to withdraw the temporary wartime regulations, the Exchange did not display the enthusiasm for vigorous competition that was necessary. Rather than enthusiasm, the Exchange demonstrated its risk aversion by delaying the return to fortnightly account trading for overseas business: a stance that hampered specialist brokers in seeking the return of international arbitrage business.

Domestically, similar forces were at work. In a marked contrast with NYSE initiatives in the early 1920s, the Exchange vetoed every proposal which would have facilitated the development of retail services for the army of small investors created during the war.[24]

These disappointments did not result from a complete absence of imagination or innovation. In the international field, the brokers who specialised in international business were ready to compete and repeatedly warned the committee of the damage that a slow return to peacetime conditions was causing. Equally, brokers who saw opportunities to develop domestic business took advantage of them where possible and regularly proposed rule changes to remove barriers where they existed. In the 1920s, Cazenove, for example, assisted in the creation of new issuing houses. Foster & Braithwaite, as another example, experimented by introducing a nominee company for temporary holdings of shares. In the 1930s, the unit trust movement was created by stockbrokers following the example of New York's experience. Failure thus sprang not from an absence of innovative spirit but from a failure of the membership at large to tolerate innovation.

In its inflexibility, the membership not only failed to tolerate innovation intended to develop new lines of business, it was also prepared to drive existing business elsewhere. Its lack of flexibility over standard rates of commission served as an encouragement for banks to clear transactions internally rather than through the Exchange. Its inflexibility over commission rates on bargains in US securities had encouraged the transfer of business from London brokers to the London offices of US brokers. The inflexible response to the nascent unit trust movement led to purchases and sales of units being effected through the unit trust managers themselves rather than through the Exchange. Its refusal to sanction direct access for provincial brokers to London jobbers encouraged the development of country jobbers: notably the development of JW Nicholson & Son of Sheffield who by the 1930s had reputedly become the largest firm of jobbers in the country (Michie, 1999, page 237). As the committee observed, perhaps ruefully:

> this firm transacts a very considerable business which otherwise would come to London . . . the gradual improvement in telephone and telegraph communications between local centres would appear to facilitate this class of business

and under existing conditions there seems no reason to believe that it will not increase in volume . . . the future will see the country brokers uniting to form an organisation of their own with their own dealers and machinery for settlement and making a market which in time may come to rival London.[25]

In other words, the membership's consistent and inflexible defence of the traditional broker's business model was pursued despite the risk that business would be lost.

Admittedly, some significant changes were made during this period. In 1930, following the Hatry crash, the cost of the deferred settlement of Hatry-related bargains was met by a temporary compensation fund contributed by members. In 1939, members accepted a proposal that members might practise as unlimited liability companies rather than in their own names individually or in partnership. These innovations were significant but neither was a sign of a willingness to be flexible. Both changes came about in reaction to a clear demonstration of an external threat. In 1930, the collapse of the 1927–1928 boom and the subsequent Hatry crash created an undeniable threat to the Exchange's autonomy. In 1939, the collapse of trading activity when having to meet tax liabilities assessed on profits earned during the 1936–1937 boom convinced members that incorporation was necessary to mitigate their exposure to Income Tax and Sur-tax. Strikingly, the report of the sub-committee which examined incorporation was candid in its admission that practice in the form of an unlimited liability company was indistinguishable from practice in the form of a partnership thus questioning whether opposition to incorporation could have been based on a principle.

The twentieth-century failure to provide an environment in which innovation was welcomed and could flourish marked a change from the nineteenth century when the Exchange had become the foremost securities market in the world. This reflected a change in the balance of power.

Originating in decisions made in 1801 to provide a market for the government debt to finance the Napoleonic War, the Exchange's constitution distinguished the powers of the proprietors of the exchange from the powers of the subscribers or members who alone had the right to trade on the Exchange floor. Neal and Davis argue persuasively that the Exchange's success as the world's leading stock exchange in the first era of global markets was attributable to this division of ownership from operation and the balance of these two different interests. (Neal and Davis, 2006, page 282)

Responsibility for construction and maintenance of the physical facilities of the Exchange was a primary responsibility of the proprietors whose powers were delegated to trustees and managers. Although all people permitted to trade through the Exchange were expected to acquire a share in the Exchange, there was no bar on shares being held by anyone who was not so involved. There was, however, a limit on the number of shares that any individual could hold. The reward for the proprietors came from the charges that could be levied for permitting access to the Exchange and its trading floor so that the proprietors had an interest in maximising the business transacted through the Exchange and the profit that could be made by those using its facilities. In practice, the proprietors' freedom to choose a marketing strategy that would maximise their return was limited by two factors. The limitation of shareholdings meant that any change of strategy needed broad support. Since all members were expected also to be proprietors, their views had to be considered,[26] and they could be relied upon to have trenchant views on whether membership should be expanded to maximise income from subscriptions or restricted to maximise the value of membership.

Moreover, as the Exchange was a private body and did not have an exclusive right to organise a market for share trading, there was a constant threat that business which would otherwise be directed to the exchange might be diverted either to informal trading between parties outside the Exchange or to competing market places such as the exchanges that existed in many provincial cities. If the Exchange were to be bypassed, the benefits of membership in the form of competitive profits or economic rents would be eroded, a danger managed by frequent reconsideration and adjustment of the Exchange's rules (Macey and Novogrod, 2011–2012, pages 963–1003).

This delicate balance had been disrupted by reforms agreed in 1904. There had for some time been concerns that the membership had grown too large. Indeed, following a decline in business, a Joint Committee of Managers and the General Purposes Committee had resolved that no one should be elected a member who had not served as clerk for two years and that the maximum number of clerks permitted to enter the House should be reduced to five per firm. In April 1904, the committee received a petition from over 3,000 members urging further restrictions which led to a drastic revision of the rules: From November 1902 candidates seeking election were obliged to acquire a 'nomination' either from a retiring member or from the legal representatives of a deceased member. The only exception was that clerks who had served four years in the House or settling room could put their names on a waiting list from which a number, fixed each year by the Committee, were elected without nomination. Clerks coming in by this route had to acquire one share and all other new members, three shares in the Stock Exchange (Morgan and Thomas, 1961, page 158).

The effect of these changes was to cap the number of members, and to ensure that, in the long run, all members would be proprietors. Moreover, the requirement that almost all new members should acquire nominations from existing members increased the likelihood that new members would share the views and ambitions of retiring members. This tendency was increased by the lack of demand for membership.

These changes disrupted the balance of power between proprietors and members. In the nineteenth century, undue defensiveness on the part of members could more easily be spotted by proprietors who were not themselves members, who could then counter balance the tendencies of existing members by using their powers to increase the size of the membership or to admit people who did not share the views of existing members. Those powers were neutered by the 1904 reforms. As the years passed, so the views of members tended to predominate so that by the 1930s, the views expressed by the Trustees and Managers were dominated by those of members. By the early 1940s there was a general acceptance that the proprietors and the membership should be merged so that the Exchange would be ruled by a single body: the Council.[27] In one further departure from precedent, members of the Council were to serve for terms of three years, with one-third of its members being re-elected in each year (Morgan and Thomas, 1961, page 232), a recognition that the previous tight control of the committee by the membership should to some extent be diluted. Although this marked the formal end of the bifurcated constitution which Neal and Davis argued was so valuable in the nineteenth century, in practice, its value had disappeared many years before (Neal and Davis, 2006, page 282).

This change in the practical balance of power might not have mattered so much if the membership had been clear-sighted about the direction of events. However, the growing polarisation of the membership and the divergence of the commercial experience of the diverging groups limited the membership's understanding. Faced with a variety of risks and threats, unconvinced by the benefit that they might obtain by encouraging innovation, a majority of the members took comfort in a risk-averse resistance to change.

During the 1920s and the 1930s, there were occasions on which the committee was able to introduce rule changes which ran counter to the membership's preferences, but only when an imminent external threat was evident to all members. As this condition was generally not fulfilled, the committee's power to make rules would only be used to serve the interests of the members as perceived by a majority of members at the time. As smaller members in a traditional way of business commanded most the membership, so it was that any rule changes which did not protect that style of business were rejected.

In an article published in 1945, *The Economist* looked back at developments since the beginning of the 1914–1918 war and observed:

> stock-broking is becoming a service industry[28]

The Economist's article went by recognising that this had led to a minimisation of risk for members and a withdrawal from competition on the basis of price. Whilst some members found this trend uncomfortable,[29] it reflected the preference for a quieter, risk-free life demonstrated by a substantial majority of members in their consistent defensiveness, careless of the cost in terms of business that was foregone.

Notes

1 There is evidence that the risk premium implicit in London share prices was lower than that for New York, but higher than in a number of other European exchanges (Dimson et al., 2002, pages 163–194).
2 Views of J Coles, Exchange Trustees and Managers minutes 18 April 1916 (Stock Exchange Archive, Guildhall Library).
3 Stock Exchange minutes, 28 February 1917 (Stock Exchange Archive, Guildhall Library).
4 The defeat of regulation 30F; see Chapter 9.
5 Stock Exchange minutes, 18 February 1920, 14 March 1921, 23 May 1921, 10 July 1922 (Stock Exchange Archive, Guildhall Library).
6 Uncertainty over the meaning of the phrase 'the end of the war' had proved troubling in many different contexts. A committee appointed to consider the issue under the

chairmanship of Mr Justice Atkin recommended that it should be defined as 'the date when treaty of peace is finally binding on the respective belligerent parties'. This proved, however, still to be vague as, in the event, there was not to be a single peace treaty but a series of treaties with each belligerent in turn. This gave the government the opportunity to delay its formal declaration of the end of the war. In the autumn of 1919, the government chose to use the possibility of delay to prolong the application of various wartime regulations rather than introducing legislation to prolong regulations: a course which would have been politically contentious (Atkin committee report, 1918).

7 Views of Gerald Williams, Stock Exchange Rules and Regulations Committee minutes, 27 November 1918 (Stock Exchange Archive, Guildhall Library).

8 The Chancellor of the Exchequer formally agreed in November 1921 to a resumption of fortnightly account settlement (Stock Exchange minutes, 7 November 1921, Stock Exchange Archive, Guildhall Library).

9 Stock Exchange minutes, 20 March 1922 (Stock Exchange Archive, Guildhall Library).

10 Stock Exchange minutes, 20 March 1922 (Stock Exchange Archive, Guildhall Library).

11 Stock Exchange minutes, 8 May 1922 (Stock Exchange Archive, Guildhall Library).

12 Stock Exchange minutes, 8 May 1922 (Stock Exchange Archive, Guildhall Library).

13 Stock Exchange minutes, 7 April 1919 (Stock Exchange Archive, Guildhall Library).

14 Report by Sir William Plender, Stock Exchange minutes, 3 November 1919, 6 November 1919, 25 November 1919 (Stock Exchange Archive, Guildhall Library).

15 Stock Exchange minutes, 3 May 1921, 12 May 1921 (Stock Exchange Archive, Guildhall Library).

16 The firm had almost failed before the war and was, in consequence, cautious in trading (Reader, 1979, pages 132, 134 and 179).

17 Stock Exchange minutes, 8 October 1923, 16 October 1923, 2 October 1923, 27 February 1928, 30 April 1928, 22 October 1928 (Stock Exchange Archive, Guildhall Library).

18 Stock Exchange minutes, 10 November 1925, 21 December 1925, 13 April 1927, 15 October 1928, 15 July 1929, 17 April 1934 (Stock Exchange Archive, Guildhall Library).

19 Stock Exchange minutes, 15 October 1928, 14 January 1929, 30 November 1936 (Stock Exchange Archive, Guildhall Library).

20 Stock Exchange minutes, 29 October 1934, 12 November 1934, 9 January 1939, 6 March 1939, 3 April 1939 (Stock Exchange Archive, Guildhall Library).

21 Stock Exchange minutes, 16 March 1936 (Stock Exchange Archive, Guildhall Library).

22 In November 1919, DA Trust Pool applied for permission to deal in units that it proposed to issue. This scheme was different from the fixed trusts of the 1930s as DA Trust Pool proposed to acquire shares in a company which would develop a new business in North America for Dunlop. The units would represent a proportion of the shares in the new business. It was promoted by James White, who was closely involved with the Beecham Estate and had been involved in an attempt to corner shares in Mexican Eagle (with Clarence Hatry) during 1919 (Applications for Listing file, Stock Exchange Archive, Guildhall Library). (Corley, 1986, pages 784–790).

23 The 'Ford Unit' was a scheme like DA Trust Pool in which a trust was alleged to own shares in Ford Company of Canada, issuing units which were alleged to convey a right to a proportion of the shares. The hawkers falsely alleged that the issue of the units in this way had been authorised by Ford Company of Canada.

24 In contrast to the London Exchange, within the NYSE commission houses which had been gaining in influence wanted to offer brokerage services to outside investors of modest means, following what would in London have been termed a 'rig' on the shares of the Stutz Motor Car Company. In 1920, the commission houses agitated for the threat of public regulation to be resisted by enlarging the number of shareholders. Although the NYSE had tended to discourage the development of retail brokerages, its policy was changed in 1921 to support members in competition with the rival Consolidated

Exchange. This led the NYSE to campaign to attract investors, presenting itself as 'the people's market', heralding universal ownership of corporate shares as the key to the equitable distribution of prosperity (Ott, 2008, pages 623–624; Ott, 2009, page 60; Ott, 2011, page 192; Holt, 2008). By comparison, the London Exchange's occasional advertisements recommending in a restrained manner that potential investors should seek the assistance of a member of the Exchange lacked enthusiasm.

25 Stock Exchange minutes, 11 March 1935 (Stock Exchange Archive, Guildhall Library).

26 In 1919, it was argued on behalf of the Stock Exchange that there was no duty to individual members beyond providing access to the facilities of the Exchange for a period of 12 months: the standard membership term (Judgment of the Lord Chancellor in *Weinberger v Inglis and Others*, *The Times*, 8 April 1919, page 6). The case arose over decisions by the committee to exclude from membership people 'of enemy birth' (including naturalised British citizens). The court did not pursue this argument but indicated that it did not accept the contention that the Exchange's obligation to members was so limited.

27 It was agreed in September 1944 that the Committee for General Purposes would cease to exist from 25 March 1945, to be replaced by a Council consisting of nine Trustees and Managers *ex officio* as foundation members and 30 ordinary members elected by ballot. In the final version of the new constitution which came into force on 1 March 1948, it was provided that one-third of the foundation members would retire on 24 June 1952 and one-third on each of 24 June 1954 and 24 June 1956 so that from that point, the Council consisted simply of elected members (with the Government broker serving *ex officio*) (Morgan and Thomas, 1961, page 232).

28 'Responsible Stockbroking', *The Economist*, 23 June 1945, page 859.

29 In a special issue of *The Banker* in 1949, Graham Greenwell argued for a return to the Exchange's sturdy laissez-faire roots, calling for the Council to 'support free trade in securities, and permit and improve every device for such trading, whether contangoes, options or dealings for the Account' (*The Banker*, March 1949, page 161 et seq.).

References

Primary works: unpublished documents

Stock Exchange Archive, Guildhall Library.

Primary works: newspapers and periodicals

The Banker.
The Economist.
The Times.

Primary works: parliamentary and government reports

Reports of the Committee Appointed by the Attorney General to Consider the Legal Interpretation of the Term 'Period of the War' (1918), (Cd 9100). (HMSO, London). (The Atkin Committee Report).

Primary works: contemporary books and articles

Lindley, N (1891), *A Treatise on the Law of Partnership* (Fifth edition, Sweet and Maxwell, London).
Sonne, HC (1915), *The City, Its Finance: July 1914 to July 1915 and Future* (Effingham Wilson, London).

Secondary works

Burhop, C, Chambers, D, Cheffins, BR (2014), 'Regulating IPOs: evidence from going public in London 1900–1913', *Explorations in Economic History*, volume 5, January 2014, pages 60–76.

Corley, TAB (1986), 'James White', in Jeremy, DJ (editor), *Dictionary of Business Biography*, volume 5, S-Z, pages 784–790 (Butterworths, London).

Dimson, E, Marsh, P and Staunton, M (2002), *Triumph of the Optimists: 101 years of global investment returns*. (Princeton University Press, Princeton, New Jersey).

Gleeson, A (1981), *People and their Money: 50 Years of Private Investment* (Privately Published, London).

Holt, DS (2008), *Acceptable Risk: Law, Regulation, and the Politics of American Financial Markets 1878–1930.* Unpublished PhD thesis, Department of History, University of Virginia.

Kinross, J (1982), *Fifty Years in the City: Financing Small Business* (John Murray, London).

Kynaston, D (1991), *Cazenove & Co: A History* (Batsford, London).

Kynaston, D (1999), *The City of London: Illusions of Gold 1914–1945*, volume 3 (Chatto & Windus, London).

Macey, JR and Novogrod, C (2011–2012), 'Enforcing Self-Regulatory Organizations' Penalties and the Nature of Self-Regulation', *Hofstra Law Review*, volume 40, pages 963–1003.

Michie, RC (1999), *The London Stock Exchange: A History* (Oxford University Press, Oxford).

Moran, M (2003), *The British Regulatory State: High Modernism and Hyper-Inflation* (Oxford University Press, Oxford).

Morgan, EV and Thomas, WA (1961), *The Stock Exchange: Its History and Functions* (Elek Books, London).

Moss, M (2000), *The Building of Europe's Largest Mutual Life Company: Standard Life, 1825–2000* (Mainstream Publishing, Edinburgh).

Neal, L and Davis, L (2006), 'The Evolution of the Structure and Performance of the London Stock Exchange in the First Global Financial Market 1812–1914', *European Review of Economic History*, volume 3, pages 279–300.

Ott, JC (June 2009), '"The Free and Open People's Market": Political Ideology and Retail Brokerage at the New York Stock Exchange, 1913–1933', *The Journal of American History*, volume 96, number 1, pages 44–71.

Ott, JC (2011), *When Wall Street Met Main Street: The Quest for an Investors' Democracy* (Harvard University Press, Cambridge, MA).

Reader, WJ (1979), *A House in the City: A Study of the City and of the Stock Exchange Based on the Records of Foster & Braithwaite, 1825–1975* (Batsford, London).

Reader, WJ and Kynaston, D (1998), *Phillips & Drew: Professionals in the City* (Robert Hale, London).

Reed, MC (1975), *A History of James Capel & Co.* (Privately Published, London).

Swinson, C (2016), *Share Trading and the London Stock Exchange 1914–1945: The Dawn of Regulation.* Unpublished PhD thesis, University of Durham.

Thomas, WA (1978), *The Finance of British Industry 1891–1976* (Methuen, London).

Worswick, GDN and Tipping, DG (1967), *Profits in the British Economy 1909–1938* (Basil Blackwell, Oxford).

6   Forced into partnership
       1914–1918

Introduction

The onset of war in July 1914 led the London Stock Exchange to close, opening again five months later in January 1915. Reopening only became possible when agreement had been reached with the government on a measure of protection for members from calls to meet liabilities contracted before the onset of war and on controls to govern wartime trading. Trading controls were unprecedented and proved dysfunctional, as they were promulgated in the form of Temporary Regulations of the Stock Exchange, which did not apply to off-market trading. They thus served as an incentive to enter into transactions off-market which were not permitted on-market, which both undermined the purpose of the controls and frustrated the Exchange's members. The experience was to confirm the Exchange's prejudice against permitting government intervention in the market.

The onset of war

Austria's ultimatum to Serbia which was communicated on 23 July 1914 and the diplomatic exchanges which followed contributed to growing international tension which was in turn reflected in volatile trading in many European exchanges[1] and in stock prices in London.[2] Between Monday 20 July 1914 and Thursday 30 July 1914, the last day for official quotations, 2.5% Consols fell by 8.9%. (Withers, 1915, page 1). Equities suffered similar falls: Great Eastern ordinary shares falling by 12.5%. The greatest falls were registered by international stocks, many of which were traded in London but held by investors outside the United Kingdom who found it convenient to trade in London. Between the same dates, Rio Tinto Copper ordinary fell by 23.6% and Canadian Pacific common fell by 14.6% as investors attempted to realise their holdings.[3]

Such rapid price falls exposed the weakness of the thin capitalisation of most members of the Exchange. Both brokers and jobbers relied on two sources of finance: bank borrowing secured on holdings of securities and the fortnightly timetable for settlement, which were both challenged by the increasing uncertainty. As stock prices fell, so did the value of the securities pledged by members as collateral for their loans, which in turn led to a demand for additional security to be pledged.[4] Quite apart from this, many members had borrowed from foreign banks to take advantage of lower interest rates and found that, with the coming of war, many foreign banks decided to terminate their loan facilities and to demand repayment. Although in many cases, English banks proved ready to replace these facilities, there was a penalty in terms of higher interest rates (Sonne, 1915, pages 11–12; Withers, 1915, pages 18–20; Roberts, 2013, page 10). As far as investors' balances were concerned, the onset of war meant that settlement became less prompt and less certain.

The inevitable consequence of this financial pressure was that members failed. On 29 July 1914, a fortnightly settlement day, seven firms were hammered: six brokers and one jobber who had specialised in Rio Tinto Copper.[5] On 30 July 1914, the Paris Bourse announced that settlement was to be postponed by one month.[6] This challenged all members involved in arbitrage business between London and Paris, for they would be obliged to wait until 31 August to receive the proceeds of sales in Paris whilst being expected to make payment immediately for purchases in London. That day brought the failure of four more firms of members (Michie, 1999, page 191). That the financial challenge arose partly from the uncertainty of international investment and settlement resulted in the failures affecting not only small firms involved only in domestic business, but also larger well-respected broking firms such as JG Eiser & Company (whose founder and senior partner was Clarence Hatry's uncle) and Derenburg & Company.[7]

At the beginning of the week, as the market was becoming more volatile, some newspapers had called for the market to be closed.[8] A proposal to this effect was considered by the Exchange's committee when it met on the afternoon of 30 July 1914; but perhaps because there was a reluctance to interrupt members' freedom to go about their business, the committee decided only that it would meet again in the morning of Friday 31 July.[9] After hours, a number of major firms told the Secretary that if the Exchange opened on 31 July, they would be obliged to default through having incurred incurred liabilities on behalf of foreign firms who could not or would not remit and option dealers who had been badly caught in the slump in prices precipitated by the onset of war (Lawson, 1915, pages 54–55).

In the face of such representations, which were reportedly supported by the Bank of England, the joint stock banks and the major merchant banks, the Chairman and Secretary determined that the Exchange should close: a view which the committee endorsed when it met at 1000 hours. Thus began a closure that was to last until Monday 4 January 1915, a period of 157 days.[10]

At first the closure was welcomed, for it brought immediate relief.[11] In a market bereft of purchasers, prices would have fallen rapidly even if members had been willing to quote prices which increasingly they were not. Business would have been thin and bank borrowings would have been uncovered by the declining value of assets pledged as security: a problem that would have affected many outside the Exchange let alone members. However, this sense of relief gradually changed. Closure meant that there was no formal trading, which in turn meant no income for members. Although there was some street trading, this was at best a poor and unsatisfactory substitute for there was no public recording of trades or prices and settlement outside the rules of the Exchange was riskier. Moreover, there was a tendency for investors to find other means of trading: such as the *Daily Mail's* service.[12] In short, as time went on, members began to press for the Exchange to reopen.

Closure also thwarted plans of people outside the Exchange who must also have supported attempts to secure an early reopening.

One such group involved Clarence Hatry, who was setting out as a company promoter. For some time, he had been planning to launch a new reinsurance company to compete with the well-established German reinsurance businesses. At the time, the British insurance companies largely relied upon reinsurance treaties with German and Austrian companies with which business amounting to about £20 million was placed each year (largely consisting of fire risks).[13] As it was, there was an opportunity for a British company to compete for this business, but the coming of war magnified this opportunity by disrupting established relationships with German insurers.[14]

In November 1913, to take advantage of these opportunities, Hatry's insurance broking company, Patmore, Logan and Hatry Limited,[15] had acquired the Planet Insurance Company Limited, a small insurance company which had been formed in 1908 by Reginald Luck, an insurance manager. In March 1914, reorganisation of the share capital was authorised by the court and in April 1914, the company had re-registered as a public company[16] in preparation for a public offering of the company's shares. In this project, Hatry was assisted by Sir Frank Crisp, the leading company lawyer and legal adviser to the Liberal Party, who was to act as Hatry's solicitor until his death soon after the end of the war.[17] Crisp invited his neighbour, Sir Douglas Dawson, who after a diplomatic career became Secretary of the Order of the Garter in 1904,[18] to become a director. On a number of occasions, Dawson had explained to Crisp his concern at he regarded as the growing 'German Menace' to peace in Europe and Crisp suggested that he might welcome a chance 'to get a score' off the German by ending the monopoly of reinsurance that to that point had been enjoyed by German and Austrian financiers. (Dawson, 1927, pages 349–350)

These plans were confirmed by a press report in January 1915 that a new reinsurance company, to be known as 'the Planet' was to be formed with a capital of £1 million.[19]

There were thus many interested in the Exchange reopening, although it was not to be straightforward. Closure had been accomplished without government action by a decision of the committee to stave off the threat of insolvency for many firms. Subsequently, pressure on settlement had been alleviated by the government's announcement of a moratorium from 4 August 1914 on settlement of debts, but only for a limited period. Reopening without making arrangements to cover firms beyond that limited period would simply have exposed firms to the same threat. Avoiding that consequence required government assistance. Unfortunately, the government was not initially enthusiastic.

By agreement, the government's general moratorium applied to Exchange commitments on 27 July 1914, rather than 4 August 1914. Restoration of Exchange business required that arrangements should be made to deal with loans and contangoes existing at the end of July carry over; differences on bargains executed between July 27 and 31 1914; and the cash bargains entered into in Throgmorton Street while the House was closed (Lawson, 1915, pages 134–135).

The first class of liability was covered initially by the general moratorium which eventually expired on 4 November 1914. Its imminent expiry represented a problem in the form of the short-term debts of London Stock Exchange members (£81 million) and provincial exchange members (£11 million).[20] As the government declined to provide direct assistance to members, this was eventually resolved by an agreement with joint stock banks that had received assistance from the government that they would not call loans until one year after the end of the war.[21] It had, however, been a condition of the government's approval of this scheme that its consent should be sought for any proposal that the Exchange should reopen. The government thus increased its power and influence over the Exchange (Morgan, 1952, page 26). Once this agreement had been reached, the outstanding settlement, which had been deferred on closure, went ahead on 18 November 1914 without significant difficulty.[22]

As for street trading while the market was closed, dealers were left to settle bargains on whatever basis had been agreed between the parties.

By chance, the deferred settlement took place on the same day as the launch of £350 million 3½% War Loan, which was to prove disappointing in that the Bank of England was obliged to subscribe for large amounts surreptitiously to create the impression that the stock had been oversubscribed (Peden, 2000, page 86; Roberts, 2013, page 186 et seq.). It had been thought feasible to launch the new stock whilst the Exchange was closed, but in retrospect this was one of the factors that had made pricing more difficult.[23] In any event, after this experience, the Treasury was more amenable to discussions of reopening, which were made easier because of a rise in the prices of shares on the street market to the levels of 27 July 1914 (Morgan, 1952, page 27). Negotiations led to an agreement which was announced on 23 December 1914. The House was to reopen on 4 January 1915, but would be subject to a number of restrictions intended to protect the market against the forced realisation of securities, to eliminate operations to depress prices and to close the market to the enemy. The Temporary Regulations (cited in Sonne, 1915) stated that trades were to be settled in cash and not 'continued from day to day'. Minimum prices were to be specified for stocks so that the value of securities lodged with banks as security could not be undermined. Admission to the Exchange was to be limited to British-born and naturalised members and clerks. Naturalised members originating in enemy countries had to satisfy the committee that they had been 'de-nationalised in their country of origin'. No dealing would be permitted in any new issue made after 4 January 1915 unless 'specially allowed by the committee and approved by the Treasury'.[24]

New issue controls

The arrangements for approving new issues were set out in a Treasury announcement on 19 January 1915 and contained four provisions. Issues for United Kingdom businesses would only be approved if they were shown to be in the national interest. Issues for businesses in the British Empire overseas would only be approved if there were shown to be urgent necessity or special circumstances. Issues for businesses outside the British Empire would not be approved. Issues relating to the renewal of instruments for foreign and colonial governments, municipal corporations, railways or other undertakings were expected to be generally exempt from these restrictions (Sonne, 1915, pages 49–50).

This agreement was embodied in the Temporary Regulations issued by the Exchange; and for effect it relied not upon public law but upon contract law as it applied to the relationship between the Exchange and its members. Although this mechanism had the advantage that its creation did not require parliamentary time and its enforcement through the Exchange's normal arrangements could be swifter than a court process, it also had disadvantages. The agreement only applied to the Exchange's members: it could not apply to others such as the members of provincial exchanges, with whom there appears to have been no attempt to negotiate parallel agreements. Neither could it apply to traders who were not members of any formal exchange.

Moreover, the approval of new issues was to be in the hands of a new committee established by the Treasury whose members were: Viscount (later Earl) St Aldwyn, a former Chancellor of the Exchequer and Chairman of the committee; Lord Cunliffe, Governor of the Bank of England; Sir Thomas Whitaker, a Liberal MP; and two Conservative MPs, Sir Frederick Banbury and Captain EG Pretyman. Inauspiciously, not one of the members had experience of the Exchange.

Above all other considerations, the December 1914 agreement showed the Exchange and the Treasury in pragmatic mood. Faced with the demands from members to reopen the market and the need to arrange some financial protection for members from the effects of the declaration of war, the Exchange's committee had compromised in accepting the Treasury's controls which in other circumstances would have been an anathema. For its part, having established the right to sanction the reopening of the Exchange, the Treasury compromised by allowing the Exchange to reopen in return for some measure of control and restriction.

Reactions to the agreement were mixed. Some welcomed it as the means of permitting the Exchange to reopen and accepted that it was reasonable to limit the risk of speculation at a time when there should be a concentration of resources on the war effort.[25] For some, the wartime regulations offered an opportunity:

> to experiment with what was called a 'practical socialism'. For many years, some had been agitating for the government to control all public issues of capital with a view to protecting unsuspecting investors from ill-considered schemes. Whilst the primary object of the Treasury regulations was to prevent the export of capital, some commentators identified a secondary object: was the prevention of loss to the average investor.[26]

> Others were concerned that the restrictions that it was going too far to attempt to forbid any new financial business to be undertaken without the government's express permission. Could this be the country of laissez-faire?
>
> (Lawson, 1915, page 234)

At the time, there was little information about the way in which the new controls would operate. Apart from the brief statement of the purpose of the new issues control, there were no statements of the policy to be followed by the new advisory committee and no guidance on the criteria which it would apply.[27] Presumably, this omission was intentional for the Chairman was strongly urged by the Chancellor of the Exchequer to approve no more than the unavoidable minimum number of issues.[28] Equally, there was no guidance on the process which it would follow and the way in which its decisions would be communicated. All of this was left to be settled in practice. This allowed the market to believe initially that new issues could still be launched as can be seen from the newspaper suggestions in February 1915 that Hatry's new insurance company, the Planet, was still to be launched.

Growing concern

As time went by and the Fresh Issues Committee's modus operandi became clearer (Kynaston, 1999, page 11), the negative voices became stronger and its Chairman came to be known as 'Black Michael' after the villain in *The Prisoner of Zenda*, the popular novel by Anthony Hope (Hicks Beach, 1932, page 355).

The first sign of concern emerged in June 1915 after the London Chamber of Commerce had established a 'financial section', whose first objective was to report on new capital issues.[29] Two weeks later, a second sign appeared in the form of a letter from Mr AA Bauman, the Chairman of the Chamber's new section, reporting his concern at the Treasury's refusal to approve an issue with which he had been involved: a proposal to amalgamate the Rubber Share Trust and the Culloden Tea and Rubber Trust. The scheme involved the shareholders of the two predecessor companies exchanging their shares for shares in a new company, the Culloden Consolidated Company, which would take over their operations. Whilst this exchange of shares did not itself require any transfer of cash, the scheme also involved the raising of some cash for working capital; and although the Treasury's Committee did not offer reasons for its decision, it was inferred that the raising of working capital had been critical.

A similar complaint emerged a few months later, over a proposal that Barclays Bank should take over the United Counties Bank. This proposal also involved a cashless exchange of shares although again the opportunity was to be taken to raise a small amount as additional capital. The Fresh Issues Committee's refusal of this proposal was excoriated by the newspapers who viewed the Barclays Bank proposal as potentially beneficial, especially when the proposal was adjusted to exclude any suggestion that additional capital was to be raised. In the eyes of the press, this decision was regarded as a blunder for which no-one was able to advance a satisfactory justification. *The Times* hinted that the members of the committee were all very busy men and implied that they had not given the matter proper consideration. An editorial observed that the offence was compounded by the committee's refusal to discuss the proposal with the directors of Barclays Bank, going on to speculate that if the directors of Barclays Bank were to be treated in so cavalier a manner, there could be no chance that 'the lower lights of the financial world' would secure reasonable consideration.[30]

The sustained strength of the reaction, coupled with the fact that it attracted political attention, led to a reversal of the decision: at least as far as the amalgamation was concerned.[31]

The force of this reaction to the decision on the Barclays proposal was undoubtedly strengthened by the collapse of the Bleriot Manufacturing Aircraft Company, whose shareholders decided on 15 January 1916 that the company should be wound up.[32] The company had survived for less than six months from the date on which its shares were offered to the public, having received the approval of the Treasury's Committee on the recommendation of the War Office which wanted to encourage the manufacture of aircraft.[33] The company's failure was widely attributed to the predations of its promoter, Harry Lawson.[34] The juxtaposition of the rejection of what was widely seen as the solid Barclays proposal and the approval of the ill-fated Bleriot issue was poisonous.

The reaction to decisions such as these which seemed inexplicable to the market was exacerbated by the manner in which both the Fresh Issues Committee and the Treasury went about their business. Applications were considered on the basis of formal submissions in response to formal questionnaires. Personal representations were not invited or permitted. Frequently, decisions were long delayed and were always issued without explanations so that the market was left to infer the grounds on which a decision had been reached and thus how any future application might be considered. Mr Bauman suggested that the committee was exercising its powers unjustly and that there was a dangerous confusion of administrative and judicial functions.[35]

Correspondents writing letters published in the *Financial Times* described the committee as a secret or Star Chamber, superior to the law, whose methods were arbitrary, and autocratic.[36]

Concern about such questions had arisen early; but it proved difficult to engage the Treasury's interest. By mid-July 1915, the new financial section of the London Chamber of Commerce had prepared a report on cases of hardship and injustice alleged to have arisen from the Treasury Committee's decisions.[37] It was not until January 1916 that the Chamber was able to report that a deputation had 'waited upon the Treasury' to discuss the complaints and that a promise had been made that the representations of the deputation would receive special consideration.'[38]

Whatever consideration may have been given to these representations, there was no discernible change in the Fresh Issues Committee's procedures and the opprobrium in which it had come to be held, as the Chairman of the London Chamber of Commerce suggested in a further letter to the *Financial Times* complaining of the arbitrary manner of committee's working, the absence of a clear line of policy guiding its decisions, and the fact, that it had no statutory sanction or legal power to enforce its views.[39]

By this stage, it had become clear that the Fresh Issues Committee was disinclined to approve any new issue which involved the subscription of cash, even where it was arguable that the issue would serve the national interest.[40] Whilst on the one hand, the London Chamber of Commerce and others campaigned against what they regarded as an unsatisfactory state of affairs, others looked for ways around the problem.

Finance-raising alternatives

Many resorted to the most obvious alternative: borrowing from banks or from the Ministry of Munitions. This was the course adopted by companies such as Spillers & Bakers Limited, Leyland Motors Limited and United Brassfounders. In each case, new manufacturing capacity to meet wartime requirements was financed by loans.[41] This represented a departure from peacetime practice by which companies would have financed investment in productive fixed assets by retaining profits or issuing shares, and implied a higher level of gearing than most would have been prepared to contemplate. Whilst this might have been relatively risk-free in a wartime context in which many companies could expect that all of their production would be bought by the government, by the end of the war, it would increase pressure to issue shares to replace borrowing as indeed was done by Spillers, Leyland Motors and United Brassfounders.[42] As a variation of this approach, some companies accepted loans or deposits from shareholders in the expectation that, at the end of the war, they would be exchanged for shares.

Bank borrowing was often not available to finance new ventures. In such cases, the purchase of an existing quoted company provided an alternative. In Hatry's instance, the Planet acquired from Austrian and German interests a controlling interest in City Equitable Fire Insurance Company, a small quoted insurance company which specialised in fire reinsurance. In short order, the company's capital was reorganised, presumably with a view to issuing shares at some stage, and the controlling interest was then sold to interests led by Gerard Lee Bevan, the senior partner of Ellis & Company, stockbrokers (Vander Weyer, 2011, page 96). Taking the profit from this sale, Hatry and his associates then used the acquisition approach again when they acquired from investment trusts controlled by Viscount St Davids[43] a controlling interest in Commercial Bank of London Limited, a small, quoted bank which had been formed in 1906 to finance trading between England and Japan. When it proved difficult to develop that business satisfactorily, it had been acquired by Viscount St Davids and his associates to concentrate on banking business within England but on the commencement of war had reduced its activities. Hatry used the bank as the main vehicle for his stock market operations, augmented by the later acquisition of Reuters Bank (Emden, 1951, page 221).

A third alternative to an issue of shares on the London Exchange was a private issue of shares outside the market, which of course remained possible because the wartime restrictions on new issues only applied to the London Exchange. This possibility was taken up quickly, especially by shipping interests, as a result of which there was revival of the one ship company that had at one time been a prominent feature of promotions

In November 1915, the *Financial Times* listed 88 such companies with a combined capitalisation of about £2.5 million.[44]

The attractions of this business had led firms to forsake membership of the Exchange. Some firms such as Helbert Wagg & Russell had followed this course before the war, commencing business as an issuing house under the name Helbert Wagg & Company.[45] In 1915, they were followed by Sperling & Company which in due course was to concentrate upon ship-building and ship-repairing companies. (Diaper, 1990, page 75) There was sufficient activity to justify the creation of new firms such as BST Limited which, in 1915, was established by a group of provincial brokers to specialise in new issues.[46]

Exchange reactions

Whilst all of this activity was helpful in sustaining businesses, it was frustrating for Exchange members. Trading in the market was in any event depressed by the war, and most of the activity that was taking place off-market would in other times have been expected to take place on-market. Pelion was heaped on Ossa by the fact that former members of the Exchange such as the partners of Sperling & Company were actively participating in the off-market activity denied to continuing members.[47]

A similar report appeared in December 1916, which complained that:

> Something more drastic than the present mild warnings which the responsible newspapers advertise gratuitously is needed.[48]

Admittedly, some members thought that the controls improved some aspects of trading:

> The one outstanding feature in dealings in the 'House' during the past four inherently difficult years has been the well-nigh perfect safety for all concerned. Not only did the cash basis of our transactions effectively reduce to – practically – zero the risk involved in the ultimate completion of each bargain, but it tended to stabilise markets in a most salutary and hitherto unknown manner.[49]

Yet in the long term, such improvements in trading did not outweigh the cost of business being diverted to off-market trading.

Treasury frustration

The Treasury was also frustrated by the extent of off-market activity, for the only device available to limit this activity was the occasional issue of public notices urging restraint.[50]

Presumably this device proved ineffective, as the Treasury appears to have consulted Parliamentary Counsel in 1916 on replacing the Stock Exchange's Temporary Regulation by a new Regulation under the Defence of the Realm Act 1914 (DORA) to control new issues. Such regulations were a straightforward and quick way of issuing legislation. At the time this was thought impracticable as the War Ministry's lawyers took the view that regulations could not be issued under DORA that were not closely related to military requirements.[51]

As a result, the Treasury was left with responsibility for a procedure that not only fell short of achieving the objective of controlling new issues and share trading but was also attracting considerable business and, at times, political criticism.

Cabinet review

Towards the end of 1917, this criticism led to a review of the controls as one element of the Cabinet's consideration of a proposal from the French government for a co-ordinated economic offensive.[52] The Cabinet committee's report accepted that:

> it is essential . . . that not merely undertakings directly connected with the war, but also others upon which the national well-being depends, or which involve expenditure of capital for urgent matters of reconstruction should receive the Treasury consent more readily and much more promptly than has been the case in the past. We have had before us various instances of delays and refusals which we cannot but regard as contrary to the national interest and indeed injurious to the successful prosecution of the war.[53]

The report went on to recommend that, as a matter of urgency, a new Cabinet committee should be established to consider appeals by government departments in cases where a new issue had been approved by a government department but not approved by the Treasury within two weeks. This recommendation was subject to the reservation that:

> It is perhaps hardly necessary to add that promoters' schemes, purchase of patents, fancy additions for the purchase of goodwill and other forms of watered capital should all be discouraged, and that only genuine issues of capital for the purposes described should be sanctioned.

In effect, criticisms of the speed with which the Fresh Issues Committee worked had been accepted by the Economic Offensive Committee whose recommendations were approved by the Cabinet after receiving a memorandum from the Ministry of Munitions:

> there is money available for speculative issues which is not attracted by war loans; if the New Issues Committee would allow issues of shares by aircraft companies and by companies requiring capital for extension of mining and certain industrial, chemical, and alloy steel processes, the speculators' money would be brought to the service of the State and relieve the Ministry of making advances to such companies, advances which have to come out of the proceeds of war loans.[54]

When announced, this change in practice was not warmly welcomed:

> The concession has not been made a day too soon and may lose much of its value if the composition of the Cabinet Committee is not more practical than that of the New Issues Committee itself . . . the best thing of course would be to reform the Committee on the lines of, say, the Board of Referees for Excess Profits Duty,[55] but not to give too great an affront to the members who are personally irreproachable, we suppose we must accept the Cabinet Committee as an Appeal Court.[56]

Thus, in the spring of 1918, none of the parties involved were entirely satisfied with the Fresh Issues Committee's operation. For businesses needing to raise money, the introduction of an appeal mechanism did little to assuage their concerns about a system that seemed to them autocratic, unfair and even capricious. For the Stock Exchange, an appeal mechanism did nothing to curb the resentment of members that their patriotic co-operation had led to difficulty for their clients (i.e. companies wishing to raise money) and had also led to a loss of business through diversion to off-market activity. For the Treasury, the review had largely accepted the market's criticisms of the way in which the Fresh Issues Committee and the department had applied the controls: an outcome that cannot have been welcomed. Moreover, the control's effectiveness was threatened by the development of off-market activity. If the Treasury considered that controlling speculative activity around new issues mattered, introduction of an appeal mechanism did nothing to correct the weakness inherent in the control.

Above all of this, experience of the control had left many businesses in a suboptimal position. Those which had not obtained approval for proposed share issues and had financed new fixed assets by bank borrowing were left with higher gearing than they desired. Many that would have preferred to issue shares through the Exchange had resorted to off-market issues. All of those businesses are likely to have looked forward to the end of the war as a moment when they could regularise their finances, assuming that the new issues control would be relaxed.

Reconsideration in 1918

Perhaps sensing that there was an opportunity for change, the Exchange chose this moment to renew its complaints to the Treasury about off-market activity. On 6 May 1918, the committee sent the Treasury a circular from Graham Marsh & Company, an outside broker;[57] a further circular from the same company was sent on 6 June 1918.[58] Finally, on 24 September 1918, the Exchange sent a letter enclosing a memorandum circulated on behalf of Sperling & Company and complaining:

> The Committee desire to point out that a considerable hardship is inflicted on Members of the Stock Exchange owing to lack of efficient Government control over outside issuing houses and that the Public are being educated

to the knowledge that issues of fresh capital can be made irrespective of the interests of the country or the wishes of the Treasury provided no use is made of recognised Stock Exchanges.[59]

The memorandum which was the subject of this letter had been circulated by Clarence Hatry on behalf of Sperling & Company, soliciting subscriptions for shares in Northumberland Shipbuilding Company (NSC).[60]

For some time, Hatry and Sperling & Company had been co-operating with each other to take advantage of commercial opportunities in ship-building and ship-repairing, and in 1917, Hatry had acquired interests in three small dockyard companies: H&C Grayson, Jos Eltringham and Irvine's (Diaper, 1990, page 80). It was expected that the end of the war would be followed by a boom in ship-building as merchant fleets sought to replace ships that had been destroyed during the war. When the acquisition of H&C Grayson had been announced, *Money Market Review* had agreed that recent losses of shipping and the accumulated backlog of repairs suggested that ship building and repairing yards would enjoy considerable prosperity after the war.[61]

NSC was owned by the Furness Withy Group, which decided that the business should be sold. In July 1918, with Sperling & Company's support, the company was acquired by Robert Workman, a London ship broker, who had family connections with ship-building in Belfast. Sperling & Company, with the support of Kleinwort Sons & Company and others, planned to use NSC as a base for rationalising the ship-building industry. Whilst Sperling & Company appears to have been a prime mover in designing the scheme, Hatry's contribution was to market the proposal to potential investors. The memorandum which attracted the Exchange's attention was a part of that marketing.[62]

The Exchange's letter was eventually considered by a then junior official, Otto Neimeyer, who recommended that, in view of the need for regulation of new issues to continue after the war, a regulation-instituting formal control should be considered:

It seems to me that we must once again consider whether strong methods should not be taken against offenders . . . I can see no administrative step that we can take on present powers which is likely to be effective.

Specific legislation forbidding capital issues except with the approval of the Treasury is I take it impractical but there still remains the possibility of a Defence of the Realm Regulation. When this was discussed in September 1916 . . . Parliamentary Counsel saw considerable objection to using the [DORA] to deal with matters only indirectly connected with the Defence of the Realm, but I am not quite sure that this objection holds, in view of the things we have done under the Act. It is not much more violent I should have thought to prevent various forms of diverting possible subscriptions to War Bonds by a regulation than it is to prevent as we do selling securities abroad unless we approve of it. I believe not only Stock Exchange but public opinion would support the rule which had the result of preventing wild cat speculations and I suggest that the question for such a rule ought now to be reconsidered. There is it seems a good deal to be said for starting the policy now, when we should have the support of the Stock Exchange Committee, in view of the possible post-war control which will surely be very necessary.[63]

With the approval of the Permanent Secretary, Sir John Bradbury, and the First Parliamentary Counsel, work on this proposal was started. In mid-December, a draft regulation was sent to the Stock Exchange for the committee's comments, and, once the committee's observations had been taken into account, a final version of a regulation was completed.

What was to become Regulation 30F prohibited the issue of shares stock or securities, for cash or otherwise, by any person unless it had been licensed by the Treasury. But in addition to this provision, which extended the remit of the existing Stock Exchange regulation to all outside issues, Regulation 30F prohibited the sale of any security which had been issued since January 1915 without Treasury sanction. In other words, Regulation 30F would have obliged companies which had issued shares since 1915 outside the Stock Exchange to seek Treasury approval retrospectively.

The new regulation was announced on 24 February 1919 in the form of a press release[64] and elicited a furious response.

The extension of the wartime regulation was not welcomed. As soon as the armistice had been signed, there had been a call for relaxation of the controls.[65] Moreover, it was known that there was pressure to make new issues[66] from businesses which had been looking forward to the end of the war as an opportunity to repair unsatisfactory financing that they had been obliged to accept during the war. But they may have been assuaged by announcement of a re-casting of the Fresh Issues Committee to include market experience which should have offered a prospect of a more pragmatic approach from the committee. Moreover, the extension of regulation to off-market issues might have been welcome as a means of discouraging abusive selling of shares to unsophisticated investors. After all, the need for this had been recognised in two recent reports.[67] But the retrospective application of the regulation to issues since January 1915 would have been a grave disappointment to businesses involved in such issues which had expected to regularise their position at the end of the war and promised to destabilise markets in a way that neither the Treasury nor the Stock Exchange had foreseen.[68]

The effect of the regulation would have been to undermine the value of any share that had been issued without Treasury sanction as it could not be sold. Consequently, such a share would not have been acceptable as security for a bank loan as it could be realised by the bank in the event of the debtor's default. As a result, Regulation 30F would have required banks that had accepted such shares as security for existing loans to oblige their debtors to provide valuable security to cover the loans or to repay them.

In the face of a storm of complaint, the government had no choice but to climb down. Three days after the announcement of Regulation 30F Bonar Law was obliged to announce that the new regulation was to be withdrawn.[69]

It then took some time for a revised version of the regulation to be published, a delay that attracted further complaint in the press. On this occasion, *Truth* complained that there was an unanswerable case for the continuation of some form of control but that doubt had arisen because of the incompetence of the controllers who had made some 'howling blunders' during the war.[70]

For the time being, the New Issues Committee[71] remained in operation, but its decisions were regularly marked by withering comment on contentious decisions such as the refusal (subsequently reversed) to approve an issue by the South Perak Rubber Syndicate,[72] its refusal to sanction a share splitting scheme proposed by Commercial Union,[73] and its approval on 6 March 1919 of an issue by the Co-operative Medical Bottle Company Limited, which *Truth* described as:

> the most recent promotion of a notorious gang (with an ex-convict among them) whose joint-stock ramps ought to have led to a prosecution long ago.[74]

When the revised Regulation 30F was issued, attempts to control domestic issues ceased immediately and attempts to control issues on behalf of overseas undertakings eventually ceased later in 1919.[75] The first domestic prospectus to appear under the new arrangements was published on 21 March 1919 on behalf of Wiggins Teape.[76]

From February 1919, for discouragement of 'wild cat speculation' such as had occurred soon after the armistice,[77] the Treasury pragmatically relied upon other restraints on Stock Exchange trading. In 1915, the Stock Exchange's Temporary Regulations, which had been agreed by the Treasury and were expected to apply until 'the end of the war', specified that trading had to be settled in cash on a day-to-day basis and options business was not permitted. In the event, although hostilities had ended in November 1918, a formal declaration of the end of the war was considerably delayed which meant that the Temporary Regulations remained in force.

At the end of March 1919, looking back at the attempt to prolong the war-time controls, *Truth* lamented:

> that the government had not been able to sustain its initial view that control of new issues should be maintained. Whilst it was recognised that some blunders had been made in granting or refusing permission for new issues, but it should not have been impossible to find men and devise means to ensure a more judicious and efficient control. As it was, *Truth* feared that a great deal of money would be diverted to unnecessary and undesirable propositions, and that the less scrupulous class of company promoters would have the time of their lives.[78]

With hindsight, it is evident that the 1914–1918 war had given fresh impetus to changes in the character of the market that had begun before 1914. In large part, the war had been financed by the issue of government stock leading to a great increase in the national debt from 25% of GDP to 135% (Skidelsky, 2014, page 167). Much of this debt had been acquired by small investors who had not previously held securities tradeable through the Stock Exchange and had been sold to them by agents such as Arthur Wheeler[79] who were not members.

At the time, there were some who understood the risks that this change would create. Reports of two of the many committees established to consider questions that would arise on the close of the war foresaw that people who had become investors through buying War Loan would be vulnerable to abusive share traders in the boom that was expected would follow the war. In July 1918, AS Comyns Carr commented in a minority reservation to the Wrenbury Committee report:

> We have seen during the war a remarkably widespread diffusion of money, and a wonderful growth in the habit of investment, among classes of the population to whom both are a novelty . . . After the war it may be expected that a large number of people who never were investors before will be willing to entrust their savings to commercial companies but will not be very well equipped to select those which are worthy of their confidence. Simultaneously there will be a large crop of new schemes . . . offering unique opportunity to the fraudulent and over-sanguine[80]

The Wrenbury Committee's majority added a waspish comment that Carr had not attended most of the meetings and took no account of his observations. Carr was at the time legal adviser to the Ministry of Reconstruction,[81] which sponsored another committee which was to comment on the risks of share trading fraud. That committee, whose members included Sir John Bradbury[82] and Sir Alexander Roger,[83] was chaired by Sir Richard Vassar-Smith, the Chairman of Lloyds Bank. Its report, published in November 1918, generally supported extension of the Treasury's control of new issues but went further, suggesting that:

> permanent measures would be taken to prevent, or make more difficult, the promotion and issue of unsound propositions.[84]

The report went on to suggest that banks:

> should undertake some responsibility for the bona fides of undertakings on behalf of which they agree to accept subscriptions.[85]

This understanding of the changing character of the market and the risks it created does not appear to have been shared widely by Exchange members. Neither was it shared by another committee that considered post-war conditions. The Commercial and Industrial Policy report recognised that it might be necessary for exceptional measures to be taken in the immediate aftermath of the war but that in general only capital issues on behalf of foreign governments or states should be controlled.[86]

Reflections

Whatever was achieved by way of avoiding the distraction of capital from the war effort, the relationship between the Exchange and the Treasury was transformed by the experience of regulating new issues. This followed from the extent to which the cost of the war was financed by borrowing (Peden, 2000, page 84). Government stock had been sold to large numbers of people who had not previously owned, or expected to own, securities tradeable through a stock exchange. The issue of the first of these securities, 3½% War Loan,[87] and its failure to attract subscriptions demonstrated that the Chancellor's borrowing ambitions could not be achieved without the assistance of a functioning stock exchange. Rather to its surprise, the Treasury had found that it needed the Stock Exchange. For its part, the Exchange had already discovered that it needed the assistance of the government as reopening the trading floor involved reassurance through the deferral of members' liabilities.

This mutual dependability was a surprise to both parties. Traditionally, the Exchange had resisted all suggestions that it should have public functions recognised in public law. It saw itself as a private club which was how it had been viewed by government. Finding how to live with mutual dependability was not straightforward.

Implicitly, the Treasury assumed that the market would comply with the new controls unquestioningly: an assumption that betrayed little understanding of the market which was adept at finding ways to achieve commercial objectives whilst either staying within the rules or working around them. Initially, the market was patriotically inclined to respect the controls, but it was unrealistic to suppose that this would endure unless care was taken to foster market support rather than squandering it by the high-handed and perverse procedure adopted by the Fresh Issues Committee.[88] As market sentiment changed, so support for the controls waned and the propensity to subvert them increased.

Matters were made more difficult by failures of foresight, such as the egregious failure to see the weakness of Regulation 30F. On this occasion, the Treasury consulted the Exchange, although at a late stage, sharing a copy of the draft regulation and inviting comments, and understandably may have been frustrated that there was no warning of the effect that would be caused by the attempt to ban off-market shares issues retrospectively. There were earlier examples. For example, neither the Treasury nor the Exchange appears to have foreseen the risk that new issues would move off-market undermining the control and depriving members of business and income. At an aggregated level, it seemed impossible to discern trends and the implications of accommodations being made in the market at a disaggregated level.

Consequently, from the Treasury's point of view, the lasting memory was that the attempt to regulate market activity had only been partially successful. The controls had gradually lost effectiveness and the Treasury's attempt to recover the position by the imposition of Regulation 30F had failed ignominiously. The implication was clear: direct regulation of the market was unlikely to be successful if managed by market outsiders and more likely to be successful if managed by insiders: it was a specialist business (Peters, 1993).

This was an early recognition of the view expressed in 1931 by the Macmillan Committee:

> The important thing to bear in mind is that financial policy can only be carried into effect by those whose business it is.
>
> (Macmillan Committee report, 1931, page 5)

It is also an echo of the conclusion reached by the Royal Commission on the Stock Exchange in 1878:

> The existing body of rules and regulations have been formed with much care, and are the result of long experience and the vigilant attention of a body of persons intimately acquainted with the needs and exigencies of the community for whom they have legislated. Any attempt to reduce these rules to the limits of the ordinary law of the land, or to abolish all checks and safeguards not to be found in that law, would in our opinion be detrimental to the honest and efficient conduct of business.
>
> (Royal Commission report, 1878, page 17)

It would be a mistake to suppose that these thoughts were just held in the impersonal corporate memory of the Treasury. The final recommendation to the Chancellor which eventually led to Regulation 30F bore the initials of the then Chief Secretary, Stanley Baldwin. In 1936, he was to be the Prime Minister who presided over the Cabinet meetings that approved an enquiry into share-pushing and the legislation that followed. He is unlikely to have forgotten the ill-starred attempt in 1919 to control new issue activity by imposing legislation on the Exchange.

From the Exchange's point of view although the experience had been an unavoidable condition of reopening in 1915 it had not been an unmitigated success. Business had been led to bypass the Exchange and there was little that the committee could do to stop it. Members' frustration at losing business added to their irritation at the haughty and, in their eyes, ignorant way in which the Treasury's committee went about its business. By 1919, members were eager for a rapid return to business as usual, not least to escape the baleful effect of the Treasury's control which had confirmed their traditional antipathy to governmental intervention in the Exchange's business.

Notes

1 The volatile trading led to decisions to suspend or close many exchanges: Vienna (26 July), Budapest (26 July), Paris (27 July), Brussels (27 July), Oslo (27 July), Lisbon (28 July), Oporto (28 July), Madrid (28 July), Montreal (28 July), Toronto (28 July), Amsterdam (29 July), Antwerp (29 July), Berlin (29 July), Milan (29 July) and Rome (29 July) (Roberts, 2013, pages 8–9).
2 *The Economist*, 8 August 1914.

3　Closing prices quoted in *The Times*.
4　'*The Bankers' Magazine* for September showed that the 387 representative securities whose movements it periodically records, marked in the ten days July 20 to 30 an average fall of 5.6%' (Withers, 1915, pages 18–19).
5　*The Times*, 30 July 1914, page 19.
6　*The Times*, 31 July 1914, page 17.
7　*Financial Times*, 30 July 1914, page 8; 31 July 1914, page 1.
8　*Financial Times*, 29 July 1914; *The Economist*, 1 August 1914.
9　Stock Exchange Committee minutes, 30 July 1914 (Stock Exchange Archive, Guildhall Library).
10　*Financial Times*, 1 August 1914.
11　*Financial News*, 1 August 1914.
12　The *Daily Mail* had for some time offered a service by which readers' transactions were matched for a cost below the commission that would be charged by a member of the Exchange.
13　There were thought to be about 40 German companies concentrating solely on reinsurance and a further 40 German companies involved in both reinsurance and direct business. There were thought to be a further 40 reinsurance companies in Austria (*Insurance Journal*, 15 October 1914, page 39).
14　*The Times*, 28 September 1914, page 14.
15　Hatry had joined a chance acquaintance, Deighton Patmore, who specialised in workmen's compensation insurance for employers. They had developed a successful business organising life insurance linked loans for young people wishing to borrow against their expectations of inheritance.
16　National Archives, file BT31/18520/99222.
17　At which point, his son, Sir John Crisp, took on the role.
18　In the Lord Chamberlain's office before the war, he had also been involved in theatre censorship.
19　*Insurance Guardian*, February 1915, page 3. In fact, the authorised share capital had been increased to £500,000 in March 1914 and again to £1 million in October 1914. The further increase in October 1914, which incurred a Stamp Duty charge of about £1,270, suggests that a public offering of the company's shares remained in contemplation: even during the Exchange's closure. Similarly, the newspaper report in February 1915 suggests that the plan had not been abandoned by that stage, notwithstanding the introduction of controls on new issues.
20　The amounts of the loans were established for the committee by circularising members (*The Economist*, 17 October 1914).
21　The assistance had been in the form of currency note facilities. For other lenders, the government arranged that the Bank of England would advance 60% of the value of securities held against outstanding loans valued at the prices ruling before closure of the Exchange. Interest was to be charged at 1% over Base Rate. The Bank also undertook not to press for repayment of the loans until 12 months after the end of the war.
22　*The Economist*, 21 November 1914; *Financial News*, 19 November 1914. One firm, Williams & Wimbrush, failed (*Financial Times*, 19 November 1914).
23　The Bank of England had wanted to offer a rate of interest high enough to ensure that the issued was a success. The Treasury was less inclined to be generous and insisted on a rate that was lower than the Governor would have preferred. In the absence of a functioning market, there was no possibility of referring to market rates (Wormell, 2000, pages 85–87).
24　Temporary Regulations dated 23 December 1914 (Sonne, 1915, pages 45–48).
25　*The Accountant*, 30 January 1915, page 149. *Money Market Review* reported that the controls had met with general approval and an acceptance that all other issues 'must be subordinated to the paramount necessity of harbouring the country's financial resources' (*Money Market Review*, 9 January 1915, page 21).

26 *The Accountant*, 5 April 1915, page 437. See also *Money Market Review*, 23 January 1915, page 50.

27 This omission was later to be compared unfavourably with the practice adopted by an equivalent committee which was later formed in New York (*Financial Times*, 9 January 1919, page 2). The US Capital Issues Committee was inaugurated in January 1918 as a committee of the Federal Reserve Board to express an opinion on whether a proposed issue was compatible with the national interest. It was in essence a voluntary arrangement without legal basis although certain stock exchanges (such as the New York Stock Exchange) made a favourable opinion a prerequisite for listing. Shortly thereafter, in March 1918, legislation was passed providing a legal framework for the committee and creating the War Finance Corporation which took over responsibility for the committee (Willoughby, 1934, Chapter 1).

28 Letter dated 17 April 1915 from the Chancellor of the Exchequer (Hicks Beach, 1932, page 329).

29 *Financial Times*, 12 June 1915, page 2.

30 Editorial, *Financial Times*, 6 November 1915, page 2.

31 *Financial Times*, 18 January 1916, page 2.

32 *Financial Times*, 14 January 1916, page 4.

33 *Financial Times*, 21 January 1916, page 2.

34 Lawson was involved in promoting many companies before the 1914–1918 war (Harrison, 1981).

35 Letter to the Editor, *Financial Times*, 22 June 1915, page 3. This description was largely consistent with a subsequent description given by the Chancellor of the Exchequer (R McKenna) in answer to a question in the House of Commons (*Financial Times*, 16 January 1916, page 2).

36 *Financial Times*, 10 June 1916, page 2.

37 *Financial Times*, 10 July 1915, page 4.

38 *Financial Times*, 14 January 1916, page 3. The delay in meeting the Treasury (and the Chamber's frustration at it) is described in a letter from the chamber's Chairman, Mr F Faithful Begg (*Financial Times*, 6 June 1916, page 2.

39 Letter from Mr F Faithful Begg, Chairman of the London Chamber of Commerce: *Financial Times*, 2 May 1916, page 2.

40 An example of the committee appearing to ignore a national interest was provided by Spillers & Bakers Limited which proposed to raise cash to increase its food manufacturing capacity, arguing it was important to support the war effort. The proposal was refused (*Financial Times*, 8 May 1916, page 2).

41 In the case of Spillers, the capacity was required to meet the food requirements of the forces in France. Leyland Motors Limited supplied all the heavy lorries required by the Royal Flying Corps in France. The whole of United Brassfounders' production was diverted to the manufacture of munitions designed for trench warfare.

42 Leyland Motors and United Brassfounders were both to become clients of Hatry. Leyland Motors became a client by the summer of 1918 at the latest (i.e. before the end of hostilities) when planning began for a public offer of shares, in part to replace bank borrowing. United Brassfounders' issue occurred somewhat later, in 1920, and was a private rather than a public issue (Memorandum by Gerard Lee Bevan dated 7 September 1920, National Archives, file HO 144/2745).

43 Viscount St Davids was a prominent supporter of the Liberal Party, and would have been known to Hatry's solicitor, Sir Frank Crisp, who was legal adviser to the Liberal Party.

44 *Financial Times*, 22 November 1915, page 3.

45 The new firm was established on 1 January 1913 (Roberts, 1992, page 364).

46 The new business was led by Edgar Crammond, who was the secretary of the Liverpool Stock Exchange, a position he left in 1918 to become Managing Director of BST.

Subsidiary companies were established in major cities around the country to secure support from provincial brokers in obtaining a bigger share of underwriting for new issues which gravitated towards London. In the mid-1920s, the network was reorganised under a new holding company and re-named British Shareholders Trust Limited (*The Times*, 26 June 1918, page 10; 20 June 1924, page 22).

47 *Money Market Review*, 16 September 1916, pages 163–164.

48 *Money Market Review*, 20 December 1916, page 371.

49 Letter from Gerald Williams to the committee, Rules and Regulations Committee minutes, 27 November 1918 (Stock Exchange Archive, Guildhall Library).

50 For examples of such warnings see *The Times*, 8 March 1917, page 12 and 10 October 1918, page 12.

51 Letter from Parliamentary Counsel dated 24 October 1918 (National Archives, file T12200/37031).

52 Appointment of a committee to consider an economic offensive (National Archives, Cabinet minutes, 20 August 1917, page 5, CAB/23/3/68).

53 Interim Report Number 7 of the Economic Offensive Committee (National Archives, Cabinet minutes, CAB/24/4/34).

54 National Archives, Cabinet minutes, 21 February 1918, CAB/23/5/43. The recommendation was approved after circulation of a memorandum by the Ministry of Munitions, which suggested that the manufacture of munitions had been held up by the Treasury control (National Archives, Cabinet minutes, CAB/24/40/82). The memorandum had been written by Sir Laming Worthington-Evans who was Parliamentary Secretary to the Ministry of Munitions but before the war had practised as a solicitor, who was knowledgeable about company law and, indeed, was a published author on the subject. In 1915 and 1916, as a backbencher, he had asked parliamentary questions about the Fresh Issues Committee's processes.

55 The Board of Referees was created to minimise parliamentary objections to the detailed provisions of Excess Profits Duty. External to the Inland Revenue, it comprised 'persons sufficiently experienced in general business to appreciate the issues involved'. Its 29 members included nine accountants and successive senior partners of Price, Waterhouse & Company served as members. The first appointments were announced on 7 December 1915 (Stamp, 1932, page 170; Billings and Oats, 2014, page 93).

56 *Financial Times*, 5 March 1918, page 2. Similar sentiments were expressed in *The Accountant*, 16 March 1918, page 227.

57 National Archives, file T18210.

58 National Archives, file T12200/22511. The Stock Exchange appears to have submitted similar circulars on other occasions as an internal Treasury memorandum refers to circulars in respect of Russo-Canadian Development Corporation Limited, Kwall Tin Fields of Nigeria and Harmony Transvaal Development Company (National Archives, file T12200/37071). Documentary evidence of these submissions does not appear to have survived.

59 National Archives, file T12200/37071.

60 Kleinwort & Sons Archive, London Metropolitan Archives.

61 *Money Market Review*, 2 June 1917, page 321.

62 *The Times*, 7 October 1918, page 12.

63 Memorandum dated 1 November 1918 (National Archives, file T12200/37071). The change in approach to DORA reflected differences in legal interpretations of the meaning of 'the necessity of war' rather than an increasing laxity in applying DORA (Hull, 2014).

64 Treasury press release C10917. Reproduced in *Sperling's Journal*, March 1919, pages 20–21.

65 *The Times*, 13 November 1918, page 13.

66 *The Times*, 6 December 1918, page 13; 10 March 1919, page 17.

67 The report of the Wrenbury Committee on Company Law Amendment included a reservation by a member, AS Comyns Carr, warning of the risk that many new investors would lose money as a result of abusive share advisers (Wrenbury Committee report, 1918, pages 13–14). The report of the Vassar-Smith Committee on Financial Facilities made a similar point (Vassar-Smith Committee report, 1918, page 8).

68 *The Times*, somewhat unpersuasively, argued that arguments about retrospection were not significant and that the prime interest lay in 'what sort of new issues are now to be much more freely sanctioned' (*The Times*, 6 March 1919, page 15).

69 Article headed 'Our Financial Muddlers' (*Truth*, 5 March 1919, page 330). A proposal to issue the regulation had been approved in November 1918 by Stanley Baldwin as Financial Secretary at the Treasury and by Bonar Law when he was still Chancellor of the Exchequer. Its announcement in February 1919 was made by Austen Chamberlain who had become Chancellor, on Bonar Law's becoming Leader of the House.

70 Article headed 'The New Issues Farce' (*Truth*, 19 March 1919, page 423).

71 The Fresh Issues Committee had been re-named the New Issues Committee.

72 *Truth*, 12 March 1919, page 375.

73 The Commercial Union proposed to divide its £10 shares into two shares of £5. *The Times*, 22 February 1922, page 1919.

74 *Truth*, 19 March 1919, page 423.

75 On 12 September 1919, letters were sent to members of the New Issues Committee thanking them for their services which would no longer be required (National Archives, file T172/1039).

76 *The Times*, 21 March 1919, page 19.

77 An example of such speculation was provided by trading in the shares of Hudson's Consolidated (*The Times*, 26 November 1918, page 11).

78 *Truth*, 26 March 1919, page 466.

79 Subsequently knighted for his efforts.

80 Wrenbury Committee report, 1918, pages 13–14.

81 The Minister responsible for the department was Dr Christopher Addison, who had contributed a foreword to Carr's 1912 book on National Insurance.

82 Permanent Secretary to the Treasury.

83 Former Chairman of Commercial Bank of London Limited, acquired by Hatry in 1916, and Director General of the unit that had been responsible for the production of munitions for trench warfare during the war.

84 Vassar-Smith Committee report, 1918, page 8.

85 Vassar-Smith Committee report, 1918, page 10.

86 Lord Balfour Committee report, 1918, page 42.

87 The Chancellor's borrowing plans and the first issue were both announced by the Chancellor in the Autumn Budget statement in November 1914.

88 Changes in the market's attitude towards the new issue controls may also have been a product of a slow realisation that whatever had been understood in January 1915, the Chancellor of the Exchequer had never intended that domestic share issues should be encouraged or even permitted.

References

Primary works: unpublished documents

Kleinwort Benson Archive, London Metropolitan Archives.
National Archives.
Stock Exchange Archive, Guildhall Library.

Primary works: newspapers and periodicals

The Accountant.
The Economist.
Financial News.
Financial Times.
Insurance Guardian.
Money Market Review.
Sperling's Journal.
The Times.
Truth.

Primary works: government and parliamentary reports

Board of Trade (1918a), *Final Report of the Committee on Commercial and Industrial Policy After the War* (Cmd 9035). (HMSO, London). ('The Lord Balfour Committee Report).

Board of Trade (1918b), *Report of the Committee on Financial Facilities* (Cmd 9227). (HMSO, London). ('The Vassar-Smith Committee Report').

Board of Trade (1918c), *Report of the Company Law Amendment Committee* (Cmd 9138). (HMSO, London). ('The Wrenbury Committee Report').

HM Treasury (1931), *Report of the Committee on Finance and Industry* (Cmd 3897). (HMSO, London). ('The Macmillan Committee Report').

Royal Commission Report (1878), *London Stock Exchange Commission: Report of the Commissioners* (Cmd 2157). (HMSO, London).

Primary works: contemporary books and articles

Dawson, Sir D (1927), *A Soldier Diplomat* (John Murray, London).

Hicks Beach, Lady Victoria (1932), *Life of Sir Michael Hicks Beach*, volume 2 (Macmillan, London).

Lawson, WR (1915), *British War Finance 1914–1915* (Constable & Company, London).

Sonne, HC (1915), *The City, Its Finance: July 1914 to July 1915 and Future* (Effingham Wilson, London).

Stamp, J (1932), *Taxation During the War* (Oxford University Press, London).

Willoughby, W (1934), *The Capital Issues Committee and War Finance Corporation* (Johns Hopkins Press, Baltimore).

Withers, H (1915), *War and Lombard Street* (EP Dutton & Company, New York).

Secondary works

Billings, M and Oats, L (2014), 'Innovation and Pragmatism in Tax Design: Excess Profits Duty in the UK During the First World War', *Accounting History Review*, volume 24, numbers 2–3, pages 83–101.

Diaper, S (1990), 'The Sperling Combine and the Shipbuilding Industry, Merchant Banking and Industrial Finance in the 1920s', in van Helten, JJ and Cassis, Y (editors), *Capitalism in a Mature Economy: Financial Institutions, Capital Exports and British Industry, 1870–1939* (Edward Elgar, Aldershot).

Emden, PH (1951–52), 'Baron Paul Julius de Reuter', *Transactions, the Jewish Historical Society of England*, volume 17, pages 215–223.

Harrison, AE (1981), 'Joint Stock Company Flotation in the Cycle Motor Vehicle and Related Industries 1882–1914', *Business History*, volume XXIII, number 2, pages 165–190.

Hull, IV (2014), *A Scrap of Paper: Breaking and Making International Law During the Great War* (Cornell University Press, Ithaca, NY).

Kynaston, D (1999), *The City of London: Illusions of Gold 1914–1945*, volume 3 (Chatto & Windus, London).

Michie, RC (1999), *The London Stock Exchange: A History* (Oxford University Press, Oxford).

Morgan, EV (1952), *Studies in British Financial Policy, 1914–1925* (Macmillan, London).

Peden, GC (2000), *The Treasury and British Public Policy, 1906–1959* (Oxford University Press, Oxford).

Peters, J (1993), 'The British Government and the City-Industry Divide: The Case of the 1914 Financial Crisis', *Twentieth Century British History*, volume 4, number 2, pages 126–142.

Roberts, R (1992), *Schroders: Merchants and Bankers* (Macmillan, London).

Roberts, R (2013), *Saving the City: The Great Financial Crisis of 1914* (Oxford University Press, Oxford).

Skidelsky, R (2014), *Britain Since 1900: A Success Story?* (Vintage Books, London).

Vander Weyer, M (2011), *Fortune's Spear: The Story of the Blue-Blooded Rogue Behind the Most Notorious City Scandal of the 1920s* (Elliott & Thompson, London).

Wormell, J (2000), *The Management of the National Debt of the United Kingdom, 1900–1932* (Routledge, London).

7   Leave it to the Exchange 1919–1929

Introduction

Speaking of regulation of share trading in the 1920s without qualifying the term is misleading. None of the organisations involved accepted responsibility for regulating share trading in the sense of managing the risks that all parties took in becoming involved in trading. Nor did they think it necessary that all such risks should be managed for all parties. The Exchange believed itself to be running a members' organisation with the narrow objectives of maximising members' business, and limiting members' counterparty risk. No corporate responsibility towards outsiders was accepted by the Exchange which assumed that outsiders should understand the basis on which the market operated and be able to afford the financial consequences of the risks of dealing. If their transactions took place through the market, outsiders were expected to manage their own risks. Implicitly, if they were incapable of doing this, they should not be dealing.

This did not mean that there was no scrutiny of new issues. For a security to be admitted to the Official List, the Exchange's rules had to be followed and mandatory disclosures had to be made, but, by means of the Special Settlement arrangements which were accompanied by less arduous requirements, a large number of riskier securities were admitted to dealing with significantly less scrutiny (Davis and Gallman, 2001, page 191). This lack of scrutiny undoubtedly reflected a concern that a more restrictive regime would have those securities to other exchanges causing a loss of business for the Exchange's members. It must also have reflected an understanding of the risk appetite of the Exchange's habitual investors coupled with a lack of any prolonged public demand for greater protection, which suggests that, before 1914, there were no, or only weak, incentives for the Exchange to regulate the quality of all securities in which dealing was permitted (Burhop et al., 2014, pages 73–74).

As for the Board of Trade, it saw itself as responsible for ensuring that proper arrangements existed for members of the public to seek redress if deals misfired. It also tried to ensure that egregiously abusive practices were punished in the hope that others might be deterred from such practices. The DPP's responsibility extended to ensuring that egregious cases were prosecuted, but no further.

The events of the 1920s challenged the limited view of their roles held by each of these three organisations.

London Stock Exchange

From the beginning of the gradual return to peacetime trading in 1919, the Exchange's committee returned to its pre-war role of policing members' compliance with the rules, amending them when necessary to reflect new peacetime arrangements and to respond to evidence of traders taking advantage of weaknesses in the rules.

For many years, company law had required that prospectuses covering new issues of shares should include various disclosures including, for example, information about goodwill, the company's contracts and promoters' profits.[1] Those requirements did not apply to offers for sale, in which another company owning shares in the company being floated offered those shares for sale. By structuring a new issue as an offer for sale, a promoter was thus given the opportunity to avoid inconvenient disclosure. A document would be published that looked like a prospectus and gave a great deal of the information that would be expected in a prospectus but left out key details.[2]

One such offer came to the committee's attention in November 1919. An application was made for permission to deal in the shares of Agricultural Industries Limited (AIL): one of Hatry's promotions. The documents were in strict compliance with the law and the rules. However, the committee's papers suggest that the committee was sceptical about the completeness of the information disclosed because the application file contains manuscript annotations suggesting that someone attempted to calculate the profit that Hatry as promoter was making from the promotion. These annotations indicate that there was no profit for the promoter: an answer that must have seemed incredible to whoever made the annotations, for the scale of promoters' profits was notorious. It was indeed incorrect. A misleading impression had been created by the non-disclosure of agreements between AIL, Hatry's company Commercial Bank of London Limited (CBL) and the farming companies being acquired by AIL from the Dennis family: disclosure that would have been required in a prospectus but was not required in an offer for sale.[3] Under these agreements, CBL was enabled to extract cash from the farming companies by way of dividend as ownership of their shares was passed from the Dennis family to AIL by way of CBL. Payment of that dividend was obscured in the published information and was the source of the promoter's profit.[4]

Realising that this inconsistency between the law and the rules was an open door for manipulation, the sub-committee that reviewed AIL's application recommended that the Exchange should reconsider its disclosure requirements in respect of offers for sale. At a subsequent meeting a week or two later, the Exchange's Committee for General Purposes approved a proposal that permission to deal in shares would only be granted in respect of shares offered for sale once all the information that would have been required in a prospectus had been published and advertised in two national newspapers.[5]

This was not quite the end of the matter. Almost a year later, the committee rejected an application for permission to deal in the shares of another Hatry promotion: Jute Industries Limited (JIL), which was also structured as an offer for sale. JIL had been formed to float six jute mills which it had acquired from the families who formerly owned them. Hatry had undertaken the negotiations to create the combine after being approached by one of the families. Towards the end of October 1920, the formal offer documents were approved by the board of JIL: a week or two before the offer for sale was announced and, crucially, a day or two before signature of the final agreement by which JIL acquired the business of Cox Brothers, the largest of the family companies. The formal offer for sale disclosed all of the acquisition agreements save one: that with Cox Brothers Limited. None of the disclosed agreements showed a profit for the promoter as the whole of the promoter's profit was to be taken in the course of transferring Cox Brothers Limited to JIL. When the formal documents were submitted to the Exchange, the agreement with Cox Brothers was omitted as it had not been signed before the formal application to the Exchange was drawn up. This failure to disclose an agreement was spotted by the Exchange's secretariat and led to the committee's rejection of the application: a rejection which the committee was later to reverse, but only on condition that the omitted agreement and the information in it should be published and advertised in every newspaper in which the original offer for sale had been advertised. This elicited the admission that the original offer for sale had been advertised in 93 newspapers, and an assurance that amending advertisements had been placed in all of them.[6]

Changing the rules without enforcing them would have been pointless, and the JIL episode demonstrates that the Exchange was, to some extent, an active enforcer: at least as far as Hatry's transactions were concerned. But there were limits to the Exchange's activism, as demonstrated by its failure to notice and prevent the decline in the quality of underwriting which led to calamitous results in 1929.

Arguably, the Exchange had been in a position to spot the dangers of a decline. The problems which were to be experienced in 1929, the year of the crash, resulted from a combination of two factors: a series of changes in the drafting of underwriting contracts, which had reduced the liabilities of lead underwriters, and the acceptance as sub-underwriters of insubstantial companies that proved unable to meet their commitments. Throughout the 1920s, when applying for permission to deal in shares, companies were required to submit copies of contracts, the existence of which had to be disclosed in a prospectus. Thus copies of underwriting contracts were made available to the Exchange and, indeed, can still be found in the applications files. As a result, even if the relevant committee's members were not personally aware of changes in underwriting practice, access to the contracts themselves should have put them on notice of the changes in the liability of lead underwriters. There is no evidence in the committee minutes of any appreciation of the exposure to poor underwriting that this was to create.

It would be unreasonable to suggest that the committee should have spotted sub-underwriters who were potentially incapable of meeting their underwriting commitments. Often, they were numerous and their financial circumstances were not known to the committee. Yet the contractual arrangements were known and the possibility that they would lead to a heightened counterparty risk could perhaps have been seen.

Of course, the implications of such a gradual weakening of contractual terms are much easier to see in retrospect; but the implication is that, for whatever reason, the Exchange was in reactive mode, acting when problems confronted a committee, as in the case of JIL. In effect, the committee was relying upon members. The rules required that for each issue, a member should be nominated to provide full information about the incorporation of the undertaking and to furnish all particulars requested by the committee.[7] It appears to have been assumed that nominated members would not associate themselves with information they knew to be incorrect, which would after all have been a criminal offence,[8] and with issues which had poor commercial prospects.

Throughout the 1920s, the Exchange made no further changes to the rules concerning and none restricting new issues, which presumably was welcome to financially stressed members keen to develop business. Newly floated companies had understandably experienced difficulty in the circumstances of 1920. Many had suffered trading losses which created the impression that they had been over-capitalised on flotation. Some indeed had failed. But the gravity of the economic circumstances of 1920 had not been foreseen, so these companies' difficulties were not automatically regarded as a demonstration of a systemic failure. Leyland's case is an example of a business with good prospects whose management, in company with many others, had made judgements that in retrospect seemed unwise.[9] Amalgamated Industrials Limited fell into insolvency in 1921, little more than a year after its flotation, because of the collapse in demand for new ships. Joseph Nathan (the manufacturers of Glaxo),[10] Handley Page (aircraft manufacturers), Austin Motors and Kommer Vehicles, all of which issued new capital in the aftermath of the war, were all later obliged to seek reductions in their capital.

A study published by the Balfour Committee observed:

> over-capitalisation is not something quite definite, recognisable at any time, to which it is possible to attach a label and in respect of which a culprit is necessarily in the background, though there can be no doubt as to the existence of culprits in some cases or as to the evil and the losses which have resulted. In so far as over-capitalisation results from normal changes in value or in profits it is inherent in business and cannot be avoided. In so far as it results from the skill of men in exploiting the cupidity and ignorance of the public it merits opprobrium.[11]

This memorandum, prepared for the committee by DH Allan, an accountant, concentrated upon the effect of over-capitalisation on the costs and competitiveness of industry because that had been the focus of campaigns in Bradford and elsewhere. It did not consider the effect on investors, especially unsophisticated investors.

Nonetheless, towards the end of 1928, it was recognised in the press which suggested that a large number of speculative issues had appeared in the autumn encouraged by the popularity of shilling shares, and investor enthusiasm for companies manufacturing safety glass, gramophones, and photographic processes. The implication was that the quality of new issues may have declined.[12] The Exchange cannot have failed to be aware of this tendency.

The Economist returned to this theme in January 1929, when it described a practice by which, once floated, a company sold some element of its business to another company whose shares were then offered for sale to the public, a process that could then be repeated. Blue Bird was one such company.[13]

Reflecting concern about the decline in quality, the committee belatedly made small changes to the rules to require more prominent disclosure of details of the capital of a company applying for permission for dealing in its shares.[14] By this stage, the damage had been done. The combination of members seeking to escape from financial pressure and the unwillingness or inability of the Exchange to curb their excesses had the result that in 1928, the brokerages paid out on worthless securities were substantial (Kinross, 1982, page 71).

Prosecution

Quite apart from the failure of the Stock Exchange rules to prevent the decline in the quality of new issues that occurred during the later 1920s, there were signs that public law generally was failing to deter abusive share promotion and selling activity. At first, reports of abusive activity appeared more regularly in periodicals such as *Truth* and *Money Market Review.* The reports began to appear in the daily newspapers. In January 1925, there were reports of the arrest of George Hills and Albert Clark who were accused of conspiracy to obtain valuable securities by false pretences with intent to defraud. George Hills, described as a company promoter, had distributed circulars purporting to have been published by Oil Leases Investment Company inviting recipients to take out plots of land in Texas which it was hoped would be oil producing. It was later estimated that this fraudulent scheme had led to receipts of £700,000.[15]

Throughout 1925, the newspapers published reports of civil actions by which duped investors aimed to recover money paid for 'Ford units' which proved to be worthless.[16] The receipts from this fraud were later estimated to have been £200,000.[17]

Between March and July 1926, the *Daily Mail* and others published articles exposing the activities of a gang of share pushers led by Jacob Factor.[18] In 1926, Bessie Watkins commenced legal action against Imperial Tobacco Company to restrain the company from registering shares obtained from her by share pushers. She had been canvassed to take up shares in the British Associated Oil Company of Canada and took up ten shares and later 40 shares. After receiving her certificates, she was again solicited and finally prevailed on to take up a further 450 shares of $1 each. She was unable to pay the price of those shares, £90, but instead handed over as security a certificate for her shares in the Imperial Tobacco Company, which were worth approximately £578. Subsequently, another representative of the Oil company persuaded her to execute a document which was later understood to be a transfer of her shares.[19]

In December 1927, the *Daily Mail* published further articles about Jacob Factor and one of his associates, Maurice Singer.[20] The headlines under which the articles appeared referred to Factor as an 'Aristocrat of the Underworld' and announced: 'Varsity Man's 50 year frauds' and 'Jacob Factor's Associate: To Prison Again'. On this occasion, Factor commenced libel proceedings against the newspaper claiming that the comment was libellous. When the *Daily Mail* published more articles in the same vein, Factor applied for a Court order claiming that the newspaper was attempting to interfere with the libel proceedings and was thus in contempt of the court.[21]

In the 1920s, the occurrence of two booms and the increase in abusive activity, which had been foreseen before the end of the war and which evidently gathered speed as the decade wore on, might have been expected to lead to an increase in prosecutions, especially of fraudulent promoters and abusive share pushers. After all, in other jurisdictions, this is precisely what happened. After a press campaign for the protection of bondholders from pushers trying to persuade them to exchange sound investments for shares in all manner of speculative ventures, the Attorney General of Ontario cracked down on promoters who failed to comply with Ontario's Companies Act by not filing prospectuses before advertising shares for sale (Armstrong, 1997, page 98). The outcome was a series of prosecutions.

In England, the level of prosecutorial activity against share pushers can be assessed from evidence provided to the Bodkin Committee in 1937. In response to a request from the committee, the Board of Trade prepared a report of action taken in respect of suspected share-pushing activities. This showed that between 1918 and 1929 no more than 34 cases had led to some form of action, including prosecution in some cases: fewer than two in each year.[22]

In most instances, cases did not proceed to trial because the suspects could not be apprehended, often because they had left the country. The report also showed that a wide range of charges was used, which may suggest that there was some difficulty in finding charges that matched precisely the activities of pushers, although the DPP appears to have believed that for most purposes the available charges were adequate.[23]

Table 7.1 Share-pushing cases reported by the DPP to the Bodkin Committee

	1919	1920	1921	1922	1923	1924	1925	1926	1927	1928	1929
Cases in which proceedings commenced	0	1	0	2	0	4	3	0	3	3	2
Abortive cases	0	0	0	0	0	2	0	0	2	2	1
Cases which proceeded to trial	0	1	0	2	0	2	3	0	1	1	1

Source: National Archives, file Bt58/302.

In addition, between 1919 and 1929, a small number of prosecutions arose from charges relating to allegedly fraudulent prospectuses. In 1920, Ernest Terah Hooley and others were prosecuted on charges relating to a fraudulent prospectus in respect of Jubilee Cotton Mills Limited. This was to be the last of Hooley's long list of company promotions. Known as the Napoleon of Finance and the Risley Squire, he had a reputation as an irrepressible salesman who:

> could sell anything: especially worthless securities.
>
> (Bell, 1939, page 165)

A year later, Isaac Hickson was prosecuted on charges arising out of the operations of the National Alliance House Purchase and Investment Company Limited.[24] In 1922, Gerard Lee Bevan was prosecuted on a number of charges including one relating to the prospectus issued by City Equitable Associated Interests Limited in 1921.[25] Albert Augustus Scanlan was prosecuted in 1924 on charges relating to a company called Marchants Limited.[26] Finally, in 1927, Colonel Edmund Eaton and others were prosecuted on charges that related to Chalk Fuel Power Gas and By-Products Corporation Limited.[27]

How effective all of this was as a deterrent is not clear as there is no way of measuring how much abusive activity there might have been had no prosecutions taken place. Anecdotal evidence suggests, however, that there was an increase in abusive share pushing after the end of the war and particularly after 1925. It also suggests that, driven out of New York by the campaign of Albert Ottinger, American share pushers found that England offered a relatively benign environment in which to ply their trade.[28] This at least suggests that in England prosecutions were not proving an effective deterrent for which the record of prosecutions may offer some explanations.

There is a parallel between the English experience in the 1890s and the New York experience in the 1920s: in both cases, the pursuit of company promoters and share pushers through the courts sprang from a person's mission, albeit springing from different motives.

In the 1890s in England, this role had been taken by John Smith, the Inspector General of Companies Liquidation, who used his power to undertake public examinations of companies in liquidation to investigate company failures and reveal potential cases for prosecution. When he left his position in 1903, his department was restructured and the series of revelations came to an end (Batzel, 1987, page 364).

Smith viewed companies as a device that the unscrupulous used to avoid the public exposure that would be given to business malpractice under the Bankruptcy Acts: a process with which he was familiar as he had for some years been Inspector General of Bankruptcy. He viewed his appointment as Inspector General in Companies Liquidation as an opportunity to close this loophole (Batzel, 1987, page 355).

In New York in the mid-1920s, Albert Ottinger was to use action against share pushers and promoters as the foundation for his campaign to secure election as

Governor of New York.[29] In this he was assisted by the NYSE, which regularly reported to him instances of traders and conduct that might warrant investigation. There is no evidence (either in the Stock Exchange Archive or the records of the DPP) that the London Stock Exchange ever considered making such reports. The Exchange only once brought the matter to public attention when it submitted evidence to the Greene Committee on the Amendment of Company Law.[30]

In England in the 1920s, there was no one with the missionary zeal in an official position with the necessary powers to act against company promoters and share-pushing fraud.

Throughout the decade, every prosecution arising from an allegedly fraudulent prospectus followed an earlier process which had attracted public attention. On 14 March 1921, Barry Police Court saw the beginning of criminal proceedings against the Chairman, Managing Director and six other officials of the National Alliance House Purchase and Investment Company which had attracted attention six months earlier. In September 1920, Laura Frish had sought the Court's permission to issue a writ against the company on the grounds that she had been induced to purchase certificates from the company by misrepresentations in a prospectus. Permission of the English Court was required because the writ would be served out of jurisdiction as the company had been registered in Scotland, although the victims of the alleged misrepresentations lived in Wales. The company argued that the application was an abuse of process: calculated to gain public attention for a violent and unjustified attack on the integrity of the company and its directors. In fearing public attention the company was proved right, for the effect of the application was to draw public attention to an allegedly fraudulent promotion which led hundreds of people to lose money.[31] In 1921, it was this reaction that led to a prosecution instigated by the DPP at which 200 witnesses provided evidence for the prosecution.

Six years later, in 1927, the Registrar of Friendly Societies appointed John Fox as an inspector to investigate the affairs of the House Coal Association Limited. Mr Fox's report found that the scheme was promoted with the sole object of putting money into their own pockets and with no regard for the interests of the subscribers. The capital was subscribed upon the faith of statements contained in the prospectuses which were false and which the scheme's promoters they knew to be false.[32] By the end, 228 people had subscribed, of whom 80 were never to see any coal at all for their money. In the midst of the attention attracted to this report, a prosecution was launched by the DPP.[33]

In part, this apparent reluctance to prosecute was due to the limited powers and resources of the DPP. It was also due to the marked reluctance of the Board of Trade to order inspections using powers under section 109 of the Companies (Consolidation) Act 1908 that were the equivalent for companies of the investigative powers of the Registrar of Friendly Societies. As the DPP observed in giving evidence to the Greene Committee:

I have cases from time to time in which I have a grave suspicion that a company is not being honestly conducted. Shareholders communicate with me – I ought to say very occasionally – and I am entirely without any powers of investigation. It is useless, as I have pointed out in this memorandum, to send anyone down to the office of the company. Why, you would be a trespasser; you would be turned out: you have no right of any sort or kind. What is the good of writing to the directors or the Secretary? That brings you no further, and the only section, apart from an investigation when criminal proceedings are intended or are instituted, is section 109, and it has been rather a matter of comment in my department that the Board of Trade are very difficult to move under section 109. It is also very hard on the shareholders to put up the money to meet the expenses of the investigation. If that could be a little more frequently put in force, I think the public would be advantaged.[34]

As a result, each instance of a public prosecution relating to an allegedly fraudulent prospectus followed public attention attracted either by a private proceeding or another investigative process. This suggests that unless there was public pressure, the DPP was reluctant to prosecute. In his review of prosecutorial practice in the late nineteenth century, Taylor suggests that the DPP's office was understaffed and under constant pressure to provide value for money. In these circumstances, it was understandable that the DPP learned to steer clear of the more complicated financial cases (Taylor, 2013b, page 248).

The Director's caution was well justified, for fraudulent promotions were expensive to investigate and then to prosecute. In the Jubilee Cotton Mills trial, there were six defendants, each legally represented. Fifty witnesses were called by the prosecution and were each subjected to cross-examination by each of the six defence teams. All of this took time, a lot of time. The trial lasted from Thursday 9 March 1922 to Saturday 8 April 1922. Moreover, it required skills beyond the normal resources of the police. Two police officers had worked on the investigation full time from September 1921, assisted by other officers within the Metropolitan Police, officers from the provincial police forces in Nottinghamshire, Derbyshire and Lancashire and external teams of company lawyers and accountants. During the trial, the team was augmented by three more officers who were assigned to observe the jury and associates of the defendants as the Director had been warned that attempts might be made to tamper with the jury.[35]

Moreover, in each of the cases prosecuted in the 1920s, the charge that a prospectus was fraudulent was accompanied by charges alleging that the defendants had personally extracted money from the transaction, so that it would not have been necessary to argue the merits of a prospectus in the absence of an allegation that a person had gained a demonstrably illegitimate personal benefit. In the Jubilee Cotton Mills case, Hooley was shown to have converted the company's funds for his private use. For the unscrupulous, the implication would have been that, provided a way could be found of extracting profit from a flotation by a legitimate means,[36] prosecution for uttering a misleading prospectus could be avoided.

Prosecution would have been even more contentious in respect of scrupulous vendors shown to have authorised a prospectus in breach of the law. Doubtless it would have been the vendors' intention to get the best price for their shares however difficult the commercial proposition may have been, but for upright respectable vendors, breach of the law would not have been acceptable. It was one of the functions of a company promoter to ensure that all of the applicable laws and rules were obeyed. If the promoter went too far and failed to comply with the law, from the vendors' point of view, this would have been unintentional.[37]

When six of the jute barons of Dundee chose Clarence Hatry to mastermind the flotation of JIL, they knew of his reputation.[38] They must also have known that the future of their mills was challenged by the growth of competition from mills in Bengal,[39] the reduction in military demand following the end of the war, the termination of wartime controls, which exposed the Dundee mills again to the volatility of raw jute prices, and the growth of unrest among workers in Dundee.[40] By the time that the JIL prospectus was published, the largest mills had reduced their working hours and their labour force to reduce production as sales were falling and losses were in prospect.[41] It is difficult to avoid the conclusion that Clarence Hatry was chosen to manage the flotation to devise a means of obtaining a satisfactory (for the vendors) price for the mills against a background of worsening prospects.

The prospectus published by JIL demonstrates why it would have been difficult to base a prosecution on the merits (or demerits) of a prospectus in the absence of evidence that cash had been extracted illegitimately.[42] In that instance, the reader was invited to concentrate on the high profits earned during the war and immediately thereafter. There was no mention in the prospectus of recent events such as the growth of international competition, the termination of wartime central purchasing, the development of labour unrest or the decline into loss-making. Nor was there any mention of the collapse in the international price of raw jute which had occurred in the summer of 1920 and threatened the balance sheet valuation of the mills' stocks of raw jute which in October 1920 were still carried at original purchase price.[43] Admittedly, the prospectus warned that the wartime profits would not necessarily be repeated; but this caution was set against the counterweight of explicit references to the wartime profits in advertisements placed by one of Hatry's companies,[44] not in the prospectus itself, for which alone the directors were responsible. Whilst in retrospect, it is evident that the families were selling their equity in the face of worsening trading conditions which they did not expect to improve in the short term, it was the company promoter's function to achieve the vendors' objectives without exposing them to a risk of legal action.[45]

Irrespective of whether the JIL prospectus was itself fraudulent, the circumstances of the flotation demonstrate why prosecution would have been fraught with difficulty and also the limitations of the suggestion that disclosure of information in a prospectus afforded protection to a potential investor. The weakness of JIL's prospects could have been spotted by an investor who was knowledgeable about the state of the jute industry, but the investor in London may not easily have had access to such knowledge.[46] A potential investor might also have paused to wonder why the conservative jute barons of Dundee had chosen the end of the 1919–1920 boom in share prices as the moment to sell their equity. In essence, these were matters of judgement which would have been problematic in criminal court proceedings.

These factors explain why prosecutors were unenthusiastic about flotation-related prosecutions, undermining any deterrent effect that prosecutions might have had. In practice, prosecution tended to result from an accident of public attention rather than being a foreseeable consequence of criminal behaviour. Of course there remained the possibility of a private prosecution, but only if the aggrieved parties were able and willing to finance it, having already lost money.

Greene Committee

The Greene Committee was to propose the addition of three new requirements for mandatory disclosure: a statement of the rights to dividend and capital of each class of a company's shares, a statement of any dividends declared during the three years before the prospectus and a statement certified by the auditors of the net profits for the three years before the prospectus.[47]

Unsurprisingly in the light of the evidence presented, concern about the effectiveness of prosecutions lay behind two other groups of recommendations made by the Greene Committee.

Having been appointed following the Court's decision in the City Equitable case, reaction to the committee's report concentrated on the position and liabilities of directors and auditors. City Equitable's Articles of Association had exempted its directors and auditors from liability for loss, except when it was due to 'wilful neglect of default'.[48] The Committee recommended that such an exemption should no longer be permitted.[49] As far as the issue of shares was concerned, the committee adopted a stance like that of the Stock Exchange, limiting itself to recommending changes to the law reflecting the Exchange's rule change in December 1919.[50]

However, in taking evidence, the committee was made aware of American share pushers who were attempting to sell 'units' in England and the response of authorities in New York when similar attempts had been made there:

> it is within our knowledge that the New York Stock Exchange are taking very vigorous measures about what they call the foisting on the public of fraudulent shares and things of that kind.[51]

The committee must have been persuaded that existing practice was incapable of dealing with this abuse, for it recommended strengthening the law so that:

> the offering from house to house of shares, stocks, bonds, debentures . . . should be made an offence[52]

This recommendation was taken up in the Companies Act 1928, although not unquestioningly, for the Board of Trade at one stage decided that the new offence should:

> not be confined to hawking 'from house to house' but cover all personal canvassing.[53]

This may suggest that the Board of Trade harboured some misgivings about prohibiting 'house to house' selling in view of the risk that defining the offence might prove problematic in practice, as indeed proved to be the case.

The new offence was regarded as being of such importance that it was the only measure to come into force immediately on the King's Assent being granted,[54] implementation of all other sections of the Act being deferred until a consolidating measure could be introduced. The new provisions were not universally welcomed, however. Periodicals such as *Money Market Review* doubted whether these new provisions would end the activities of the vendors of worthless shares in the light of the eagerness of many investors to buy them.[55]

Although the new legislation had been expedited, it was more than a year before the first prosecution took place: the new offences were difficult to prove and easy to circumvent.

In support of the Director's efforts, the committee made a second group of recommendations that were intended to deal with the difficulty of investigating cases. It was proposed that section 109 of the Companies (Consolidation) Act, 1908 (which dealt with Board of Trade inspections) should be amended to remove the practical difficulties of which the Director had complained and it was urged that the Director should be given new duties to prosecute. Some of these changes were made in the new Companies Act, although the Board of Trade was nervous of the cost:

> It was thought that the result of amending Section 109 of the Companies Act so as to fix the security at a nominal sum and provide that costs, when the investigation is followed by a prosecution, shall be defrayed out of public funds, would be to increase the number of applications, the expenditure of money and the work of the Department.

After consideration, however, it appeared to the Council to be desirable on the whole to put the recommendation in the Bill.[56]

Nonetheless there remained a marked difference between the amended powers of the Director and the powers that had been used elsewhere. To American share pushers in particular, the new Companies Act 1928 offences must have seemed tame by comparison. In New York, the Attorney General had been given broad and drastic powers of investigation, of subpoenaing witnesses, examining them and compelling the production of books and papers. Mere suspicion was sufficient to warrant investigation. Severe penalties were provided for unco-operative witnesses, who risked arrest and a fine of $5,000 or two years' imprisonment for refusing to attend, answer questions or produce necessary documents (Winter, 1927, page 520).

These powers were created by the Martin Act in 1921[57] and were used effectively by Albert Ottinger.[58] The key to the effectiveness of these powers of investigation is that they could be employed on the basis simply of suspicion that a fraud may have been committed or may be about to be committed, thus avoiding the need for cause to be shown before intrusive investigations of a company's records could begin.[59]

Although the vigorous action taken in New York was mentioned to the Greene Committee, there is no evidence that they inquired what that action was or under what powers it was being taken, or that there was any inquiry into developments in other jurisdictions such as Canada where, in 1926, licensing share salesmen was being actively considered.[60] By comparison, the creation of a new, flawed offence of door-to-door selling of shares was an inadequate response which manifestly failed to deal with the difficulties of exposing potential cases.[61]

Even jurisdictions that were believed to have used the Greene Committee's recommendation as a basis for new legislation went further. In 1929, France adopted similar legislation prohibiting the practice of '*démarchage financier*'.[62] The measure required that sales, purchases and every other operation in connection with shares or bonds should take place on premises used for banking purposes to the exclusion of all other commercial premises.[63]

An alternative approach, involving registration of immigrant share traders, was considered but rejected by the Greene Committee partly because it was not considered appropriate for introduction by way of amendment of company law.

How anticlimactic this outcome must have been. The committee had accepted that in some forms share promotion represented an abuse that required a response. It had also accepted that the existing response was inadequate. Implicitly it had accepted that current prosecutorial practice was not a satisfactory deterrent. In effect, it had seen that the dangers of which AS Comyns Carr had warned in his reservation to the Wrenbury Report had come to pass. Moreover, the government had accepted that the problem was of sufficient importance to require urgent action in the form of expedited legislation.

Yet the result was a disappointing change to the law which many believed was no improvement.

Reflections

For the Exchange, returning to business as usual involved the committee in managing the market as it had always done: in the interests of the members on the assumption that third parties (i.e. investors) would be responsible for managing their own risks. This did not mean that the committee was inactive, but its actions were designed principally to manage relationships between members. This is demonstrated by the committee's change of the rules concerning 'offers for sale'. Having realised that company promoters could manipulate the law's asymmetrical treatment of 'offers for sale', to ensure that even market insiders could not work out how much profit was being taken by the promoter, the Exchange's rules were amended to ensure that 'offers for sale' were accompanied by the information that the law would have required to be provided in a prospectus. A year later, on discovering that in managing the flotation of Jute Industries Clarence Hatry had tried to manipulate the new rules to avoid disclosure, the committee refused permission to deal unless the missing information was published.

Whilst superficially this decision favoured transparency in the interest of investors, it was intended to protect members. The committee recognised no obligation to non-members. After the supplementary information had been published disclosing the profit that Hatry had made from the flotation, an investor wrote to the Exchange complaining that had she known of Hatry's profit she would not have bought the shares and asking how she could obtain redress. The file's record suggests that she received no response of any kind.[64]

In other respects, the Exchange was less vigilant as was to be realised in 1929 when the 1928 boom came to an end. Having seen an end to the wartime controls of new issues and Treasury intervention, there had been no enthusiasm for the Exchange to impose its own restrictions. Consistent with this approach, there is no evidence that the Exchange took any steps to assist the criminal justice authorities in dealing with abusive off-market share pushers apart from pointing out to the Greene Committee that there appeared to be a problem.

This attitude contrasts sharply with the approach adopted by the NYSE. In the early 1920s, to stave off the threat of state regulation, the NYSE decided that it must be able to demonstrate that its self-regulatory mechanisms were working successfully and that it must co-operate with the criminal justice authorities to deal with abusive off-market operators.

A number of stock frauds in the summer of 1919 which led the Bureau of Commercial Frauds to investigate the operations of stock promoters[65] had attracted attention but did not lead to consensus support for any particular course of action.[66] Attention was again attracted by a conflict between the NYSE and the head of the Stutz Motor Company. After Stutz managed to corner the stock of his own company early in 1920, the NYSE intervened by suspending trading because an open and fair market had ceased to exist, an action which led Stutz to campaign against the NYSE for infringing his rights of free contract. In this campaign, Stutz proposed that the NYSE should be incorporated and that its rule-making powers should be transferred to the state of New York.[67]

The outcome of this campaign and a number of false starts was that additional legislation was passed in the form of the Martin Act which did not introduce regulation of share trading but instead strengthened the investigative powers of the NYAG.[68] At this point, the NYSE realised that if it did not act purposefully, its position and independence would be at risk. To preserve both, the NYSE determined to demonstrate that its self-regulatory mechanism was effective and to support the criminal justice system in eliminating off-market abuse. Its aim was to deprive campaigners of justification for introducing state oversight or regulation[69]

Whilst these sentiments are remarkably similar to the views held by the London Exchange which had been shared by the Royal Commission in 1878 and were to be expressed by the Macmillan Committee in 1931,[70] the two exchanges were adopting radically different strategies towards the regulation of their markets. Whereas the NYSE aimed to demonstrate the effectiveness of self-regulation in achieving the objectives of the proponents of state regulation, the London Exchange was withdrawing into a traditional view of its oversight of the market:

a view which did not admit any obligations beyond the actors within the market. These divergent strategies reflected major differences between the views of the two exchanges about the threats they faced.

Whilst in London, there was a boom in 1919 and 1920, and there had been irregular trading, the effect had not been as extreme as in New York. London's equivalent to the Stutz Motor Company corner was an attempt by a syndicate led by the company promoter James White to corner the shares of Mexican Eagle. This had not been so successful, did not lead to suspension and did not become a cause célèbre. To match the complaints about oil stock promotions in New York, there were complaints that many companies in the cotton industry had been re-capitalised during the post-war boom. However, these complaints took some time to emerge and were focussed not on the abuse of unsuspecting shareholders but on the alleged inflation of the companies' cost base to the disadvantage of workers in the industry.

In New York, the public outcry over fraud and market manipulation immediately after the end of the war had focussed on New York's failure to implement 'Blue Sky' legislation similar to that already passed by many other states. There was a public willingness to believe that the practice of share trading was at fault and that New York's failure to legislate had exacerbated the problem. In London, there was no comparable critique. Indeed, when government enquiries examined the subject, they tended to the view that the financial system had been operating successfully and did not require major reform.[71]

Admittedly, political criticism of the financial system was growing in England, but this was not principally directed towards the Exchange.

Initially, at the end of the war, complaints about the capitalist system had limited appeal. The Labour Party's political programme, outlined in 1918, built on the experience of government intervention during the 1914–1918 war and spoke of democratic control of finance and the nationalisation of financial institutions.[72] It did not command broad political support, however, for the Labour Party won only 22.2% of the votes cast in the December 1918 General Election. But gradually, as people realised that their post-war expectations would remain unrealised (Eliot, 1922; Bowra, 1949, pages 160–161). As a result of disappointing economic performance, support grew for critiques of capitalism. From the notion that capitalist civilisation was decaying, developed by the Webbs in 1923 (Webb and Webb, 1923, page 86) by way of Keynes in 1924 (Keynes, 1924), support grew for modifying capitalist markets by the creation or reform of central institutions, until by 1928, it was supported by elements in all of the main political parties. In 1928, the Liberal Industrial Inquiry concluded that:

> In large companies of diffuse ownership, where the shares are mainly held by the general public and not by interests represented by the directors, abuses are increasingly frequent, for which the secrecy of accounts is at least partly responsible. The common practice of publishing balance sheets which convey entirely inadequate information to the shareholders themselves or can only mislead them, facilitates the continuance of mismanagement, and is the cause

of loss and deception for the investing public by placing a premium on 'inside information, gossip, and breach of confidence'.

(Liberal Party, 1928, page 85)

The Inquiry suggested that the necessary rationalisation of industry would involve the national direction of financial resources through a Board of National Investment which would direct public sector investment and raise money by loans as needed (Liberal Party, 1928, page 111 et seq).

Even if they would not have supported the proposals of the Liberal Industrial inquiry, there were Conservative Members of Parliament who recognised that radical change should be considered:

The war period shattered preconceived economic notions, proved possible theoretic impossibilities, removed irremovable barriers, created new and undreamt-of situations. Yet by far the greater part of the legislation which today governs trade and industry dates from before that period. We are surely entitled to ask whether it is now adequate to meet the vastly changed conditions of the modern economic era.

(Boothby et al., 1927, page 35)

They proposed that obstacles to rationalisation should be removed and that compulsory powers should be given to those promoting rationalisation. Co-partnership schemes would be introduced in the larger industrial units thus created, and in banks.

In 1926, the Independent Labour Party had published a report entitled *Socialism in Our Time*,[73] which proposed not only the nationalisation of certain major industries but also the nationalisation of the banking industry. In 1928, the Labour Party published a pamphlet written by RH Tawney at the invitation of the party conference to encapsulate the party's programme, which observed:

with grave concern the present diversion of a considerable proportion of the national credit and national savings into enterprises which, from a public point of view, are at best useless, and at worst, mischievous. It holds that any sane method of allocating them among different undertakings should be based on qualitative, as well as quantitative, considerations and that services of national importance must be adequately financed before resources are placed at the disposal of enterprises concerned with luxuries or amusements.

(Labour Party, 1928, page 26)

For most of the 1920s, although these critiques were gaining support, there was no urgent reason for the members of the London Exchange to fear political intervention and to reassess the effectiveness of their management of the market.

Equally, there was little to encourage the London Exchange to support the criminal justice system in dealing with abusive off-market trading in the manner adopted by the NYSE. In New York, there was considerable share-trading activity outside the NYSE both formally through the Consolidated Exchange or informally. The NYSE had a clear interest in defeating the Consolidated Exchange which, to the NYSE's annoyance, acted as a free-rider making use of prices set on the NYSE.

The London Exchange faced different circumstances. There appears to have been proportionately less trading off-market than in New York and although there were competing exchanges and trading platforms, members did not consider that their interests were threatened by them. As for off-market traders, although there had always been abuse, the anecdotal evidence is that it did not become a serious problem in England until the late 1920s after a number of New York operators led by Jacob Factor moved to London.

As far as members of the London Exchange were concerned, there were no urgent threats which required or justified any change in policy and no change was made.

Notes

1 Section 81, Companies (Consolidation) Act, 1908.
2 Of the 78 issues announced in *The Times* in October and November 1919, ten took the form of offers for sale.
3 Sections 81(j) and (k), Companies (Consolidation) Act, 1908.
4 Confirmed by comparison of the Board of Trade Inspector's report which was not published, and the Exchange's application file (National Archives, file COS 2424/45; Application for Listing file, Stock Exchange Archive, Guildhall Library). The Board of Trade Inspector's report appears to have been the first issued under the provisions of the Companies Act 1948 which gave inspectors powers to investigate subsidiaries of a company under investigation. The Board of Trade's policy with regard to publication of such reports changed subsequently.
5 Stock Exchange minutes (Stock Exchange Archive, Guildhall Library).
6 Application for Listing file (Stock Exchange Archive, Guildhall Library).
7 Rule 136(viii).
8 *R v Aspinal*, 1876.
9 The company had anticipated a surge in demand after the war but this proved short-lived. Moreover, when the company's plans were undermined by the government's sale of Leyland lorries which had been bought for use by the Royal Flying Corps during the war, the company decided to buy and refurbish all of the war surplus lorries to prevent its own sales and reputation being undermined by poorly maintained secondhand vehicles. It took the company many years to sell the refurbished vehicles and to recover from this unexpected burden.
10 Glaxo was a dried milk baby food marketed under the slogan: 'Glaxo builds bonny babies'.
11 Balfour Committee, 1929, page 174. The examples of capital reductions are taken from a list of capital reductions that was presented to the committee with the draft report but was not published (National Archives, file COS 5288).
12 *The Economist*, 10 November 1929, page 830.
13 *The Economist*, 19 January 1929, page 112. The original 'Blue Bird' business was established by Malcolm Campbell, the racing driver and speed record holder.
14 *The Economist*, 5 January 1929, page 5.

15 *The Times*, 21 January 1925, page 18; 17 January 1925, page 7; 21 January 1925, page 11; 27 January 1925, page 5. The estimate of receipts was quoted later in a House of Commons debate (*The Times*, 22 February 1928, page 8).

16 The units in question were said to be issued with the authority of the Ford Motor Company of Canada, carrying an entitlement to share in the ownership of shares in that company (*Harvey v Hoshor Montayne Limited*, *The Times*, 11 January 1925, page 16; 25 June 1925, page 24; 15 October 1925, page 9; *Catton v British American Securities Limited*, 28 July 1925, page 11; *Parkhouse v British American Securities Limited*, 13 January 1926, page 5). The sale of 'Ford Units' had been reported on numerous occasions by *Money Market Review* and *Truth*.

17 The estimate of receipts was quoted later in a House of Commons debate (*The Times*, 22 February 1928, page 8). In error, the newspaper report refers to 'Four Units' rather than 'Ford Units'.

18 *Daily Mail*, 30 March 1926; 24 July 1926; *Continental Daily Mail*, 24 July 1926; *Evening News*, 31 March 1926.

19 *Watkins v Singer and others* (*The Times*, 19 November 1926, page 5; 7 July 1927, page 5).

20 *Daily Mail*, 15 December 1927; 23 December 1927.

21 *The Times*, 12 January 1928, page 5; 31 January 1928, page 5; 7 February 1928, page 5; 11 February 1928, page 4. The court noted that Factor had not commenced libel proceedings in respect of the articles published in 1926. The application was refused.

22 National Archives, file BT 298/69.

23 The Director gave evidence on this point to the Greene Committee. He suggested that the provisions of the Larceny Acts generally sufficed: adducing necessary evidence was a greater problem (Answer to Question 1741, 13 May 1925, Minutes of Evidence of the Greene Committee, 1925).

24 *The Times*, 28 October 1921, page 4.

25 *The Times*, 21 November 1922, page 6, and subsequently; Vander Weyer (2011, page 216 et seq).

26 *The Times*, 15 April 1924, page 5.

27 *The Times*, 22 June 1927, page 28, and subsequently.

28 Interestingly, although there was a history of American share pushers extending their activities to Canada, Armstrong (1997 does not suggest that the exodus of share pushers from New York in the mid-1920s led to an increase in their activity in Canada, which may suggest that the prosecution activity in England was also viewed by share pushers to be more benign than in Canada.

29 He was to fail in this. He marginally lost the election to FD Roosevelt by 25,000 votes in 1928 (Ott, 2011).

30 Greene Committee Minutes of Evidence, 29 April 1925.

31 *Frish v National Alliance House Purchase and Investment Company* (*The Times*, 9 September 1920, page 4; 16 September 1920, page 4).

32 *The Times*, 12 November 1927, page 4.

33 *The Times*, 30 January 1928, page 9. Throughout the 1920s, there is not a single example of a prosecution following the appointment of an inspector by the Board of Trade under the equivalent powers within the Companies Acts.

34 Answer to Question 1812, Evidence of Sir Archibald Bodkin, Director of Public Prosecutions (Minutes of Evidence of the Greene Committee, 13 May 1925).

35 DI Collins's report dated 16 April 1922 (National Archives, file MEPO 3/518).

36 Hatry was often able to extract cash by paying out the accumulated profit of a company by way of dividend. Alternatively, a profit might be realised by using his own company to acquire the business to be floated, selling it at a profit to a company whose shares would then be offered for sale.

37 The difficulty of proving intent is the source of the development in the sphere of factory law of strict liability for charges which were regarded not so much as 'crimes' but as 'regulatory offences' (Croall, 2003, page 45).

38 Correspondence between Robert Fleming and John Cox (Dundee University Archives, reference MS 66/II/10/50).

39 Shares in three prominent Bengal mills were quoted on the Dundee Stock Exchange (Dundee Stock Exchange Archive, Dundee University Archives, reference MS 69).

40 The Bengal mills had been developed using money from the Dundee jute barons themselves. Three Bengal mill companies were quoted on the Dundee Stock Exchange. The Government's wartime jute purchasing scheme was ended early in 1920 (Dundee University Archives). For the growth of worker activism in Dundee, see Walker (1979).

41 The accounting records of the largest of the six mill companies, Cox Brothers Limited, suggest that the company began to record gross losses in mid-October 1920, a month before the offer for sale was published. At that point, Cox Brothers Limited began to reduce its workforce to stabilise the average cost of production (Dundee University Archives, reference MS 66/II/4). Manufacturing cloth from jute was sensitive to cyclical fluctuations in the price of the raw fibre. Traditionally, the jute mill barons of Dundee had managed this problem by rapidly reducing or expanding the workforce (Lenman et al., 1969; Walker, 1979).

42 There is no suggestion that cash was extracted illegitimately in the case of JIL. Hatry took his profit as a promoter by way of a dividend paid legitimately by Cox Brothers Limited as it passed through the hands of CBL, his company. The vendors all received their consideration in the form of cash paid to them by CBL as purchaser of their shares (Analysis of payments due to former shareholders, Cox Brothers Limited Archive, Dundee University Archives, reference MS 66/II/10).

43 The accounting practice followed, for example, by Cox Brothers, was that during an accounting period raw jute would be valued at purchase price: an adjustment to current market price being made at the end of the period when a balance sheet was drawn up. Thus, once a substantial fall in the market price had occurred, the directors would have expected a material loss to be recognised at the end of the accounting period, as indeed happened in the spring of 1921. This prospect would therefore have been known to the directors of Cox Brothers Limited in November 1920 when the JIL prospectus was published (Dundee University Archives, reference MS 66/II/11/20).

44 General Publicity Agency: a company originally established by Charles Duguid, a former City Editor of the *Daily Mail* who, earlier in 1920, had become the head of the issues department of Hatry's organisation.

45 The analysis of the company's trading position is based on the accounting records of Cox Brothers Limited, the largest of JIL's predecessor companies, a large collection of which is held by Dundee University Archives (reference MS 66/II/3–8). A book containing various memorandum accounts includes a weekly analysis of production costs and average cost per unit of production. The account shows that total labour costs were falling, as the company reduced its workforce, and that average costs were static. The implication is that costs were being managed in the face of falling sales so that average costs per unit did not rise. That average costs were static when total production was falling dramatically cannot have been an accident and demonstrates that the company's management must have been aware of the true trading position.

46 The share registers of JIL have not survived. However, the Dundee Textile Workers' Union published a list of shareholders in its regular newsletter. This shows that no substantial shareholdings were registered at addresses in Scotland. Although some shareholdings may have been registered at the addresses of London-based nominees, this is consistent with Scottish investors being better informed about the state of the jute trade.

47 Greene Committee report, 1926, pages 16–17.
48 *Re City Equitable Fire Insurance*, 1925, ChD 407.
49 Greene Committee report, 1926, pages 19–21 and 37–38.
50 Greene Committee report, 1926, pages 17–18.
51 Answer to Question 1073 (Minutes of Evidence of the Greene Committee, 29 April 1925, page 55).
52 Greene Committee report, 1926, paragraph 93.
53 Draft minutes of Board of Trade Council, 10 June 1926 (National Archives, file COS 2964).
54 This was the government's intention when the bill was first presented in the House of Commons (Statement of the President of the Board of Trade in the Second Reading debate, House of Commons Hansard, 21 February 1928).
55 *Money Market Review*, 11 August 1926, page 299.
56 Draft minutes of Board of Trade Council, 10 June 1926 (National Archives, file COS 2964).
57 New York was the 41st state to introduce legislation on this subject, referred to as 'Blue-Sky Laws'. Mahoney (2003) identifies three general approaches adopted in these laws. He identifies 12 states that required a public official to review the merits of a proposed issue ('merit review'). In 29 states, a public official was empowered to veto issues that appeared fraudulent ('ex ante fraud'). In seven states, including New York, issues were not required to be approved in advance but securities fraud was prohibited and a public official was empowered to investigate (Mahoney, 2003, page 232).
58 Indeed, they remain in force ('New York Supreme Court denies Barclays' motion to dismiss NYAG's Martin Act claim', headline dated 24 February 2015. Downloaded from www.lexology.com).
59 Loss and Cowett (1958, page 22). 'The section has a majestic one-sentence sweep.'
60 Armstrong (1997, page 130). The papers of the Greene Committee held by the National Archives do not include the briefing and research papers that would have been made available to the committee.
61 Even the provisions of the Martin Act were to be found wanting. Ottinger's successor as NYAG observed in 1929 that 'the Martin Act is no protection against the common thief who claims to be a broker or salesman and deals in worthless securities. From the petty grafter to the gang of high-pressure salesmen with plenty of money who open a big office, there is a large field in which the remedies provided by the Martin Act help but little' (cited in Balleisen, 2017, page 249).
62 The legislation was passed as a reaction to the arrest of Marthe Hanau in respect of share-pushing charges. It was believed that she was connected to the group led by Jacob Factor who had also been active in England (Guilleminault and Singer-Lecocq, 1975, pages 351–363; Desanti, 1968).
63 *The Economist*, 5 January 1929, page 30.
64 Application for Listing file (Stock Exchange Archive, Guildhall Library).
65 *New York Times*, 3 June 1919.
66 A committee appointed by the Governor to consider securities regulation could not reach agreement and published two mutually contradictory reports. One proposed that the state of New York should create administrative machinery to prevent fraud and the other favoured strengthened criminal penalties against fraud (*New York Times*, 25 December 1919).
67 *New York Times*, 16 April 1920.
68 The Act empowered the NYAG to commence investigations when there was a suspicion that there may be an intention to commit fraud and required co-operation with the NYAG's enquiries by people thought to hold relevant information or documents. It was no longer necessary for the NYAG to wait until there was evidence that a fraud had been committed.

69 Memorandum in Opposition to Incorporation of the New York Stock Exchange, undated (cited by Holt, 2008, page 349).
70 Royal Commission report, 1878 page 17; Macmillan Committee report, 1931, page 5.
71 Wrenbury Committee report, 1918. Although the report included AS Comyns Carr's reservation that there was a need for amendments to the law to avoid abuse of investors, a majority of the committee did not share Carr's views (Greene Committee report, 1926; Balfour Committee report, 1929
72 Labour Party (1918).
73 Written by JA Hobson, HN Brailsford, EF Wise and A Creech Jones.

References

Primary works: unpublished documents

Dundee University Archives.
National Archives.
Stock Exchange Archive, Guildhall Library.

Primary works: newspapers and periodicals

Continental Daily Mail.
Daily Mail.
The Economist.
Evening News.
Money Market Review.
New York Times.
The Times.
Truth.

Primary works: government and parliamentary reports

Board of Trade (1918b), *Report of the Company Law Amendment Committee* (Cd 9138). (HMSO, London). ('The Wrenbury Committee Report').
Board of Trade (1926), *Report of the Company Law Amendment Committee* (Cmd 2657). (HMSO, London). ('The Greene Committee Report').
Board of Trade (1929), *Final Report of the Committee on Industry and Trade* (Cmd 3282). (HMSO, London).
Greene Committee Minutes of Evidence (1926), *Minutes of Evidence of the Company Law Amendment Committee* (HMSO, London).
HM Treasury (1931), *Report of the Committee on Finance and Industry* (Cmd 3897). (HMSO, London). ('The Macmillan Committee Report').
London Stock Exchange Commission (1878), *Report of the Commissioners* (C2157). (HMSO, London). ('The Royal Commission Report').

Primary works: contemporary books and articles

Bell, EA (1939), *Those Meddlesome Attorneys* (Richards Press, London).

Boothby, R, Macmillan, H, Loder, J and Stanley, O (1927), *Industry and the State: A Conservative View* (Macmillan, London).

Eliot, TS (1922), *The Waste Land*. Reprinted in Eliot, TS (1962), *Collected Poems 1909–1962* (Faber and Faber, London).

Independent Labour Party (1926), *Socialism in Our Time* (Privately Published, London).

Keynes, JM (1924), '*The End of Laissez-Faire*', The Syndey Ball Lecture published separately as a pamphlet in 1926. Reprinted in Keynes, JM (1965), *Essays in Persuasion* (WW Norton Company, New York).

Labour Party (1918), *Labour and the New Social Order* (Labour Party, London).

Labour Party (1928), *Labour and the Nation* (Labour Party, London).

Liberal Party (1928), *Britain's Industrial Future: Being the Report of the Liberal Industrial Inquiry* (Ernest Benn, London).

Webb, S and Webb, B (1923), *The Decay of Capitalist Civilisation* (Fabian Society, London).

Winter, K (November 1927), 'Parasites of Finance', *The North American Review*, volume 224, number 837, pages 516–521.

Secondary works

Armstrong, C (1997), *Blue Skies and Boiler Rooms: Buying and Selling Securities in Canada, 1870–1940* (University of Toronto Press, Toronto).

Balleisen, EJ (2017), *Fraud: An American History From Barnum to Madoff* (Princeton University Press, Princeton).

Batzel, VM (1987), 'The General Scope of the Act: A Study of Law, Moralism and Administration in England, 1844–1910', *Canadian Journal of History/Annales Canadiennes d'Histoire*, volume 22, number 3, page 349.

Bowra, CM (1949), *The Creative Experiment* (Macmillan, London).

Burhop, C, Chambers, D and Cheffins, B (2014), 'Regulating IPOs: Evidence From Going Public in London, 1900–1913', *Explorations in Economic History*, volume 51, pages 60–76.

Croall, H (2003), 'Combating Financial Crime: Regulatory Versus Crime Control Approaches', *Journal of Financial Crime*, volume 11, number 1, pages 45–55.

Davis, LE and Gallman, RE (2001), *Evolving Financial Markets and International Capital Flows: Britain, the Americas, and Australia, 1865–1914* (Cambridge University Press, Cambridge).

Desanti, D (1968), *La Banquière des Années Folles: Marthe Hanau* (Fayard, Paris).

Guilleminault, G and Singer-Lecocq, Y (1975), *La France des Gogos: trois siècles de scandales financiers* (Librairie Arthème Fayard, Paris).

Holt, DS (2008), *Acceptable Risk: Law, Regulation and the Politics of American Financial Markets 1878–1930*. Unpublished PhD thesis, Department of History, University of Virginia.

Kinross, J (1982), *Fifty Years in the City: Financing Small Business* (John Murray, London).

Lenman, B, Lythe C and Gauldie, E (1969), *Dundee and Its Textile Industry 1850–1914* (Abertay Historical Society, Dundee).

Loss, L and Cowett, EM (1958), *Blue Sky Law* (Little Brown & Company, Boston).

Mahoney, PG (2003), 'The Origins of the Blue-Sky Laws: A Test of Competing Hypotheses', *Journal of Law and Economics*, volume 46, number 1, pages 229–251.

Ott, JC (2011), *When Wall Street Met Main Street: The Quest for an Investors' Democracy* (Harvard University Press, Cambridge, MA).

Taylor, J (2013b), *Boardroom Scandal: The Criminalisation of Fraud in Nineteenth-Century Britain* (Oxford University Press, Oxford).

Vander Weyer, M (2011), *Fortune's Spear: The Story of the Blue-Blooded Rogue Behind the Most Notorious City Scandal of the 1920s* (Elliott & Thompson, London).

Walker, WM (1979), *Juteopolis: Dundee and Its Textile Workers 1885–1923* (Scottish Academic Press, Edinburgh).

8   On the brink of the abyss, 1929

Introduction

As so often, in its first issue of 1929, a *Punch* cartoon captured the prevailing mood. A sailor, labelled 'Optimist', was shown drifting on an exiguous raft which had no sail or rudder, accompanied by nothing more than a small barrel (of rum?) and a tin (of biscuits?). He is waving a pipe: for cartoonists of the day, the usual signifier of Stanley Baldwin, the Prime Minister. He has no human company, but the raft is encircled by menacing sharks whose mouths are full of the sharpest teeth. The cartoonist did not label the sharks but there were many reasons for uncertainty. Unemployment remained high and threatened to rise. Industrial rationalisation was understood to be necessary but threatened heightened industrial tension (Williamson, 1982, page 368). Internationally, arguments over post-war reparations threatened monetary disruption. Above all, the outcome of an impending general election on a wider franchise could not be foreseen, and the King had fallen seriously ill.

The cartoonist's uneasy portrayal of optimism at the mercy of the elements was reflected in many places.

In 1928, it had seemed more difficult to make money in the City's markets than it was in 1927. For the first four months of 1928 everything had been plain sailing. Every investor had made money. But a general reaction in October saw a slump in the smaller gramophone shares and the one shilling gambles.[1] In other words, a bubble was following the usual pattern. Initial price increases had attracted investor interest and demand. That new demand led to more price increases which could not go on forever. After the halt to price increases, investors were being forced to reconsider their motivation for holding highly priced stocks. The risk was that new shocks would lead to a dramatic price reversal (Shiller, 2003, page 38).

In 1929, matters were brought to a head in two crashes: the first in the spring, which saw the failure of many companies floated in 1928, and the second in September, precipitated by the collapse of Clarence Hatry's companies. The crashes were to become an existential threat to the Exchange as they coincided with the election of a minority Labour government on a manifesto that envisaged radical reform to reduce unemployment (Labour Party, 1929).

The first crash of 1929

By the end of January 1929, there was bad news of two speculative promotions. At the adjourned annual meeting of Ner Sag Limited, the directors reported that the published accounts could not be trusted and that the company had probably made a loss of about £24,000 rather than a profit of about £104,000. The whereabouts of the Managing Director, Charles Brandreth, were unknown.[2]

Ner Sag was one of the more notorious issues of the 1928 boom. Originally founded in 1925 to take over the nascent business of Charles Brandreth and his wife, it aimed to exploit patents for a new type of mattress which it boasted would never sag. Dealing in the company's shares had been permitted by the Exchange since the autumn of 1927, but its profits and dividends had been small. In mid-1928, a second company, Ner Sag Overseas Limited, had been floated and the issue had been heavily over-subscribed in response to ambitious promises of overseas sales to Germany and the US. The result had been that the market price for the shares of both Ner Sag companies had risen to exceptional levels.[3] A few months later, in October 1928, newspapers began to report rumours that Ner Sag could not have achieved the level of sales and business which had been claimed and the share prices could not be justified asking whether Ner Sag shares could honestly be said to be worth £8 10s each.[4]

In response, Ner Sag issued a statement[5] and placed advertisements[6] asserting that the company had been trading profitably and promising that audited accounts would soon be published. When the accounts were published early in December, they showed that Ner Sag had made a profit of £104,166 (compared with £14,821 in the previous year), proposed a final dividend of 50% and presaged a bonus share issue. At the subsequent annual meeting of shareholders, the public rumours were put to directors, but save for the appointment of two new directors, no decisions had been taken before the meeting was adjourned. There matters rested at the end of the year.

When the annual meeting resumed on 23 January 1929, the directors reported the result of their investigations. The company had not made a profit. Indeed, it seemed likely that a loss of about £43,000 had been made. Moreover, it was known that Mr Brandreth had placed substantial orders for goods and machinery without keeping records of the orders. It was thus impossible to assess the company's true liabilities and to prepare reliable accounts. Unfortunately, after the investigation had begun, Mr Brandreth had disappeared and his current whereabouts were unknown.[7] A week later, a warrant was issued for Mr Brandreth's arrest[8] and he was duly arrested on 9 February 1929.[9] Mr Brandreth's crime was that throughout 1928 he had knowingly exaggerated the trading results of the two Ner Sag companies and when accounts had to be published for the year to 30 September 1928 included fictitious sales of about £100,000. He had profited partly by taking some of the money subscribed for the shares of Ner Sag Overseas and partly by trading in the shares at the exaggerated prices he engineered.[10]

On the same day as *The Times* reported Ner Sag's adjourned annual meeting, Blue Bird Holdings, a company whose shares had been offered for sale as recently as 17 December 1928,[11] was reported to have failed to make expected cash payments. It had been created to acquire shares in other Blue Bird petrol companies that had been promoted in the previous two years and the cash payments were due to former shareholders. At a meeting at the end of January, the promoter, Mr Francis Lorang, attempted to explain why the cash raised by the flotation of Blue Bird Holdings had not been available. *The Economist* doubted whether Lorang's explanation had cleared the confusion in any way.[12]

It was quickly apparent that the shareholders' funds could not be found. This was just the beginning of yet another series of depressing news reports as one after another, the individual Blue Bird companies were wound up, all without convincing explanations from Mr Lorang. To escape questioning in the Bankruptcy Court, which needed his assistance to unravel his financing schemes, Lorang escaped to Paris. Although he was eventually traced and arrested, extradition proved so slow that he did not stand trial until the autumn of 1930.[13] The money was never to be recovered.

Blue Bird was an example of what *The Economist* called 'parent finance': a technique for milking the maximum cash from highly speculative promotions. Companies would be formed, allegedly to exploit a new invention or process, and then floated. After flotation, the company would sell some of its entitlement to exploit rights within a particular territory to another company whose shares would in turn be offered to the public. In Blue Bird's case, if an offer of shares was not fully subscribed, one of the existing Blue Bird companies would buy the remainder of the shares to create the impression that the issue had been fully subscribed.[14] Apart from Blue Bird, there were many examples of this practice, including some floated by Clarence Hatry.[15]

The effect of these well-publicised debacles and the subsequent stream of dispiriting newspaper reports was to discourage investors and force them 'to reconsider their motivation' (Shiller, 2003, page 38).

Table 8.1 Shares issued in February–March 1929. Proportion of issue left with underwriters – five largest

Company	Nature of offer	Proportion left with underwriters %
Roadway Time Tables	320,000 5 shilling shares	92%
Trowbridge Tyre & Rubber	550,000 5 shilling ordinary	90%
Curzon Bros & Maxims	594,000 5 shilling ordinary	90%
Walls & Highley Theatres	95,000 8% £1 cumulative participating preference	82%
	400,000 1 shilling ordinary	
Multidoor	580,000 5 shilling ordinary	80%

Source: The Economist, 6 April 1929, page 756.

Nervousness about speculative promotions was heightened in February[16] by an increase in Bank Rate from 4½ to 5½%. Moreover, there was a growing realisation that no party might be able to win an overall majority in the General Election, which in turn contributed to speculation about the process by which a government might be formed after an inconclusive election and what its programme might be.[17] Inevitably, the heightened uncertainty led to a fall in share prices, which disproportionately affected shares floated in 1927 and 1928. It also led to new issues in February and March proving unsuccessful, especially the more speculative promotions. A number failed lamentably to attract subscriptions so that large numbers of shares were left with underwriters.

After Easter, the prices of shares floated in the 1928 boom continued to fall.

None of this can have been helped by the fact that some of the weakest companies floated in 1928 and early 1929 were already being wound up.[18] Nor was the position improved by court hearings in which companies tried, often vainly,

Table 8.2 Low denomination shares issued in 1927 and 1928: market price changes January–June 1929

	1929		14 Jan 1929	27 June 1929	Jan– June 1929
	Highest price	Lowest price	Price	Price	Rise or fall %
Duophone	12/=	1/6	6/3	1/7½	−74.5
Electramonic	3/8	1/=	2/=	1/=	−50.0
Dominion Records	2/1¾	6¾	2/1½	10½ d	−58.8
Photomaton Parent	15/7½	12/3	15/=	13/9	−8.3
Far Eastern Photomaton	3/9¼	4½ d	3/6	1/=	−71.4
Ner Sag	£4/0/0	4/1½	50/=	12/6	−75.0
Ner Sag (Overseas)	9/6	5d	7/6	9d	−90.0
Photomatik Portraits	1/2½	1½ d	10½ d	2½ d	−76.2
British Filmcraft	2/9	6 d	2/4 ½	10 ½ d	−63.2
British Lion Film Corp.	41/6	4 ½ d	1/4 ½	6 ¾ d	−59.1
Whitehall Films	7 ½ d	1 d	–	–	–
Waste Food Products	18/9	2/=	15/=	3/11 ½	−75.3

Source: Table reproduced from *The Economist*, 29 June 1929, page 1461.

to insist on underwriters taking up their shares.[19] The North British Artificial Silks case attracted particular attention, as it was found that the issuing house, Token-house Securities, had agreed with the company that it should not be liable for non-performance by sub-underwriters. Within the Exchange, the committee was receiving a series of requests for it to adjudicate on disputes between members arising from underwriters and others seeking to avoid liabilities.[20]

These public and private disputes fed public outrage which was reflected in the editorial columns of the *Financial Times* which drew the obvious conclusion suggesting that those responsible for floating shares, including the issuing houses, have not discharged their duties to potential investors as a whole. For *The Economist's* leader writer, anyone launching a public company should make sure that its finances were properly secured. Neglecting this duty would bring discredit not only to the defaulters but also to anyone who had not exercised due care in placing the underwriting. Proper care had to be be taken if the spread of investment were to be fostered.[21]

In campaigning mode, for a week at the end of July, the *Financial Times* ran a series of articles examining cases which had come to public attention and identifying the people who should be acting to stamp out the abuse arguing that if a finance house was not able to procure genuine and honest sub-underwriters, then the Stock Exchange's Committee should not permit it to float companies.[22]

Unbeknown to the press, action had already been taken as the Sub-Committee on New Issues and Official Quotations had been asked to investigate instances in which sub-underwriters had defaulted and issues which had shown other unsatisfactory features. The sub-committee's report, dated 9 August 1929, which was limited to an examination of public documents, listed 29 cases that warranted further investigation and suggested that there were probably other cases that had not been identified because the appropriate reports had not been published. In each of these cases, subscription of a material amount of the company's capital was in arrears: the highest being Transmutograph Limited with subscribed capital of £83,000 of which 78.36% was in arrears.[23] The report noted that the paid up capital of the syndicate that had underwritten the shares was merely £9. In some of the cases, preliminary expenses represented a substantial proportion of the subscribed capital: the highest being Universal Refrigerators Limited whose preliminary expenses represented 43.9% of subscribed capital.[24] Ten firms of brokers were involved in the cases named by the committee, including the two firms that had been most active during the boom: T Gordon Hensler & Company (18 flotations in 1928) and Charles Stanley & Company (16 flotations in 1928).[25]

The number of cases and firms identified in the report suggested that there was a significant problem. It was plain that a significant number of issues listed by the sub-committee were of little commercial merit and that this may have been appreciated by the members who had sponsored Applications for Permission to Deal in these shares. This raised the possibility that the members involved had colluded with outside interests to take advantage of potential investors and suggested that the Exchange's rules had proved inadequate.

The report recommended that, in view of the number of cases, the brokers in question should be 'seen' or, in other words, interviewed and asked for an explanation. It also recommended that the rules should require that brokers sponsoring an issue should confirm that they had satisfied themselves that underwriters and sub-underwriters were good for their commitments.[26]

On reading this report, it was clear to the Exchange's committee that in policing the rules there had been a failure to safeguard the Exchange and its members from abusive issues and that, as a result, investors had incurred losses by buying shares in companies which had little hope of survival. The full extent of those losses would not become apparent for some years,[27] but it was quickly evident that they were substantial, as *The Economist* recognised in August:

Table 8.3 Speculative shares issued to the public in 1928

Market categories	Par value £m	Market valuation at highest prices in 1928 £m	Market valuation in August 1929 £m	Discount in August 1929 compared with par value %
Artificial silk companies	8.3	8.8	3.2	61.4
Film companies	1.7	1.9	.7	58.9
Gramophone companies	3.5	6.4	1.4	60.0
Patent companies	2.5	5.1	1.2	52.0
Safety glass companies	.9	1.1	.3	66.6
Miscellaneous companies	13.3	15.2	10.6	20.3
TOTALS	30.2	38.5	17.4	42.4

Source: Based on a table published in *The Economist*, 17 August 1929, page 317.

The Horne group

Before the Exchange could act on its sub-committee's recommendations, the market's attention had passed to a different issue. Up to this point, attention had been taken by companies that had issued shares: not so much by the people or businesses promoting them. At the beginning of August, *The Economist* drew attention to a company whose business was reorganising companies and floating issues: British Cement Products and Finance Company Limited. The company had been formed in 1926 by HS Horne, a former stockbroker, to take interests in independent cement manufacturers which he formed into a group trading under the brand 'Red Triangle' in competition with O'Hagan's 'Blue Circle' group. He had gone on to form Associated Anglo-American Corporation, Carmelite Trust and Anglo-Foreign Newspapers, all of which took interests in newspaper companies.

All of these companies were intended to exploit Mr Horne's theory that by acquiring substantial share interests, financial trusts staffed by progressive thinkers and advised by technical experts could use their voting power to maximise industrial efficiency. Each of the companies was financed by loans secured on the share interests being acquired. As market prices fell, so rumours spread that banks were demanding that the group should provide additional collateral to replace the reduction in the value of the shares which had been pledged to the banks as security. The air of uncertainty was encouraged by the fact that publication of the company's accounts was overdue and by fresh approaches to existing shareholders to raise additional capital: approaches that were accompanied by extraordinary requests that the prospectus circulated to shareholders should be returned to the company.[28] By mid-September 1929, the Horne companies' share prices had fallen by more than 75% from the highest prices they had reached during 1929.[29]

The Hatry group and the United Steel scheme

It was natural that the market should then look for other companies in a similar position, and that attention should turn to the Hatry group which was also known to borrow money to finance share interests, and had been slow in publishing accounts.

From the beginning of 1929, Hatry's companies had been short of cash. This may have been caused by the fall in share prices, as in 1921, but as his companies' accounting records have not survived, the precise cause cannot be known. In the following months, Hatry was to resort to increasingly desperate measures to raise money.

In January and February 1929, on the acquisition of British Automatic Company (BAC) by Associated Automatic Machine Corporation, the BAC pension scheme's trustees were immediately replaced by Hatry's associates. The funds' investments were swapped for Hatry group securities and realised for cash, which was then used by other Hatry companies.[30]

At the same time, Hatry formed Iron Industries Limited with a nominal capital of £650,000. On 4 February 1929, Austin Friars Trust (AFT) applied for 500,000 of the 650,000 £1 shares paid for by a cheque drawn by AFT which was immediately loaned back by Iron Industries. Iron Industries' only asset was the debt due from AFT. Without delay, AFT's shares in this newly created shell company were used as security for bank loans amounting to £600,000. (Manley, 1976, pages 54–55).

In May 1929, Hatry sought the agreement of the directors of CGS to make a public offer of £400,000 of its shares but was opposed by Frederick Braithwaite of Foster & Braithwaite, the stockbrokers whose support in 1925 had been critical to the success of CGS.[31] The directors rejected Hatry's proposed issue, and no public offer was made. However, assuming that the directors would approve the issue, underwriting contracts had already been agreed with the proposed underwriters and were used as security for a loan of £400,000 from Westminster Bank.[32]

In August 1929, another Photomaton company, British Photomaton Trading Company Limited, was formed to develop the Photomaton business in the United Kingdom and whose shares were distributed to shareholders in existing Photomaton companies.[33] Another example of what *The Economist* had termed 'parent finance'.

Meanwhile, having organised the flotation of Allied Ironfounders Limited, which brought together 15 English and Scottish foundries engaged in making light castings,[34] Hatry conceived the idea of a similar amalgamation of heavy iron and steel companies and, in the process, writing off their accumulated losses. In February 1929, he began soliciting support for his scheme,[35] which envisaged that a new company would acquire the share capital of the companies being amalgamated, and that subsequently the new holding company would issue its own shares to meet the cost of acquisition. It was planned that the nominal value of the new company's share capital would be considerably smaller than that of the predecessor companies so that the underlying businesses would be relieved of the servicing cost. Between the original acquisition and the share issue, the scheme, which was expected to cost about £7 million, would be financed partly by bank borrowing and partly by cash deposited by members of a syndicate created for the purpose.[36] Hatry envisaged that once the initial transaction had been completed, the new company would acquire controlling interests in other steel companies, thus leading in time to the amalgamation of the whole industry.

The scheme went through a number of iterations, but was eventually announced on 16 April 1929 when the directors of United Steel Companies circulated a letter to shareholders setting out the terms of the offer which was conditional upon acceptance by 90% of each class of shares. Although the required acceptances had not been received by the deadline, the acceptance period was extended and the condition was satisfied by the new deadline: 19 May 1929. As a result, the transaction went ahead; the due date for payments to be made to shareholders was set as 19 June 1929.

Hatry had not been able to settle the financing arrangements for the transaction before 19 May 1929. Indeed, it was not until 24 June 1929 that he reported to M Samuel & Company that he had placed the preference shares to be issued by the new holding company:[37] Steel Industries of Great Britain Limited. He explained that:

> he had faced considerable personal opposition from several quarters, chiefly Vickers and Nivisons and the Governor of the Bank of England.[38]

Vickers was involved in other schemes to rationalise the steel industry. Nivisons had suffered from Hatry's competition as they had been one of the three firms of brokers who had monopolised local authority loan issues before Hatry had turned his attention to that market. Moreover, at the beginning of 1929 he had been responsible for floating a loan for the City of Melbourne. This was Hatry's first Empire issue[39] and thus was a new threat to Nivisons' business. For his part, the Governor had his own interest in industrial reorganisation, and may have believed that Hatry's intervention was inconvenient. He was also close to Nivisons and the other firms that handled Empire issues, for they managed a queuing system that controlled the flow of Empire issues and was approved by the Bank of England.

To stem this opposition, on 29 May 1929 Hatry had visited the Governor who told him:

> so far as it was possible for him to comment on Mr Hatry's proposals, he was not satisfied that:
>
> (1) a project on this scale (i.e. to embrace 60% of the whole Steel Industry of the country) was feasible or immediately desirable:
> (2) a sound valuation and examination of the conditions of the Companies and of the Plant &c both from a financial and industrial point of view, had been made:
> (3) the people were ready at hand to run the nationalized industry.[40]

The Governor went on to say that he had been responding to questions from bankers by telling them that he opposed the scheme (Wood and Wood, 1954, page 152). Three days later, the Governor described his impression of this meeting in a letter to Frank Tiarks, a director of Schroders:

> The impression left on my mind is something like this: he has already bitten off a scheme as large as (or larger than) he can chew: if he could further actualise a dream and join the two together on your and my backs, he would be relieved – and also successful. For the moment he is absorbed by the prospect of this relief and success – to it he would give up profit and leadership, just as he has already given up other good things. A dangerous and perhaps an ailing Mr Hatry.[41]

In the face of the Governor's opposition, Hatry might have considered aborting his scheme, not least because any technical difficulties had been magnified by the result of the General Election at which a minority Labour government was elected on a manifesto envisaging government direction of investment. It was expected that share prices would fall in reaction to the outcome of the election and this would make it more difficult for Hatry to raise further bank loans using share holdings as security. Perhaps Hatry had lost the ability to be objective about the scheme, an opinion formed by Hubert Meredith when he discussed the steel scheme with Hatry:

> As he sat opposite to me, smoking away at his pipe, the financier disappeared and in his place there seemed to me to be a very vain man undertaking a colossal task, not with the idea of making money out of it, but with the object of showing the world what a great man Clarence Hatry really was.
>
> (Meredith, 1931, page 309)

For whatever reason Hatry continued, but although he was able to place the new preference shares, he was unable to arrange the loans that the new holding company would require in the interim. Hatry's later recollection, which was to be hotly disputed, was that at a meeting of the four key directors on Sunday 23 June 1929, one of them, John Gialdini, had suggested that they could create documents that would serve as collateral for bank loans by duplicating receipts for subscriptions to local authority loan issues and certified share transfers. The Hatry companies would then be able to raise the necessary money.[42] Recognising that the steel scheme would fail unless the necessary cash was found, the four directors agreed to take this course, and proceeded to duplicate documents and use them as collateral for new short-term loans.[43] Hatry later suggested that the directors were partly moved to adopt this course of action by a somewhat emotional outburst by Gialdini:

> Gialdini, however, persisted and said that we were within an ace of success after colossal efforts . . . and that the alternative meant failure and with it a big crash in which enormous sums would be lost by the public. He had thought seriously about the whole position and rather than face such a crash he had made up his mind that he would blow out his brains.[44]

This stratagem did not satisfy the banks. One effect of Hatry's increasingly desperate efforts to raise money was that a growing number of houses were aware of his cash shortage which made banks even less enthusiastic about lending to him. M Samuel & Company for one declined to extend their exposure to his companies by refusing to advance new money until the repayment terms of an old loan had been honoured, which he proved unable to do.[45]

The September 1929 crash

By September, Hatry's financial position was becoming critical. Whilst he was expecting that the steel scheme would lead to his realising a substantial profit, that was not expected to materialise until October[46] and thus would not be available to meet either loan repayments due in September or to replace the duplicate receipts that had been created in June and would also expire in September.[47] In the end, Hatry's banks lost patience, and on Monday, 16 September 1929, Lloyds Bank and Westminster Bank decided to commission an investigation into the financial condition of Hatry's companies. Sir Gilbert Garnsey of Price, Waterhouse & Company was appointed on Wednesday 18 September.[48]

On the market, prices of Hatry-related shares began to fall, suggesting that news of Sir Gilbert's appointment had leaked. For Hatry, a fall in the prices of his companies' shares threatened a repeat of 1921, when price falls had reduced the value of investments deposited as security for bank loans. By mid-September 1929, he had already taken steps to support the price of his companies' shares and he now redoubled these efforts. Under his influence, a number of trust companies placed purchase orders with country brokers for shares in Hatry-related companies. Simultaneously, sale instructions were given to London brokers. The overall effect was intended to be a demonstration of purchasing pressure that would support the shares' prices. In this it failed, for the price of Hatry-related shares continued to fall.

If the banks had thought they were dealing with a localised liquidity issue they were about to be disabused. For some time, Hatry and his colleagues had known that a collapse was inevitable and had prepared themselves; during the previous weekend, one of them, Gialdini, converted his assets into cash and left for Paris. For his part, Hatry resolved to stay and save what could be saved. On learning of the banks' appointment of an investigator, Hatry asked to meet Sir Gilbert and gave him two pieces of information: that his group's deficiency was of the order of £20 million and that local authority loan receipts and certified share transfers had been duplicated irregularly. A deficiency of £20 million would have been shocking as it was larger than Lloyds Bank's issued share capital and implied a potentially disabling loss for the bank.[49] But the duplication of loan and share certificates also was equally troubling, for it suggested that banks and others had been trading in worthless paper and might mistakenly have accepted false documents as collateral for loans.

On being persuaded by Hatry that his assertions were serious, Garnsey reported to his two instructing banks who then reported to the Governor of the Bank of England, who in turn convened a small group which met on Thursday 19 September to consider the problem.

In the meantime, share prices continued to fall.[50]

Reflections

The events of 1929 had transformed the LSE's understanding of its position.

By the end of September 1929, many small investors had already suffered heavy losses on their holdings of shares floated in the 1928 boom. With the collapse in the prices of shares in the Horne group and of Clarence Hatry's companies, further losses were in prospect. As the Governor's group met on 19 September, they cannot have known how many companies might eventually be affected. They were aware, however, that the losses caused by the Hatry collapse might prove troublesome for at least two clearing banks: Lloyds and Westminster.

From the Exchange's point of view, there was a potentially serious embarrassment for there must have been a suspicion that it had itself contributed to the financial consequences of the crashes. The report of the sub-committee which had examined evidence for weak underwriting had shown that members had, presumably knowingly, sponsored weakly underwritten new issues with unsatisfactory commercial prospects. In addition, Hatry had admitted that he had traded in duplicate securities. This implied that experienced securities clerks had not been able to distinguish his duplicate scrip from legitimate scrip, but also that the Exchange's normal processes had not been adequate to exclude illegitimate scrip from trading. As the Governor's group was meeting, they cannot have been sure what the limits of these problems were.

They were sure, however, that these problems threatened to validate the growing political criticism of the Exchange and the City. In 1926, the Greene Committee on Company Law Amendment had endorsed the existing legal framework for new issues and in 1929 that endorsement had largely been supported by the conclusions of the Balfour Committee.

The effect of the events of 1929 was to invalidate and discredit these conclusions: how could a system be said to be working satisfactorily when so much money had been lost so quickly on shares floated as recently as 1928? Carelessly, by its failure to be alert to changing conditions, the Exchange had created a platform for its critics. The collapse of 1928 issues in the spring had already been seized upon by campaigners seeking reform.[51] The Hatry collapse would increase the pressure.

To make matters worse, a minority Labour government had taken power at the 1929 General Election. Its manifesto for the election had not proposed far-reaching financial reform (Labour Party, 1928, 1929), but as the Governor had known for some months, the Chancellor of the Exchequer proposed to appoint a committee to inquire into the financial system. Although the proposal originated in a suggestion that there should be an inquiry into monetary policy,[52] it was expected that the terms of reference would be broader as indeed turned out to be the case.[53]

Although the Labour government was hindered by not having a majority in the House of Commons, there were many who believed that institutional reform of the City was a serious and immediate threat.

The London Exchange was facing a situation similar to that which had confronted the NYSE a few years earlier, in which defeating an existential threat to its independence would depend upon demonstrating that its self-regulatory mechanism could serve the interests of outsiders and not simply its members.

Notes

1 *The Nation and Athenaeum*, 5 January 1929, page 506.
2 *The Economist*, 26 January 1929, page 172. He was subsequently apprehended and prosecuted (*The Times*, 18 February 1929, page 7).
3 Dealings had been marked at £2 5 shillings per share on 31 December 1927 and at £9 2 shillings 6 pennies in October 1928 (*Stock Exchange Times*, 31 October 1928, page 5).
4 Advance notice of articles to be published in the 31 October issue of *Stock Exchange Times* (held in the Application for Listing file of Ner Sag Limited, Stock Exchange Archive, Guildhall Library).
5 *The Times*, 27 October 1928, page 21.
6 *The Times*, 30 October 1928, page 25.
7 Directors' statement to shareholders (*The Times*, 25 January 1929, page 24).
8 *The Times*, 4 February 1929, page 9.
9 *The Times*, 11 February 1929, page 11.
10 The case for the prosecution (*The Times*, 23 April 1929, page 13; 24 April 1929, page 5).
11 *The Times*, 27 December 1929, page 22,
12 *The Economist*, 26 January 1929, page 169.
13 *The Times*, 19 November 1930, page 5, and on subsequent days.
14 As alleged in the prosecution's case (*The Times*, 19 November 1930, page 5).
15 *The Economist*, 19 January 1929, page 111. Hatry had floated Photomaton Parent Corporation Limited, Far Eastern Photomaton Limited and Photomaton (Lancashire and Midlands) Limited.

16 7 February 1929.
17 'The Minority Dilemma' (*The Economist*, 16 February 1929, page 327).
18 Apart from various of the Blue Bird companies, for example Poso-graph Great Britain Distributing which had been floated on 25 October 1928.
19 *FA Hales Limited v Cross Keys Trust Limited* (*Financial Times*, 2 July 1929, page 11); *North British Artificial Silk v Tokenhouse Securities* (*Financial Times*, 26 July 1929, page 10).
20 *Hoblyn & King v Pike & Bryant: re Poso-Graph Parent Corporation*, 9 May 1929; *CH Eden v J Joseph & Company: re American and Dominions Unbreakable Records (ADUR)*, 17 May 1929; *J Joseph & Company v Higginson Wallis & Company: re ADUR*, 4 June 1929.
21 *Financial Times*, 21 June 1929, page 6.
22 *Financial Times*, 25 July 1929, page 7.
23 The company had been floated in March 1929. The brokers responsible were Simpson Miller & Springer.
24 The company had been floated in December 1928. The brokers responsible were T Gordon Hensler & Company.
25 The ten brokers named in the report had been responsible for 67 out of the 288 new issues in 1928.
26 Stock Exchange minutes, 12 August 1929 (Stock Exchange Archive, Guildhall Library).
27 See the speech of Henry Morgan, President of the Society of Incorporated Accountants at Sheffield (*The Accountant*, 23 October 1930, page 305 et seq; Anonymous, 1931; Cole, 1935, pages 103–138).
28 Circular letter (Fremantle papers, Buckinghamshire County Records Centre, Aylesbury). The prospectus in question is not with the Fremantle papers so was, presumably, returned as requested. The Stock Exchange Archive does not hold a copy of this prospectus which suggests that there was no application to deal in the shares concerned.
29 *The Economist*, 20 July 1929, pages 126–7; 3 August 1929, page 230–1; 14 September 1929, page 485.
30 National Archives, file DPP 1/91.
31 After the collapse of Hatry's companies, Braithwaite explained his connection to Hatry when interviewed by the Governor of the Bank of England. He told the Government he had only acted for Hatry in connection with local authority loan issues and had never supported any of Hatry's other issues (Braithwaite's pencil note of the interview, Foster & Braithwaite Archive, Guildhall Library).
32 Note dated 28 May 1929 of a meeting on 17 May 1929 (Foster & Braithwaite Archive, Guildhall Library; CGS Companies' House file, National Archives, file BT31/218878/203047).
33 *The Times*, 8 August 1929, page 16.
34 The issued share capital of Allied Ironfounders Limited was £1.6 million. In addition, the flotation was to raise £748,800 through an offer of £780,000 6% Convertible Debenture Stock at 96% (*The Times*, 13 May 1929, page 24).
35 M Samuel Private Office memorandum, 18 February 1929 (Lloyds Bank Archive).
36 M Samuel Private Office memoranda, 8 April 1929 and October 1929 (Lloyds Bank Archive, File S/1/1/6/228). The total amount required for the purchase of the debentures and shares of United Steel and United Strip & Bar was £4.2 million. In addition, Hatry undertook to repay the bank overdrafts of these companies which amounted to approximately £2.9 million (Memorandum of Sir Gilbert Garnsey to form the basis of a Proof of Evidence, National Archives, file DPP1/91).
37 This completed the financing of the streel scheme. It was once thought that Hatry was not able to complete the financing; but that misunderstanding was dispelled when Sir Gilbert Garnsey's report became available on the opening by the National Archives of the files of the Director of Public Prosecutions. Sir Gilbert's memorandum makes

clear that the steel scheme financing was completed and that Hatry's companies must therefore have been short of cash before the steel scheme was conceived (Manley, 1976, page 81; Walker, 1977, page 81; Jones, 1981, page 150; Jones, 1985, page 143 et seq.).

38 M Samuel Private Office memorandum, 24 June 1929 (Lloyds Bank Archive).

39 The transaction was a direct result of an initiative in 1928 when CGS's board was joined by Sir Archibald Weigall, a former Governor of South Australia. Hatry appointed an agent in Australia, Sir James Connolly who had served in London as Agent-General of Western Australia. Connolly was instrumental in forming the connection with Melbourne (Memorandum to Australian Loan Council dated 3 October 1929, Connolly papers, National Library of Australia).

40 Bank of England Archive, file ADM 1 /2. The difficulty is unlikely to have been caused wholly by the Governor as the failure of the Conservative Party to win a majority in the General Election on 30 May 1929 will have contributed. Frederick Szarvasy's opinion had been that 'if the Conservative Government got back with a majority of 40 he was certain there would be a considerable boom in such shares as these' (M Samuel & Company Private Office memorandum, 22 May 1929, Lloyds Bank Archive).

41 Letter dated 1 June 1929 (Bank of England Archive, file SMT 118/7). Similar letters were sent to Edward Peacock, a partner in Barings, and Sir Guy Granet of Higginsons. These letters are part of a continuing correspondence between the Governor and others concerning Hatry's steel scheme.

42 Some have suggested that this was not the first occasion on which Hatry and his associates had done this (Michie, 1999, page 262). This study has only found evidence of one previous anomaly that may have been the result of irregular use of loan certificates. That occasion appears also to have been Gialdini's responsibility (Sir Gilbert Garnsey's memorandum, pages 15–16, National Archives, file DPP 1/91). If the issue of supernumerary receipts had been a regular feature of Hatry's operation, it might have been normal practice to print sufficient blank receipts in advance for this to happen. At Hatry's trial, evidence was adduced that it was necessary for additional blank receipts to be printed for Gialdini's scheme to be implemented. This also suggests that the issue of additional receipts in 1929 was exceptional.

43 Hatry Trial Transcript, Norman Birkett's speech, 24 January 1930 (National Archives, file DPP 1/91, page 33 et seq.).

44 Statement prepared by Hatry for use in litigation concerning irregular Drapery Trust share certificates (National Archives, file HO 144/17846, page 20). As for the contentious nature of these assertions, see letter dated 29 January 1931 from Hatry to his solicitor, Atherton Powys (National Archives, file HO 144/17846).

45 A £500,000 loan to Austin Friars Trust due 9 August 1929 (M Samuel & Company Private Office memorandum, 8 August 1929, Lloyds Bank Archive).

46 The expected net profit was £1,400,000, which, it was hoped, would be realised in the first half of October (M Samuel & Company, Private Office memorandum, 12 September 1929, Lloyds Bank Archive).

47 The receipts in question related to a City of Wakefield loan for which the period for conversion of subscription receipts into formal certificates was to expire at the end of September.

48 Sir Gilbert Garnsey's memorandum (Lloyds Bank Archive, National Archives, file DPP 1/91).

49 As at 31 December 1928, the total of the bank's issued share capital was £15,810,282. Shareholders' equity (i.e. issued share capital and reserves) amounted to £27,287,231.

50 Jones, 1985, page 144. Jones cites an unpublished memoir by (later Sir) Thomas Robson, who undertook the detailed investigation for Garnsey (Bank of England Archive, file ADM 33/10).

51 Parliamentary questions were asked repeatedly. For example, on 16 July 1929, questions had been asked on the appointment of a committee to inquire into promotion of

industrial issues and their effect on employment, wages and public confidence, and prosecutions of share pushers under section 92 of the Companies Act 1928.

52 An inquiry into monetary policy was originally proposed in April 1928 by Sir Alfred Mond and Ben Turner (who was to be appointed Minister for Mines in the 1929 government) as joint chairmen of the Conference of Industrial Re-organisation and Industrial Relations (Bank of England archive, file ADM 33/10).

53 The MacMillan Committee was appointed 'to inquire into banking, finance and credit, paying regard to the factors both internal and international which govern their operation and to make recommendations calculated to enable these agencies to promote the development of trade and commerce and the employment of labour' (Treasury minute dated 5 November 1929, Macmillan Committee report, 1931, page 1).

References

Primary works: unpublished documents

Bank of England Archive.
Buckinghamshire County Records Centre: Fremantle Papers.
Guildhall Library: Foster & Braithwaite Papers.
Lloyds Bank Archive: M Samuel Papers.
National Archives.
National Library of Australia: Connolly Papers.
Stock Exchange Archive, Guildhall Library.

Primary works: newspapers and periodicals

The Accountant.
The Economist.
Financial Times.
The Nation and Athenaeum.
Stock Exchange Times.
The Times.

Primary works: government and parliamentary reports

HM Treasury (1931), *Report of the Committee on Finance and Industry* (Cmd 3897). (HMSO, London). ('The Macmillan Committee Report').

Primary works: contemporary books and articles

Anonymous (December 1931), 'The Results of the 1928 New Issue Boom', *The Economic Journal*, volume 41, number 164, pages 577–583.
Labour Party (1928), *Labour and the Nation* (Labour Party, London).
Labour Party (1929), *Labour's Appeal to the Nation* (Labour Party, London).
Meredith, H (1931), *The Drama of Moneymaking: Tragedy and Comedy of the London Stock Exchange* (Sampson Low, London).

Secondary works

Jones, E (1981), *Accountancy and the British Economy 1840–1980: The Evolution of Ernst & Whinney* (Batsford, London).

Jones, E (1985), *True and Fair: A History of Price Waterhouse* (Hamish Hamilton, London).

Manley, PS (1976), 'Clarence Hatry', *Abacus*, volume 12, number 1, pages 49–60.

Michie, RC (1999), *The London Stock Exchange: A History* (Oxford University Press, Oxford).

Shiller, RJ (2003), 'Diverse Views on Asset Bubbles', in Hunter, WC, Kaufman, GG and Pomerleano, M (editors), *Asset Bubbles: The Implications for Monetary, Regulatory, and International Policies* (MIT Press, Cambridge, MA).

Walker, RG (1977), 'The Hatry Affair', *Abacus*, volume 13, number 1, pages 78–82.

Williamson, P (1982), '"Safety First": Baldwin, the Conservative Party, and the 1929 General Election', *The Historical Journal*, volume 25, number 2, pages 385–409.

Wood, M and Wood, A (1954), *Silver Spoon: Being Extracts From the Random Reminiscences of Lord Grantley* (Hutchinson, London).

9   Managing the Hatry crisis, 1929

Introduction

The group convened by the Governor and which met at the end of Thursday 19 September included not only the principal clearing banks but also the Chairman of the Exchange and a representative of the Board of Trade. During that afternoon, the Governor had also met Lord Bearsted (Jones, 1986, pages 37–43), the Chairman of M Samuel, Hatry's principal non-clearing bank creditor, but he did not join the group.

At this early stage, the Governor's group knew little. They knew that a decision to investigate the Hatry group had led to confirmation that Hatry's group was probably beyond rescue, that for the banks, the resulting losses could be considerable, and the revelation that there had been improper handling of scrip. They would have feared that when news of these problems leaked, the uncertainty would cause a further fall in prices: not least because there would be doubt over the reliability of scrip, the title documents in which the Exchange traded. The Governor's group may also have been conscious of the political risk that news of Hatry's attempt to avoid failure by creating false documents would confirm suspicions of the poor standards of behaviour in the City.

A strategy adopted and implemented

In the face of these threats, at the Governor's suggestion, the group adopted a two-fold strategy: to limit market disruption and to localise responsibility for the crisis.

To limit disruption, it was agreed that trading in the stocks and securities mentioned by Hatry would be suspended as soon as practicable; that banks would be encouraged not to do anything that would precipitate further disruption in the market, by, for example, foreclosing on brokers who were financially embarrassed;[1] and that Sir Gilbert should be appointed liquidator of Hatry's principal companies to give him the authority necessary to investigate without delay.[2]

At 1100 hours the next morning, the Exchange's committee met to consider the position and agreed to suspend seven securities believed to be involved in Hatry's fraud.[3] The decision was announced formally at 1120 hours. Almost immediately, it became clear that this action was not sufficient to deal with the consequences of the fraud. Members reported suspicions that Hatry and his associates had placed a large volume of circular transactions which would fall due for settlement in a few days. They suspected that Hatry and companies under his influence had instructed country brokers to sell shares and London brokers to buy. As the Exchange's normal practice would have required the brokers to settle the deals and then account to their clients, the London brokers would be obliged to pay for the shares they had bought even though there was no prospect of recovering the money from their client (a Hatry company which was insolvent). Meanwhile, the money would be passed by the country brokers to their clients, the same Hatry company which could not reimburse the London brokers. To deal with these reports, the committee met again at 1500 hours on the same day and agreed that the Exchange's Settlement Department would undertake the settlement of all the stocks mentioned in the 1120 announcement, adding the shares and debentures of Far Eastern Photomaton Corporation Limited. All members having bargains in these securities were required to send a list to the committee by the end of Monday 23 September.[4]

At two further meetings on that day, the committee received further representations from members about the consequences of Hatry's share price support operation and agreed to appoint a sub-committee to examine the outstanding bargains and the problems that would be created if settlement proceeded on Thursday 26 September as normal.[5] The sub-committee reported on 25 September that it had discovered that:

> the bulk of the account could not be settled owing to names not being forthcoming. The Sub-Committee were convinced that it was impossible to isolate transactions and order a partial postponement of settlement. The Sub-Committee also thought that if the settlement was allowed to go through in the normal course, many purchasers of shares would run a grave risk of having to take delivery of shares and stock the genuineness of which was doubtful and there was the further risk that money paid would reach the hands of parties who were involved in the irregularities which had taken place.[6]

Although the Settlement Department's information was incomplete, Hatry's operation was known to be considerable:

Table 9.1 Bargains in Hatry securities by Dundee Trust Limited and associates

Company	Buyers (number)	Sellers (number)
Associated Automatic Machine Corporation Limited	403,875	544,200
Retail Trade Securities Limited	255,585	296,425
Corporation & General Securities Limited	73,600	76,700
Photomaton Parent Corporation Limited	249,985	242,500

Source: As reported to the Settlement Department. Stock Exchange minutes, 25 September 1929 (Stock Exchange Archive, Guildhall Library).

Faced with this information and the impossibility of resolving the position overnight, the committee had little option but to defer settlement of all outstanding bargains in Hatry securities.

The actions of the Stock Exchange in managing the practical problems of settlement and of the banks in managing members' financial embarrassments went a long way towards keeping order in the market although problems remained to be resolved. Members remained nervous, however. During the week, rumours spread that shares in Haslam & Newton Limited, a company not related to Hatry, may have been forged. Fearing that the frauds might have gone beyond the Hatry group, the committee immediately decided to suspend the shares, only to find itself meeting 90 minutes later to hear that the company's broker was convinced that there were no irregularities and no forged certificates. The suspension did not go ahead.[7]

These first actions were paralleled by a master-stroke: when the Governor's group met on 19 September 1929, it was agreed that Sir Gilbert should persuade Hatry and his associates to confess to the Director of Public Prosecutions. This they did, somewhat to the Director's embarrassment, on Friday, 20 September 1929.[8]

Hatry had known for some time that his frauds were likely to be discovered by the banks. That became clear during a last visit to Paris during the previous weekend when he had failed to persuade his supporters to lend him more money. Although Hatry and Daniels had returned to London, Gialdini, sensing failure, had travelled from Paris to Switzerland and then Italy, which had no extradition treaty with England. At this point, without taking the advice of his lawyers, Hatry seems to have decided that, on discovery, he would make a full confession.

It is not obvious why Hatry and his associates should have agreed to confess. Hatry must have known that if he did not confess the authorities would not have been able to prosecute immediately, if at all. They had no information on which to base charges other than any admissions he himself made. As the Jubilee Cotton Mills case demonstrated, substantial amounts of police work would be necessary to supplement an accountant's investigation. Even if Hatry did not appreciate the difficulty that stood in the way of prosecution without a confession, it seems probable that his solicitors would have advised him.[9] It is possible that Hatry believed that in confession lay the only way by which he might one day return to his business; but if so, there is no record of this having been the case.[10]

The manner of the confession was also exceptional. For most malefactors, the first encounter with a law enforcement agency would not be an interview with the Director of Public Prosecutions. Quite apart from any other consideration, a Director would be careful to avoid an early involvement that might undermine the objectivity of a decision on whether a prosecution should proceed. Having obtained Hatry's signature to a statement confirming his confession,[11] the Director and the police arranged for Hatry and his associates to appear before the City magistrates on the next day, a Saturday. That day's newspapers bore the news of Hatry's arrest. On Sunday and Monday, the newspapers bore the news of the first hearing and the bare facts of the charges brought against the directors.

For the next few months, news of the crisis within the Exchange was dominated by reports of the prosecution which was to be advantageous for the Governor in managing the aftermath as the newspapers were constrained by the restrictions on reporting cases which were before the courts.

Hatry's trial

By acting with such speed and such flexibility, the Director achieved what the Governor and his group must have hoped. The speed was to be maintained. Hatry and his associates stood trial at the Old Bailey in January: only three-and-a-half months later.[12] On the fifth day of the trial they changed their pleas to guilty and were sentenced.[13] In sentencing Hatry, the judge told him:

> You stand convicted of the most appalling frauds that have ever disfigured the commercial reputation of this country; frauds more serious than any of the great frauds upon the public which have been committed over the past 50 years, according to my personal experience, for they have been carried out by means of wholesale forgeries of Bearer Securities in Trustee Stocks which neither banker nor broker or any member of the public would ever dream of suspecting to be otherwise than genuine . . . I am unable to imagine any worse case than yours[14]

Coming from Mr Justice Avory, these words were telling. At the time, he was the senior King's Bench judge and in one capacity or another had been involved in almost all major fraud trials since 1900. He was later to admit that he enjoyed fraud trials above others.[15] He was well connected in the City, frequently presiding at the swearing in of the Lord Mayor. His words, conveyed in what one witness recalls was a 'cruel and ice-cold' voice,[16] articulated precisely the message that the City and the Governor would have wished to convey, and the sentence was condign. At 14 years with hard labour, this was not only the maximum sentence for forgery,[17] it was also the longest sentence handed down for a non-capital crime in 1930 (Home Office, 1931).[18] This seems to have been more than Hatry had been led to expect, for one of the spectators in court later recalled that he reeled when it was handed down (Kinross, 1982, page 57).

Hatry was later to maintain that, although he had pleaded guilty, he was in fact not guilty of forgery. In a letter dated 30 March 1930, to the Marquess of Winchester who had served as Chairman of Austin Friars Trust, Hatry wrote:

> the Corporation Stocks (the subject of the prosecution) had become irregular and were *never forged*[19]

This perhaps surprising contention appears to depend on the fact that corporation loan certificates were indeed not issued by Hatry's company: the local authorities themselves did that. Hatry's company was issuing receipts on its own authority allegedly for cash subscribed which it was legally entitled to do. In other words, the receipts may have been fraudulent but were not forgeries. As Hatry and his associates pleaded guilty before their defence could be presented at the trial, this argument was not deployed. The Marquess of Winchester for one was not convinced by Hatry's claim to be innocent of forgery, although, in company with many others, he believed that the sentence handed down was excessive (Winchester, 1934, page 275).

Immediate prosecution of Hatry and most of his associates[20] served as a dramatic and unmissable sign that the authorities had established who was to blame for the problem that had occurred and that any market difficulty was limited to securities that had been within Hatry's reach. This diverted the thrust of what otherwise would have been a campaign for further investigation and, subsequently, wider reform articulated by JL Garvin in an article in *The Observer* at the end of September under the title 'Other People's Money', an explicit reference to the polemic in which before the 1914–1918 war Louis Brandeis had argued for new laws to bring an end to the scandalous practices of Wall Street. Garvin demanded a special public inquiry to supplement to the usual processes of financial and legal investigation. For him, prosecution of Hatry would not alone suffice. A commercial and social calamity had been caused by the intermingling of financial speculation with the Lancashire cotton trade. Hatry's excesses had affected municipal finance as well as industrial finance. According to Garvin, the consequences would be felt by every investor and family in the land.[21]

On this occasion, Garvin's campaigning was short-lived and did not lead immediately to government action. Hatry's conviction implied that the market's problems could not have been systemic because they resulted from the criminal activity of a single promoter against which no system could be entirely proof. What is more, it implied that the market's systems had worked well for they had led to the swiftest action against the person who was to blame. Indeed, the newspapers commented favourably on how well London compared with New York.[22]

Dealing with the aftermath

By deferring settlement, the Exchange gained time to resolve the market's practical problems. By arranging Hatry's prosecution, the Governor's group ensured that the Stock Exchange, the Bank, the Board of Trade and the Ministry of Health were left free of public attention when dealing with the weaknesses exposed by the crash.

Settlement of Hatry-related deals

Attending to the deferred settlement came first. At first the Exchange expected that when any uncertainty about allegedly false certificates had been resolved, settlement could be achieved by normal processes: any disputes being finally determined by the courts. This option soon proved unattractive for it was quickly realised that it would be expensive and take a long time to deal with every case. During that time, the uncertainty would overhang the market.[23] But there was another disadvantage, for the outcome of this process was likely to be that all of the losses caused by the Hatry frauds would be borne by parties outside the Exchange as members resorted to law to oblige their clients to pay for transactions undertaken on their instructions. The committee quickly concluded that the Exchange's reputation would be harmed if small investors were to be penalised for these frauds: they would be seen as bearing the brunt of the excesses of City traders. But the alternative of indemnifying investors[24] was not straightforward for it would require members to meet losses for which they were not personally responsible.[25] Gradually, the committee came to the view that the Exchange had been the victim of a conspiracy and that in equity the loss should be shared among the parties'(Stock Exchange, 1930a, page 6).

The difficulty lay in finding a means of doing this[26] and persuading members to share that view.

On 25 November 1929, the Chairman and Deputy Chairman convened an unofficial meeting with a number of members at which it was suggested that a fund should be established to take responsibility for settling the disputed trades in the interest of preserving the credit of the City of London and the good name of the Stock Exchange. He appealed to the parties to try and find some solution of the problem and to include provincial Brokers in any arrangement effected (Stock Exchange, 1930a, page 7).

The implication is that although the Chairman and Deputy Chairman had formed a shrewd view of the steps that were necessary, they believed it would not be wise for the committee to act without prior confirmation of members' support.

From this initiative sprang agreement to create by subscription a fund that would settle bargains deferred from 26 September in respect of five Hatry-related companies.[27] The purpose was to ensure that all liabilities to the public would be met in full and to this end the fund would take delivery of all the shares that would have to be delivered on settlement day. Of the total amount estimated to be required by the fund (£1 million), £200,000 was contributed by members and others (including banks) who had no commitments under outstanding bargains involved in the settlement. The balance was to be met by brokers (both members of the Exchange and country brokers) and dealers in agreed proportions (Stock Exchange, 1930a, pages 10–15). By the middle of January 1920, the fund had been established,[28] so that on 22 January 1930, as Hatry's trial was under way, the committee was able to agree that settlement would take place on 13 February 1930. It went through 'without a hitch' (Stock Exchange, 1930a, page 9).

This agreement was innovative, for it was an acknowledgement that liability should not fall upon outside interests, thus abrogating the principle of *caveat emptor*. Furthermore, it involved members who had no personal exposure to the outstanding Hatry settlement and involved country brokers from whom the London Exchange would customarily have stood aloof. It could hardly do otherwise, as Hatry's price support scheme had involved provincial brokers. Thus, there was a recognition that the London and the provincial exchanges shared a joint interest in avoiding further disruption and ensuring that the losses that would be crystallised on settlement should not fall upon the public. Acceptance of this joint interest was not uncontentious, and resulted from a series of short-term motives. London members wished to ensure that members of the public did not suffer losses and were doubtless grateful for the provincial brokers' contributions to the fund which otherwise would have been a charge to London members. For their part, country brokers wished to avoid insolvency.

Nonetheless, the agreement involved, however momentarily, an acceptance that for some purposes the market had to be viewed as a whole. Traditionally, the Exchange had sought to control a segment of the national share-trading market in the interests of its members: emphasising the distinctiveness of its membership and their trading standards especially by comparison with other traders and exchanges. Hatry's share price support scheme had exploited these distinctions; and, to manage its consequences, the Exchange had been obliged to compromise.

Neither the fund nor the acceptance of provincial exchanges were to last.

Systems and processes

The Exchange next set up a working party to examine the implications of the crash for the integrity of its systems and processes. It discovered that Gialdini's scheme of creating duplicate loan and share documents exploited weaknesses in the Stock Exchange's processes, firstly in respect of quoted companies and secondly in respect of local authority loans.

It was Hatry's normal practice to persuade companies that he floated to appoint one of his companies, Secretarial Services Limited (SSL), as company secretary and registrar. Quite apart from making the management of the flotation easier, it ensured that after flotation there was a continuing relationship between Hatry's group and the companies that were floated. As registrar, SSL was responsible for recording share transfers and issuing replacement share certificates to the new shareholders. In days of paper-bound processes, this was laborious, and transferees could wait for a long time before their new certificates were issued. This was especially difficult for anyone who was an active trader especially at times of heightened activity. The scale of the difficulty can be judged from the guidance given to bank securities clerks in the many textbooks on the subject (Lewcock, 1931, pages 44–90; Kiddy, n.d.; Head, 1912).

For securities admitted to the Official List, the difficulty was managed by the use of share transfers certified by the Exchange's Settlement Department. Endorsement of a transfer by the Department would signify that a valid share certificate had been received with the transfer form which would then be used by the transferee as a substitute for the certificate which would subsequently be issued by the company's registrar. In effect, transfer forms certified by the Settlement Department were regarded as tantamount to bearer securities. This facility had proved so useful that, for securities that were not included in the Official List, it had become common to treat share transfers certified by a company's own registrar as the equivalent of transfers certified by the Settlement Department. In practice, the issue of certified share transfers had become somewhat abused, as bank securities departments had found that it was easier to honour bargains by handing over certified transfer forms rather than attempting to register each transfer which was time-consuming and wearisome.[29]

Gialdini's scheme involved duplicating share transfers and falsely certifying them, which was not a difficult matter as certification only involved a rubber stamp and a signature.[30] The falsely certified share transfers were then submitted to banks as collateral for loans.

To deal with these problems, the working party proposed that company registrars should be required to speed up the issue of new certificates and that only transfers certified by the Settlement Department should be accepted as 'good delivery'. Although this recommendation was diluted to discourage rather than ban certification by company registrars, the practical effect was that certification by company registrars became much less common, not least because the banks' securities departments tightened their own procedures.[31]

As far as local authority loans were concerned, Gialdini's scheme took advantage of a change in the process of issuing local authority loans which Hatry had engineered by insisting that when a new local authority loan was offered publicly, applicants should send their application forms and any accompanying cash payment to one of his companies. That company would then issue a receipt that would certify both that the money had been received and that the holder of the receipt would receive a loan certificate from the authority concerned on presentation of the receipt (generally within six months).

Before Hatry had become involved in the issue of local authority loans, a bank would normally have acted in the capacity of receiving agent, in return for a commission. By substituting one of his own companies for a bank, Hatry had been able to cut the cost of issuing loans and to undercut the orthodox brokers who had previously enjoyed a monopoly of this activity. On receiving applications, Hatry's company would then hold the cash received until it was required by the local authority. Many wanted the money immediately after issue, but others did not want all of the money immediately and were happy to leave it on deposit with Hatry's company, C&GS, even though it did not profess to be a bank. The benefit to the authority was that Hatry offered a slightly higher rate than the clearing banks. The benefit to Hatry was that he was in effect borrowing money but at a lower rate than he would have had to pay a bank.

All local authority loans were required to comply with the 'Stock Regulations' issued by the Ministry of Health, which approved each issue and the draft notices inviting applications. All of the loans issued through C&GS were approved in this way. Although the Ministry of Health appear to have regarded this approval process as largely an administrative matter, from the perspective of the local authorities concerned it will have seemed that the receiving procedure proposed by Hatry was both known to and approved by the Ministry. There is no evidence that the Ministry ever inquired into these arrangements when considering requests for approval.

Gialdini's scheme involved using the company that received loan applications to issue duplicate receipts, i.e. receipts for more than the total nominal sum of a local authority's loan stock. The receipts were treated by bank security departments as bearer securities and thus would be accepted as proof of ownership for the purposes of lodging security for new bank loans. This was another instance of bank security departments having become careless as they found temporary cash receipts less troublesome to manage than formal loan certificates.[32] Gialdini argued that use of the receipts in this way was relatively risk-free, provided that the receipts were recycled before the deadline by which receipts had to be submitted to the local authority for issue of loan certificates in their place.

Eliminating these weaknesses required action by the Ministry of Health as well as the Exchange. In principle, the Exchange wanted to ensure that its rules for certification applied equally to local authority issues as well as to corporate securities, but the local authority loans were subject to the Stock Regulations, which first required amendment.

On investigation, it was found that the regulations existed in two forms (having initially been issued under two separate Acts of Parliament applying to different groups of authorities) and had not been reviewed for many years. When the Exchange working party had finished its work, the Ministry of Health revisited the Stock Regulations, amending them to reflect the latest Exchange practice and replacing them with new, consolidated regulations. In addition, the regulations imposed requirements concerning the appointment of receiving agents and the deposit of funds received from applicants.[33]

Weak underwriting

Having dealt with weaknesses in the procedures for dealing with share and loan transfers, the working party dealt with the implications of the August 1929 report on weak underwriting which arose from the first crash of 1929 and was not related to the Hatry crash in September 1929. Consideration was given to ways in which insubstantial issues could be avoided and ways in which underwriting arrangements could be strengthened. In both respects, the working party chose an approach that placed responsibility upon directors, advisers and brokers to ensure that arrangements for a proposed issue were appropriately strong, coupled with disclosure of the judgements they had made.

It was first proposed that permission to deal would generally not be granted in a series of circumstances that had caused particular difficulty. For example, where preliminary expenses formed an undue percentage of the proposed capital, applications for permission to deal would not be considered until after publication of the first annual report and accounts. Similarly, applications from subsidiary companies would probably not be considered until after publication of the holding company's first annual report, especially where the company's principal asset is a patent, new process or invention or an undeveloped commercial enterprise. It was also suggested that the committee responsible would look more cautiously at applications to record bargains in the Supplementary List from companies that had not published a prospectus (Stock Exchange, 1930b, page 11).

The committee proposed that whenever an unquoted company applied for permission to deal for its shares but had not published a prospectus and, furthermore, accounts for at least two years had not been made up and audited, an advertisement should be published containing specified details about the company for which the directors were to be collectively and individually responsible. Among other details, the advertisement was to include:

> A statement setting out clearly the working capital with which the Company started or is to start business, additions (if any) since made and whence derived, and the amount available at the date of the statement of working capital, after providing for all purchase considerations, promotion profits, preliminary expenses, losses, and interest or dividend payments to date, with a statement by the Directors that in their opinion the working capital available is sufficient, or, if not, how it is proposed to provide the additional working capital thought by the Directors to be necessary.
>
> (Stock Exchange, 1930b, page 16)

As far as underwriting arrangements were concerned, the working party explicitly rejected suggestions that new rules could bar undesirable underwriting. The solution in this instance lay in re-emphasising what the committee had believed was already established practice. Companies and authorities seeking permission to deal in their securities were required by the Exchange's rules to appoint a broker to furnish any information that the committee might require.[34] Although the rule did not expressly address the broker's responsibility for the quality of the information thus transmitted, it was established law that the communication of false or misleading information in this context was an offence,[35] and some textbooks suggested that brokers were under a duty to consider the quality of the information transmitted (Varley, 1925, page 143). Following the committee's 1930 reforms, there could be no doubt:

> The Committee can only impress upon Members, especially those who sponsor an issue, that it is their obvious duty to examine carefully the quality of the underwriting and sub-underwriting.
>
> (Stock Exchange, 1930b, page 5)

The committee also proposed that the required advertisements should be expected to include information concerning 'small or unknown underwriting companies': an expectation to be given force by empowering the committee to require disclosure of other particulars which it thought necessary (Stock Exchange, 1930b, page 5 and 16).

To support the committee's assessment of these matters when considering applications, it was given power to commission an independent accountant to verify a company's statements and to defer decisions on whether to grant permission to deal until after receiving the accountant's report.[36] These recommendations represented significant departures from existing practice. The new rules empowered the Exchange to use discretion in considering whether disclosure was appropriate, emphasis being placed on the adequacy of disclosure rather than on formal compliance.

Moreover, straightforward disclosure was no longer to be regarded as sufficient protection for investors: directors were to be expected to take responsibility publicly for ensuring that arrangements were sound. Coupled with this was a larger role for professional advisers: partly in taking responsibility for advising on the adequacy of disclosure in prospectuses and related documents but also in providing assurance on the adequacy of the judgements that directors and others were being called upon to make. For example, it became good practice for directors making a statement on the adequacy of the company's working capital to commission auditors to investigate the working capital and to report to them on its adequacy. This enabled the directors and other advisers to demonstrate both to the Exchange and, if challenged, to others that due care and attention had been applied in making their judgements. This development in practice was encouraged by the empowerment of the committee to commission a report from an independent accountant.

In short, these changes represented a turning from an approach based on formal compliance in the interest of maximising the number of securities in which members could trade. In its place, there was a marked encouragement for the role and responsibility of professional advisers, but also of sponsoring brokers, as gatekeepers acting increasingly to protect members of the public rather than the narrower interests of members.[37]

It remained for the Exchange to deal with members who had been associated with weak underwriting.

In August 1929, before the crash, the Exchange's sub-committee had recommended that the members concerned should 'be seen' and asked for an explanation. This had not happened before the crash, but the meetings duly took place after March 1930, i.e. involving the new committee that had been elected in March 1930. When these meetings took place, further reports were submitted giving details of the outcome of issues with which the members concerned had been associated. In the case of Charles Stanley & Sons, the report considered on 7 April 1930 listed 32 issues with which the firm had been associated since 1926. In most cases, subscription of the capital due had been in arrears: the highest reported case had been 45% in arrears. The implication was that some capital had been subscribed by the public and accepted, but that underwriters had not contributed the amounts due from them. Thus, the company had not received all the capital that it would have said in its prospectus was necessary, but the public subscribers had nonetheless been deprived of the money they had contributed. In many of the cases reported, preliminary expenses represented a high proportion of the company's capital, and reports, when submitted, were late.

The committee's minutes do not record in full what was said to each member save that whilst the member's membership would be renewed for the current year, renewal in 1931 would receive special attention from the committee. In the event, memberships were renewed. The implication, however, was that the quality of the business that the member had introduced to the House had not been satisfactory. In one instance, the minutes record that:

> Mr James was admitted & told that the Committee had received a very serious report of companies which he had been the means of introducing to the Stock Exchange. The Report would be considered by the new Committee: in the meantime he was warned to be very careful as to the class of business he transacted.[38]

Whatever was said, none of the members identified in the August 1929 report on weak underwriting sponsored any new issues between 1930 and 1939. Thus, whether by reason of changes in trading or of action by the committee, this business was stopped.

Reflections

The scale of the threat which the LSE believed it faced following the Hatry crash is evident from the scale of the action taken to deal with it.

Undoubtedly the most significant action was the organisation of a fund to meet the costs of settling outstanding transactions in Hatry-related securities. Whilst this was important to avoid the costs of settlement being borne by unsuspecting investors and to remove the threat of long-lasting legal disputes, it was the first occasion on which members had been asked to meet the costs of settling the obligations of fellow members for which most had not been personally responsible. As the LSE's senior officers must have been concerned that this variation of the traditional business model might not be supported by the generality of members, it was presented as the outcome of a consultative process managed by individual members rather than as a formal proposal by the committee. Although this initiative proved successful, the members agreed to it reluctantly with the result it was necessary for the Bank of England to make good a small shortfall in members' subscriptions to the fund, and they resisted a proposal that a permanent fund should be established.

The failure to create a permanent fund was not to be important. Once a precedent had been set by meeting the Hatry settlement, members knew that if ever similar conditions were to recur, it would be difficult to resist demands for a new fund to be created. This changed the relationship between members and led members to have greater expectations of the committee whose duty it became to avoid a recurrence and thus to avoid members having to meet similar liabilities in future. In this way, it made good commercial sense for members to support the committee in monitoring their fellow members more closely to ensure that they did not find themselves bearing the cost of other members failing to observe the club's rules.

Equally, members supported the other actions taken by the committee. In effect, members who had sponsored weakly underwritten new issues were told to stop. In parallel, the LSE's processes and practices were reformed to eliminate the weaknesses that Hatry and his associates had exploited which coincidentally increased the role of the LSE's secretariat in processing stock transfers. To support its oversight of new issues, the committee took powers to commission accountants to investigate sponsoring members' assertions about the quality of an issue. All of these changes involved departures from the traditional relationship between the LSE and its members. The members involved in weak underwriting cases were being told to terminate a profitable line of business. The oversight and validation of transfers was being centralised in a growing secretariat. The committee was acknowledging that it could no longer accept unquestioningly members' assertions about the quality of new issues. All of these were well debated within the LSE's committees but did not become the subjects of controversy among members generally. Understanding the political threat that the LSE faced, members accepted almost all of the reforms that were proposed in spite of their scale and provided support for the political claim that the LSE's self-regulatory arrangements could serve the interests of outsiders as well as those of the members themselves.

In securing this result, the Exchange's committee was assisted by good fortune. The collapse of the 1928 boom could be attributed to the failure to exclude weak and unprepossessing issues from flotation, and the collusion of some members with a number of disreputable outside elements. As far as public attention was concerned, the significance of these failures was obscured by Hatry's later collapse. Hatry's confession of guilt enabled the prosecution to begin immediately before any detailed investigation had begun and for the impression to be created that he (with his associates) bore sole responsibility for the ill that had befallen the Exchange. What was more, the words used by Sir Horace Avory in sentencing Hatry implied that no system could be guaranteed to be proof against such 'appalling frauds'. When combined with the severity of the sentence, the effect of the judge's words was to distract attention away from the possibility that the Exchange might have borne some responsibility and to allow the committee time to consider the reforms that were necessary to avoid any recurrence.

In managing these events, the Exchange was assisted by the Governor of the Bank of England who had taken a focal position in the relationship between the City and the government partly because of the importance to government of servicing the national debt. As Montagu Norman remained in his position, he became the central point for a wide network which enabled him to draw people and institutions together in support of joint plans to deal with crises. When Lloyds Bank and Westminster Bank first went to him to discuss the Hatry collapse, he was able quickly to bring together the principal clearing banks, the Exchange and the Board of Trade to agree how to respond. When the first meeting was over, his next meeting was with Lord Bearsted, the chairman of M Samuel, Hatry's principal non-clearing bank loan creditor. It was Norman who proposed the strategy of calming the markets, avoiding unnecessary financial pressure on Exchange members who faced losses and of arranging a quick prosecution to distract public attention. As the weeks passed, Norman monitored progress, ensuring that promises of action were honoured and making sure that the DPP had the evidence he needed from banks and others. When the Chairman of the Exchange needed to talk to the Board of Trade, Norman effected an introduction.[39] When the Permanent Secretary of the Ministry of Health needed to talk to the Exchange about reforming local authority loan regulations, it was to Norman he went for advice. In effect, the Bank of England was serving as the channel through which the City communicated with government and vice versa. This arrangement implicitly accepted that managing the individual markets and exchanges within the City was a technical matter best left to market specialists: an assumption that the Treasury was prepared to accept after its experience of regulating new issues during the war. Serving as a channel, the Governor would interpret the expectations of each side to the other so that when the Exchange was considering its reforms in 1931, various drafts of the proposals were reviewed by the Bank to check that they promised to achieve their objectives. In this way, the markets and exchanges were enabled to regulate their own affairs without the threat of political intervention.

Playing this pivotal role was important not only for the City but also for the Bank itself, not simply because it cemented its leadership within the City but also because Norman well knew that its own independence was also in question.

Notes

1 Eventually agreed at a meeting of clearing banks (including those not represented in the Governor's group) on Tuesday, 24 September 1929.
2 To this point, Sir Gilbert had been operating on behalf of the banks that had instructed him and required the acquiescence of the companies he was investigating to gain access to records.
3 The shares concerned were: Associated Automatic Machine Corporation Limited shares, Corporation & General Securities ordinary shares, Drapery Trust ordinary shares, Photomaton Parent Corporation Limited shares, Oak Investment Corporation Limited shares, Retail Trade Securities shares and Wakefield Corporation 4½% Redeemable Stock 1949/1959.
4 Letter dated 20 September 1929 from EN Vowler & Company to the committee. Stock Exchange minutes, 20 September 1929 (Stock Exchange Archive, Guildhall Library).
5 Letters dated 20 September 1929 from Weddle Beck & Company, Woollan & Company and Smith Brothers. Stock Exchange minutes, 23 September 1929 (Stock Exchange Archive, Guildhall Library).
6 Stock Exchange minutes, 25 September 1929 (Stock Exchange Archive, Guildhall Library).
7 Stock Exchange minutes, 1100 hours and 1240 hours, 25 September 1929 (Stock Exchange Archive, Guildhall Library).
8 In the brief to counsel to appear at the magistrate's hearing, the Director stressed that to ensure that proper formalities were observed, he had arranged for a police presence at the interview (National Archives, file DPP 1/91) Subsequent letters from the Director confirm that he was aware of the Governor's interest.
9 The Director's brief to counsel records that Hatry and his associates had been advised by Wontners. However, it is unlikely that Wontners were involved in drafting the confession (National Archives, file DPP 1/91).
10 Notably, other commentators have failed to offer convincing explanations for the confession. Kynaston (1999, page 179) refers to Hatry's confession as either 'vainglorious' or 'selfless' according to taste. However, Kynaston's account of these events does not refer to the meeting on Thursday 19 September at which the Governor urged Garnsey to persuade Hatry to confess to the DPP and thus does not take this pressure into account.

Manley (1976, page 57) does not offer an explanation. Pearson (1961, page 125) suggests that Hatry 'no longer cared'. There is some suggestion that Hatry and his colleagues had decided to confess at least one week before the events of Thursday 19 September; but apart from a single reference in a document prepared by the DPP, this suggestion is not corroborated. Statement of Case prepared by the DPP against John Gialdini for use in extradition proceedings (National Archives, file HO144/17846 page 51).

11 Copy statement (National Archives, file DPP 1/91).

12 In fraud trials during the 1930s, the typical delay between the events leading to charges and a trial was two years.

13 One of the curiosities surrounding the trial is that although they had signed confession statements on 20 September 1929, Hatry and his co-defendants pleaded not guilty, only to change those pleas at the close of the prosecution's evidence. Had they pleaded guilty on the first day of the trial, it would not have been necessary for the prosecution's case to be presented in detail and the trial would have been foreshortened. However, it was convenient for those safeguarding the City's interests that the details of Hatry's fraud should been exposed for this distracted blame from the City, justifying the judge's condemnatory remarks and the severe sentence. It is also possible that Hatry's barristers wanted the prosecution evidence to be given in full as a basis for their plea in mitigation. If Hatry supposed that he might be treated leniently if he assisted the City's cause, he was to be disabused, which might explain why he and his wife were shocked by his sentence.

14 Trial Transcript, Day Five (National Archives, file DPP 1/91).

15 Sir Home Gordon recalled: 'he twice told me that of all the cases he tried, the one that interested him most was Hatry's. He really preferred the intricacies of a financial case to the human tragedy connected with murder trials' (*The Times*, 17 June 1935, page 21).

16 Hutchinson (2015, page 362).

17 It is possible that Hatry expected a sentence of no more than seven years, which was the maximum sentence for fraud. However, in addition to fraud he was charged with forgery, for which the maximum sentence was 14 years. Moreover, there was a precedent for a promoter/fraudster being sentenced to imprisonment for more than seven years. In 1895, Jabez Balfour, when convicted on several counts of fraud, was handed down two maximum terms of seven years, to be served consecutively (McKie, 2004, page 220). As a junior barrister, Sir Horace Avory had been a member of the prosecution team at Balfour's trial.

18 Home Office (1931).

19 Underlining in original. Facsimile letter reproduced in Winchester (1934), insert after page 272. This suggestion is consistent with an assertion made by Hatry in a statement prepared for use in litigation concerning irregular Drapery Trust transfers: '*It is important to note that all scrip certificates issued in respect of stock issues sponsored by C&GS were their own documents of title issued by them at Pinners Hall and not by the Corporation*' (underlining in original: National Archives, file HO 144/17846). Pearson (1961, page 125) maintains that the charge of forgery against Hatry was based on assertions in his original confession statement dated 20 September 1929 which was signed without the benefit of legal advice on the precise wording of the statement which, as a result, included misrepresentations of the true position. Consistently with Pearson's suggestion, Hatry's first statement suggests that it was loan stock certificates which had been forged which was incorrect (National Archives; file DPP 1/91).

20 John Gialdini escaped to Italy where he was able to stay as the existing extradition arrangements did not extend to the offences with which he was charged. Following diplomatic pressure, and the personal intervention of Mussolini, he was prosecuted in Italy and convicted: only to be released in a general amnesty a year later (National Archives, file HO 144/17846). The file also contains a letter dated 29 January 1931 from Hatry to his solicitor, Atherton Powys, suggesting ways in which the case against Gialdini could be strengthened and dealing in particular with the circumstances of the meeting on 23 June 1929.

21 JL Garvin, 'Other People's Money', *The Observer*, 29 September 1929, page 16.
22 *The Observer*, 26 January 1930, page 15, reporting *The Evening World* in New York.
23 For example, the investigations into registration of share transfers undertaken by Sir Basil Mayhew for Associated Automatic Machine Corporation continued into 1930 with the result that the company was not able to recommence share registration until January 1930. Only at this point could disputes be defined and dispute resolution begin. This led to an action by Kleinwort & Sons against Associated Automatic Machine Corporation on the grounds that the bank had advanced money against transfers of the company's shares that had been falsely certified by the company's secretary (one of Hatry's companies). At first instance, the judge (in fact Mr Justice Avory) found in favour of Kleinwort, but this judgment was overturned on appeal over an interpretation of the law of agency. The case was concluded in February 1934 (i.e. after more than three years) by a judgment of the House of Lords, thus vindicating the Stock Exchange's assessment in October 1930 that waiting for legal determination of all outstanding disputes would be time-consuming (Kleinwort Archive, London Metropolitan Archives, file 02–08–01–002–0012).
24 Another alternative was canvassed: the annulment of outstanding transactions under the provisions of Rule 74. This rule provided that a transaction could be annulled by the committee where it could be shown that it resulted from fraud or willful misrepresentation. Transactions undertaken for the purpose of 'rigging' a market by creating a false price were regarded as fraudulent. Schwabe (1905), page 238, citing the Court of Appeal judgment in *Scott v Brown* (1892): 'the sole object of the purchase was to cheat and mislead the public'. Thus, superficially, Rule 74 appeared to give the committee power to annul Hatry's share support deals. This option was, however, rejected because it would have required a separate demonstration of fraud in respect of each transaction. As the share price support scheme implemented by Hatry had involved a large number of trust companies and others, this process also threatened to be lengthy and expensive. It would also have thrown all of the losses on people outside the Exchange.
25 In other words, most of the members who had been principally involved in Hatry's share price support schemes had gone out of business after the crash so it was other, surviving, members of the Exchange who would bear the cost of an indemnity for investors.
26 Stock Exchange minutes, 9 October 1929 (Stock Exchange Archive, Guildhall Library).
27 Associated Automatic Machine Corporation, Photomaton (Parent) Corporation, Corporation & General Securities, Retail Trade Securities and Oak Investment Trust.
28 Members' subscriptions fell short of the total required. The total was achieved by a final contribution by the Bank of England (£25,000) on condition that it should not be mentioned in public (Bank of England Archive, file ADM 33/10).
29 On occasion, it might also have been necessary to notify a company's registrar of the bank's security interest in a holding represented by a particular certificate. These administrative chores were avoided if the security was held in bearer form (Internal reports on secretarial practice in the light of the Hatry collapse, Lloyds Bank Archive; Lewcock, 1931, pages 59–60).
30 Examples of these documents exist in the Hatry Trial Exhibits (National Archives, file DPP 1/91).
31 Stock Exchange minutes (Stock Exchange Archive, Guildhall Library).
32 For reasons similar to those for share certificates.
33 Original regulations: 3 August 1897, S&RO 1897 Number 614 applying to County Councils and S&RO 1897 Number 615 applying to District Councils. Subsequently amended. New Regulations: SR&O 1932 Number 438, subsequently consolidated in S&RO 1934 Number 619. The need for regulation of the appointment of receiving agents and the deposit of funds received was reviewed by the House of Lords Committee considering the Wakefield Corporation Bill on 15 March 1930. Wakefield had left substantial funds on deposit with Corporation & General Securities Limited following

a loan issue early in 1929. Throughout September 1929, it had been attempting to obtain a promised payment from CGS but failed and incurred a substantial loss, which it met in part by levying a special rate (Bank of England Archive, file C40/634).

34 Rule 162(4).
35 *R v Aspinall*, 1876. This case arose from an attempted fraud on the Exchange's members concerning the issue of shares by the Eupion Power company.
36 This recommendation appeared in the private version of the committee's report considered by the Committee for General Purposes, but not in the published version of the report (Stock Exchange, 1930b, page 11; Stock Exchange minutes, 21 July 1930, Stock Exchange Archive, Guildhall Library).
37 The role is described and analysed in Coffee (2006, page 3 et seq).
38 Stock Exchange minutes, March 1930 (Stock Exchange Archive, Guildhall Library).
39 The implication of the need for this introduction is that the chairman of the Stock Exchange did not have a relationship with senior officials at the Board of Trade.

References

Primary works: unpublished documents

Bank of England Archive.
Kleinwort Benson Archive, London Metropolitan Archives.
Lloyds Bank Archive.
National Archives.
Stock Exchange Archive, Guildhall Library.

Primary works: newspapers and periodicals

The Evening World.
The New York Times.
The Observer.
The Times.

Primary works: government and parliamentary reports

Home Office (1931), *Criminal Statistics for England and Wales, 1930* (Cmd. 4036). (HMSO, London).

Primary works: contemporary books and articles

Head, FD (1912), *Transfer of Stocks, Shares, and Other Marketable Securities* (Second edition, Sir Isaac Pitman & Sons, London).
Kiddy, JG (n.d.), *The Country Banker's Handbook* (Sir Isaac Pitman & Sons, London).
Lewcock, FJ (1931), *The Securities Clerk in a Branch Bank* (Sir Isaac Pitman & Sons, London).
Schwabe, WGS (1905), *A Treatise on the Laws of the Stock Exchange* (Stevens & Sons, London).
Stock Exchange (1930a), *The Hatry Crisis* (Privately Published, London).

Stock Exchange (1930b), *Report of the Special Sub-Committee on New Issues and Official Quotations of the 21st July 1930* (Privately Published, London).

Varley, FJ (1925), *Rules and Regulations of the Stock Exchange, With Notes and References to Decided Cases* (Effingham Wilson, London).

Winchester, Marquess of (1934), *Statemen, Financiers and Felons* (Privately Published, London).

Secondary works

Coffee, JC (2006), *Gatekeepers: The Professions and Corporate Governance* (Oxford University Press, Oxford).

Hutchinson, J (2015), 'Postscript', in Grant, T (editor), *Jeremy Hutchinson's Case Histories* (John Murray, London).

Jones, G (1986), 'Marcus Samuel', in Jeremy, DJ (editor), *Dictionary of Business Biography*, volume 5, S-Z, pages 43–46 (Butterworths, London).

Kinross, J (1982), *Fifty Years in the City: Financing Small Business* (John Murray, London).

Kynaston, D (1999), *The City of London: Illusions of Gold 1914–1945*, volume 3 (Chatto & Windus, London).

Manley, PS (1976), 'Clarence Hatry', *Abacus*, volume 12, number 1, pages 49–60.

McKie, D (2004), *Jabez: The Rise and Fall of a Victorian Rogue* (Atlantic Books, London).

Pearson, M (1961), *The Millionaire Mentality* (Secker & Warburg, London).

10 Towards another boom 1930–1936

Introduction

The arrival of another boom in 1936 brought the risk that it might be accompanied by abuses such as those which had accompanied the booms of 1920 and 1928. It proved to be another test of the Exchange's system of self-regulation and the criminal justice system.

London Stock Exchange regulations

The reforms introduced by the Exchange in 1930 worked well. There was no recurrence of Hatry's manipulation of the settlement system, and there was no repetition of the spate of worthless and weakly underwritten share issues floated in 1928.

Harold Wincott, the long-term editor of *Investors' Chronicle* that was responsible for many exposés of unattractive issues and promoters, observed that there had been 'a vast improvement' in the quality of new issues made in the 1936–37 boom by comparison with those made in earlier booms, and that in only a small proportion of the 1936–37 flotations had investors lost the money they put up. Wincott attributed some of the improvement to the Companies Act of 1929, but, in his view, most of the credit attached to the Stock Exchange committee.[1]

Wincott's observation was confirmed by Chambers's analysis of survival rates for IPOs, which showed a material improvement in five-year survival rates for IPOs between 1930 and 1938 compared with IPOs in the 1920s:

Table 10.1 Five-year survival rates by industry 1919–1938 (%)

	All	Foreign	New mfg	Trad mfg	Other mfg	Non-mfg
1919–1920	71	67	83	80	73	64
1921–1926	85	83	92	79	88	84
1927–1929	64	55	50	71	67	74
1930–1933	100	100	100	100	100	100
1934–1938	96	92	94	100	98	95

Source: Chambers (2010, page 58). The percentages quoted show the number of surviving firms divided by the total number of IPOs deducting those firms liquidated and acquired for value both from the numerator and the denominator.

Chambers (2010, pages 66–70) attributes this improvement in survival rates to the action taken by the Exchange combined with economic factors including tariff protection, collusion and rearmament spending. He also suggests that the Exchange heeded the advice of the Macmillan Committee although the key reforms had been introduced before publication of the report.

The practical effect of these changes was that the Exchange's committee was more ready to reject or defer applications for permission to deal. As Chambers (2010, page 69) observes, between 1927 and 1929, the rejection rate had been 2%. Between 1934 and 1938, the rejection rate was 7%.

Elsewhere, Chambers (2009, page 1423) presents data which suggest that the degree of price volatility also fell after 1930.

In spite of these indications of the success of the Exchange's reforms, some forms of abuse continued. Perhaps the most notable example involved a public offer of shares by James & Shakspeare Limited whose prospectus was issued on 3 September 1934 and became a new cause for critics of the Stock Exchange:

> In this way does the City of London provide investors with security!
>
> (Labour Party, 1935, page 13)

However, the Labour Party pamphlet in which this comment appeared could not identify any other examples of fraudulent issues from the years after the Hatry crash. With this single exception, its complaints about investors' losses all referred to shilling shares issued in 1928.[2]

A number of other transactions were criticised in the pamphlet, but not on the ground that they were fraudulent or that investors had lost money by investing them. Rather, four transactions were criticised because City houses had allegedly made too much money from them.

Whilst criticism continued, it had changed. The criticism which followed the collapse of shilling shares in 1929 was embarrassing for the Exchange because the collapse and the consequent losses arose from the willingness of the Exchange's members to collude in reducing the protection provided to investors by weakening underwriting contracts and in introducing worthless shares. In the criticisms current in 1935, there was no suggestion of collusion. Even in the case of the shares issued by James & Shakspeare, although there had been fraud, there had been no

Table 10.2 Issues criticised in Labour Party pamphlet, July 1935

	Profit made by issuing house on sale of its interest
Griffiths Hughes Proprietaries Limited	£450,000
Eno Proprietaries Limited	£350,000
OK Bazaars (1929) Limited	£160,000
Aspro Limited	£87,500

Source: Labour Party (1935, pages 14–15).

collusion between the fraudsters and the sponsoring brokers. Now the thrust of the criticism was that the profits that could be made legitimately by promoting new issues were too big.

To this extent, the 1930 reforms had been successful.

Government interventions – the case of the Royal Mail

The reforms were also successful in restraining any temptation for the government to intervene by contributing to the Macmillan Committee's conclusion that financial policy was best implemented by those whose business it is (Macmillan Committee report, 1931, page 5), a conclusion with which the Royal Commission of 1878 would have concurred (Royal Commission report, 1878). If the Exchange had felt complacent about the effect of its reforms, it was to be disabused.

In January 1931, Sir William McLintock, an eminent Chartered Accountant, released the report of his investigation into the affairs of the Royal Mail Steam Packet Company (RMSP).

At the end of the 1920s, this had been one of the largest enterprises in England, owning about 15% of the British merchant fleet at a time when over half of the world's shipping was in British hands. Its total capital exceeded £120 million. It had grown to this size by a series of acquisitions, the most recent of which was the acquisition of the White Star line in 1927. It was a feature of these acquisitions that shares in the target company would be purchased by a number of companies associated with RMSP so that the final group structure became convoluted and opaque.[3]

That the group was in financial difficulty had begun to emerge in the summer of 1929 when the chairman, Lord Kylsant, was not able to deal with questions raised by shareholders about the auditor's report.[4] This had led to calls for the company to provide a comprehensive statement of the group's financial position which were repeated when the company failed to respond.[5] Finally, on 9 November 1929, RMSP announced that it would not be able to pay the half-yearly dividends on its preference stocks and an interim dividend on its ordinary shares. It also announced that it would not be able to repay government loans due for repayment in September/October 1930 without raising additional capital, which, it had been advised, would be impossible in view of the recent fall in its share price. Sir William's investigation had been commissioned by the government's Trade Facilities Advisory Committee to provide a basis for considering its response to RMSP's request to re-schedule the loan repayments.

Sir William reported that the White Star Line was already insolvent and that as RMSP had guaranteed the payment of dividends and any deficiency on White Star's preference shares it would itself be insolvent if any claim were to be made under that guarantee. RMSP had arrived at this position because for some years it had been trading at a loss and, in effect, for some years had been trading in the hope that 'something would turn up', hiding its true position from shareholders by what Sir William described as the 'transfer of large sums from internal reserves'.

The collapse of RMSP was a profound shock. RMSP had been a substantial company, managed by people of apparently unimpeachable respectability, which had achieved an impressive trading record. That it should collapse without warning was alarming as there seemed no doubt that even the most attentive and informed shareholder could not have inferred from RMSP's accounts that such an event was possible. This focussed attention on the practices by which RMSP's true state of affairs had been obscured and led to political pressure for those responsible to be prosecuted.[6] Eventually, charges were brought against the chairman, Lord Kylsant, and the auditor, Harold Morland that in 1926 and 1927 by the profit and loss accounts and the balance sheets, the public was led to believe that the RMSP group had made large trading profits whereas in fact the group made serious losses. Lord Kylsant was alleged to havce bene responsible for the form of the accounts whilst it was suggested that the auditor to the company, knowing perfectly well what had been done, had condoned the deception and signed reports stating that a true and correct view of the state of the company's affairs had been given. Lord Kylsant faced a similar charge relating to the prospectus although Morland was not involved, as company law had not required the prospectus to include a report by the auditor, as far as the prospectus was concerned, it was alleged that the document contained a false statement with regard to the group's financial condition and was intended to induce people to entrust or advance money to the company (Brooks, 1933, pages xxii–xxiii).

Although the disclosures which gave rise to the charges were similar in both the accounts and the prospectus, there were two critical differences. In the accounts, as a result of a suggestion made by Harold Morland,[7] the auditor, the disclosed profit was described using the words:

> BALANCE FOR THE YEAR; including Dividends on shares in Allied and other Companies, adjustment of taxation reserves, less Depreciation of Fleet etc.[8]

At the time the prospectus was published, company law did not require that accounting information disclosed in a prospectus should be accompanied by an accountant's report. Without the involvement of Harold Morland, the prospectus omitted the words 'adjustment of taxation reserves'. The prospectus also omitted to refer to dividends received from other group companies thus giving the impression that the disclosed profits had accrued from the holding company's own trading.

Superficially, the outcome of the trial appeared to vindicate the City's integrity. Both defendants were acquitted on the charges relating to the annual accounts: they were not guilty of attempting to mislead shareholders. Although Lord Kylsant was convicted of the charge relating to a prospectus, he had acted without professional advice which, had it been taken, would doubtless have ensured that the prospectus had followed normal and acceptable practice. yet although the trial appeared to acquit the defendants of an intent to mislead, as the judge observed in his summing up, it had exposed a gap between the Exchange's view of acceptable disclosure and outsiders' expectations:

It was never brought to the shareholders' knowledge what the position was. It may seem incredible that this could go on in a big company for all those years, but so it was . . . .. It is a little astounding and one cannot help wondering whether those who manage big companies do not forget sometimes that the body of directors of a company are the agents and the trustees of the shareholders, that they owe them full information . . . and it is their interests they have to study.

(Brooks, 1933, page 224)

In the Royal Mail case, the general obligations of the Larceny Act were set against the commonly accepted disclosure practices which underlay companies' compliance with the company law requirement to publish audited accounts.[9] The tension between the two sets of expectations became clear in Harold Morland's answers when under cross-examination:

Q: Do you think that when an ordinary, intelligent . . . shareholder, looked carefully through the accounts for 1926 and 1927 he would have a true picture of the company's position?
A: The balance sheet gave him a perfectly true picture of the company's position.
Q: It is very important for a shareholder to know . . . what earnings his company is making.
A: I do not see why . . . .
Q: Do you agree that one of the most material circumstances which every shareholder has a right to know is the earning capacity of the company?
A: Of course I do not agree with that.

(Brooks, 1933, page 187)

In the City, there was considerable unease about the case. Although the effect may have been that the published accounts were misleading, Kylsant and Morland had been prosecuted for practices employed by many companies and directors. In conformity with convention, Kylsant resigned from his club, but the club's committee declined to accept the resignation.[10] Slaughter & May, the solicitors who acted for Harold Morland, refused a fee:

the partners sharing the widespread feeling in the City that there had been an element of unfairness in the charges laid against Kylsant and Morland.

(Dennett, 1989, page 50)

Sir Patrick Hastings, the barrister who had represented Morland, later admitted:

As a mere observer my opinion is completely valueless, but I was never completely satisfied of the justice of that conviction. I was very sorry for Lord Kylsant.

(Hastings, 1949, page 346)

From the very moment that the case had been brought to him by the DPP, it had been clear to the Attorney General that a prosecution would present difficulties. As Jowitt later recalled:

> I realised that the proposition which the Director of Public Prosecutions . . . had put before me was that I should launch a prosecution against two distinguished men for issuing false accounts, knowing them to be false, although they had no motive in doing any such thing,[11] and although no particular statement in the accounts could be shown to be inaccurate.
>
> (Jowitt, 1954, page 166)

In response, whilst acknowledging the difficulty, the DPP had suggested that if the accounts were false, and were known to be false, it followed that they were issued with the intention of deceiving somebody. The DPP went on to suggest that the somebody who it was intended to deceive could only be the shareholders of the company, even if the only motive was to gain time in the hope that things would work out satisfactorily (Jowitt, 1954, page 167).

Yet Kylsant and Morland were acquitted of the charges relating to the accounts having defended themselves on the ground that they had followed acceptable current practice in complying with the law. The practice of manipulating transfers from inner reserves to smooth dividend payments was indeed widely used by directors to meet shareholders' expectations and to avoid disputes with shareholders.[12] Directors saw the trial as validating a practice that was critical to preserving their control, so there was no immediate change in practice (Arnold and Matthews, 2002, page 14; Arnold and Collier, 2007, executive summary, pages unnumbered).

Although the practices employed by the Royal Mail continued, there were few who sought to defend them in public. There are only two reports of company chairmen defending secret reserves after the end of the trial.[13] Lord Plender, who was chairman of the Trade Facilities Advisory Committee and had given evidence at the trial, was the foremost accountant to defend secret reserves, and was even moved to remark that he was surprised that directors of public companies stayed silent.[14] Perhaps the directors recognised that the trial had fatefully exposed the unacceptability of a mandatory disclosure system which permitted the provision of accounting information to shareholders whose overall effect might be misleading. The point was made most pungently by *The Economist* which had publicly demanded the disclosure by RMSP of more information and more particularly consolidated accounts in the months before its collapse when its dire financial position was first suspected. Its editorial castigated directors for treating shareholders as schoolboys who should be disciplined, but fellow proprietors entitled to share in the control of their companies.[15]

The prolonged campaign which was to follow featured a number of committed protagonists: Henry Morgan, President of the Society of Incorporated Accountants; Henry Hill, President of the Institute of Chartered Accountants; Horace

Samuel, lawyer; Sir Arthur Samuels, MP; and Hargreaves Parkinson, journalist. Whilst the proposals of these campaigners differed in detail, they were united in opposing the continued use of secret reserves and in supporting the publication of detailed profit and loss accounts and consolidated accounts.

Although this campaigning did not lead to immediate action, there was a gradual acceptance that the existing state of affairs was unacceptable and that, left to their own devices, directors would not voluntarily disclose information not required by the law. The tide turned in 1939.

Towards the end of 1938, the Stock Exchange's Quotations Committee considered applications for permission to deal from three companies, none of which published consolidated accounts.[16] In response, the committee asked the sponsoring brokers to point out that the Exchange preferred the publication of consolidated accounts. In response, Express Dairy said politely that they would not oblige. The committee's request was repeated with no better result. Faced with this refusal the committee decided to recommend that future applications would be denied unless the applicant company were to publish consolidated accounts. With the support of a number of bodies, including the British Trust Association, the Exchange's Committee for General Purposes accepted the recommendation which became a requirement for new listings.

Government interventions – new issues

A second intervention was made in the early summer of 1932 in connection with the conversion of War Loan. To facilitate the conversion scheme and to prevent the sterling exchange, the Chancellor of the Exchequer announced an embargo on all new issues. The government did not issue new regulations nor did it request the Exchange to introduce temporary regulations such as those which had been introduced in January 1915: the embargo was an entirely voluntary matter. Whilst the reason for the embargo was clear, and it was understood that it would only be temporary, it is interesting that there was no initial dissent. When the embargo was eased at the end of September 1932, there was some satisfaction that the voluntary approach had been so successful.[17]

From 1 October 1932, only issues on behalf of borrowers domiciled outside the Empire and issues whose proceeds were to be remitted abroad were restricted: a restraint that was to continue for some years. In 1936, marking the longevity of the scheme, the Foreign Transactions Advisory Committee was created to advise the government on the principles of the scheme and also individual transactions. Although the scope of the scheme was again reduced in 1937,[18] so that it concentrated on public issues foreign governments, states and other public authorities, the scheme and the advisory committee were still in existence at the beginning of the 1939–1945 war.

The mood of the Exchange's relationship had changed. For both sides, co-operation proved expedient.

Criminal justice system – market activity

The criminal justice system was comparatively successful in dealing with other market activity in large part because conviction of a member of the Exchange would involve exclusion from membership.[19] As a result, anyone concerned to remain active in the Exchange and the City aimed to comply with the law. Of course, on occasion, they might test the limits of the law's requirements and in so doing break the law, but the infraction would be inadvertent. In contrast, for the convicted off-market share pusher, there was nothing to prevent a return to active share pushing. For anyone who was not concerned to remain active in the Exchange or the City, being reckless of the law's requirements carried few long-term consequences and in view of the uncertainty of prosecution, might carry no short-term consequences.

The practical effect of these distinctions is demonstrated by two contemporary cases: the James & Shakspeare trial in 1936, and the Royal Mail trial in 1931.

Garabed Bishirgian, a produce broker, conceived a plan to corner the market in shellac and pepper by making substantial forward purchases through his company Williams, Henry & Company. By the autumn of 1934, the scale of these forward commitments had out-stripped the company's financial resources and this threatened the company's ability to complete and benefit from cornering shellac and pepper. To deal with this embarrassment, Bishirgian and his associates took a controlling interest in an old-established private company, James & Shakspeare Limited, with a view to re-registering as a public company and offering its shares to the public.

The offer was announced in a prospectus issued on September 1934 which suggested that the funds to be raised by the share issue would be used to provide working capital and to acquire shares in Williams, Henry & Company. There was no suggestion that the funds were required to finance purchases of shellac and pepper or, indeed, that its trading was in any way exceptional or speculative. The public offer was successful, raising about £400,000.

In February 1935, five months later, the company was declared to be in default by the General Produce Brokers Association and by the end of the month had gone into liquidation. There had been a miscalculation. Bishirgian and his associates had estimated that the supply of pepper was about 12,000 tons and entered into forward contracts to buy more than 8,200 tons. As the market price had risen so it had become economic to decortify black pepper to produce white pepper with the result that supply had considerably exceeded expectations and the market price had fallen. All of the money subscribed following the public offer had been lost.

None of the City professionals who had collaborated in organising the share issue were prosecuted. Bishirgian and his co-conspirators calculated that the professionals they needed would be deterred if they knew the real purpose of the share issue. For whatever reason, Mawby & Barrie, the solicitors who drafted the prospectus, were ignorant of the shellac and pepper trading, as were H Vigne & Sons, the brokers who sponsored the issue. Although Cull & Company, the issuing house which organised the underwriting for the issue, were ignorant of Bishirgian's plan, they were suspicious enough to require undertakings from Bishirgian that the funds would not be used for speculative purposes: undertakings that were not honoured. The three defendants were sentenced to terms of imprisonment of between nine months and two years.

Although the Labour Party used the case in its campaigns, the City professionals involved were all shown to have attempted to comply with the law as they
understood it.

Criminal justice system – off-market activity

In parallel, the criminal justice system failed to respond comprehensively to an
explosion of abusive off-market promotion by share pushers.

As a perverse consequence of the Stock Exchange's action to exclude insubstantial company promotions, there was even more abusive activity outside.
Although the *Daily Mail* later estimated that share pushers benefited each year
by five or six million pounds.[20]No justification for this estimate was ever published and members of the Bodkin Committee suggested that it was exaggerated
although without questioning that there had been a material increase.

As in the previous decade, one indication of the scale of activity is that the number
of reports of abuse in the columns of *Money Market Review*, *Truth* and *John Bull*
increased. For example, in its 1 March 1930 edition, *Money Market Review* warned
readers of the activities of Gilbert Lycett & Company who described themselves as
'stock and share brokers'. The business's technique was to gain the confidence of
investors by recommending substantial shares such as Cunard and then to move on
to less attractive securities such as Canadian Kevin Oils, which were being offered
for sale in advance of the opening of a public market. Mention was also made of circulars produced by R Kenworthy & Company which was assumed to be connected
to Gilbert Lycett & Company because the circulars seemed to be identical. Finally,
a warning was issued in respect of Whitehall & Kingsway Investment Trust's circulars offering shares in New Age Patent Writing Ink Syndicate.[21]

Typically, such warnings identified a series of allegedly bogus financial newspapers and circulars:

Table 10.3 Exposés of allegedly bogus financial newspapers and circulars 1930–1937

Exposed by	Date	Title of allegedly bogus financial newspaper or circular
Money Market Review (i.e. Investors Chronicle)	18 January 1930	Investment Service
Money Market Review (i.e. Investors Chronicle)	18 January 1930	Finance and Stock Exchange Observer
Truth	29 January 1930	Common Sense
Truth	29 January 1930	Money in the Making
Truth	1 February 1930	Stock Market Summary
Truth	19 March 1930	Finance (formerly City News)
Money Market Review (i.e. Investors Chronicle)	5 April 1930	Financial Telegraph
Money Market Review (i.e. Investors Chronicle)	5 April 1930	Financial Empire

Exposed by	Date	Title of allegedly bogus financial newspaper or circular
Money Market Review (i.e. Investors Chronicle)	18 October 1930	Financial Chronicle
Money Market Review (i.e. Investors Chronicle)	18 October 1930	Motor Finance
Money Market Review (i.e. Investors Chronicle)	18 October 1930	The Stock and Shareholder
Money Market Review (i.e. Investors Chronicle)	25 October 1930	Stock Market Record
Daily Mail	25 October 1930	Financial Telegraph
Daily Mail	25 October 1930	Finance
Money Market Review (i.e. Investors Chronicle)	15 November 1930	Financial Observer
Money Market Review (i.e. Investors Chronicle)	15 November 1930	Stock Exchange Analyst
Truth	10 June 1931	Investment Facts
Truth	2 September 1931	Bankers Gazette
Truth	2 September 1931	Market Notes
Truth	18 April 1934	The Financial Guide
Truth	14 August 1935	Market News
Truth	14 August 1935	The Financial Forum & Investors Guide
Truth	14 August 1935	Financial Express
Truth	15 April 1936	Stock Exchange Times
Financial Times	13 May 1936	The Financial Press
Financial News	25 November 1937	The Shareholder

Source: Table reproduced from Newman (1984, page 65).

Porter (2006) suggested it was likely that there were more such newspapers and circulars than Newman identified.

In the early 1930s, exposés were helpful to newspapers as weapons in a circulation war. As they had come to depend to an increasing extent on the revenue they received from advertisements, larger circulation meant higher advertising rates and hence more income. Each newspaper tried to attract readers by offering gifts of various sorts, e.g., silk stockings, encyclopaedias or sets of classic novels (Taylor, 1965, page 311). All titles competed to publish features that would appeal to readers, and, for the *Daily Mail*, share-pusher exposés were especially interesting as they appealed to a readership that had sufficient resources to be interested in investment.[22]

Apart from showing that the Exchange was unable to influence off-market activity, the explosion of off-market abuse demonstrated that the criminal justice system was failing to cope and that the changes made as a result of the Greene Committee's recommendations had not been successful.

The Greene Committee's report had proposed measures aimed at providing more information to the DPP and had suggested that prosecutions initiated on the basis of information provided by Board of Trade Inspectors should be conducted at the public's expense and not the shareholders' (Greene Committee report, 1926, page 27). In practice, no additional funds were forthcoming. It had also suggested that the law should restrict use of the word 'bank' in a company's name, a trick beloved of share pushers and company promoters.[23] This change was not implemented.[24] Finally, the Greene Committee had proposed that door-to-door selling should be made an offence and that offers of shares should be accompanied by written statements of prescribed particulars (Greene Committee report, 1926, pages 50–51). Although implemented urgently in the Companies Act 1928, the proposed new offence proved ineffective because it had been too rigidly defined and because the necessary investigative resources were not made available. It could be avoided by a number of simple devices: one of which was already being used by many share pushers. Mailing circulars to members of the public could not be construed as door-to-door selling and thus did not fall within the newly created offence. If a member of the public then responded to an invitation in a circular and in return received a call from a share pusher, it would not attract prosecution under the new offence for it was not unsolicited.[25]

Alternatively, a caller who visited houses in alternate villages or towns would not strictly be selling door-to-door and so would argue that the new offence had not been committed. In one instance, magistrates appear not to have accepted this argument, but only on hearing evidence from the chauffeur who had driven the share pushers 'through England'.[26]

There were few prosecutions under the new law.

The ineffectiveness of these measures was reflected in evidence that was to be given to the Bodkin Committee appointed by the Board of Trade in 1936 to inquire into share pushing. The information, which appears to have been based on the registers maintained by the DPP, listed 29 cases which arose between January 1930 and the end of 1935. Of those listed, only four cases that were brought to trial involved charges under the Companies Act 1929.[27] Moreover, in 16 of the remaining cases, it had either been decided that no further action should be taken, or trials had not commenced. In other words, between 1930 and 1935, a time when there had been growing public concern, only 13 cases had proceeded to trial.[28]

This evidence is supported by an analysis of the share-pushing exposés listed by Newman. In only six of the 26 cases mentioned were there subsequent prosecutions.[29] Since Jacob Factor and his associates accounted for four cases, the six prosecutions represented a marked failure to cover the pushers who were active.

Confirming the impression that prosecutorial activity was limited, a newspaper search, which included both civil and criminal actions, identified only 66 cases between 1930 and 1938 (31 before the end of 1935, and 35 between January 1936 and December 1938). Admittedly, this search may not have traced all instances of prosecutions of fraudulent company promoters and share pushers, because the cases may not have been reported under headlines using the relevant words. Omissions may also have occurred because the three newspapers searched did not report a case such as the prosecution of three defendants in 1934 over the promotion of RMC Textiles (1928) Limited which was reported in *The Accountant.*[30]

Variations in the annual numbers of cases identified by this newspaper search and those reported to the Bodkin Committee suggest that the diligence of the authorities in chasing offenders varied from year to year.

Coverage of abusive trading in publications such as *Money Market Review* and *Truth* appears to have been reasonably constant between 1930 and 1936. This suggests that the increase in the number of cases arising in 1936–1937 did not result from a marked increase in the activity of share pushers and is more likely to have resulted from a marked increase in police activity which is consistent with the City of London Police in 1936 creating a specialist team to deal with such cases. Twelve officers were trained in company law and set to 'clean up' the City. It was claimed that by February 1937, 40 arrest warrants had been issued as a result of this team's work.[31] This suggests that police activity in previous years had been limited.

Even when a crime was investigated and suspects identified, it was not straightforward to apprehend them. In a number of the cases reported to the Bodkin Committee, the suspects had not been apprehended:

Table 10.4 Number of abusive share-pushing cases arising 1930–1938

	1930	1931	1932	1933	1934	1935	1936	1937	1938	Totals
Bodkin Committee data	8	1	4	6	4	6	0	0	0	29
Newspaper search	10	6	6	4	1	4	9	17	9	66

Source: Bodkin Committee data: National Archives, file BT 58/302.

Newspaper search: digital search of *The Times*, and *Financial Times.*

One of these cases, the Broad Street Press case, illustrates some of the difficulties that were faced in apprehending suspects. Jacob Factor, an American who was the prime mover in this affair, operated under a series of aliases. It is known, for example, that he held a bank account in the North of Scotland Bank in the name of H Guest and took residence in London under the name of J Wise (McConnell, 1943, pages 9 and 12). As identification depended on written descriptions and photographs, it was not easy to pursue a suspect through changes in alias. In Factor's case, he was known to have left the country with an allegedly substantial amount of money and was eventually traced to Chicago where he was living openly. Attempts to extradite him failed. Factor had been careful to avoid direct meetings with potential investors and the handling of their money, so that it was believed that on the available evidence a prosecution on charges of obtaining money with false pretences would be unlikely to succeed.[32] As a result, the warrant for his arrest was issued for the crime of 'receiving property knowing the same to have been fraudulently obtained'.[33] Factor's lawyers contended that there was no crime in the Illinois criminal code that matched this offence and that there was

Table 10.5 Abusive share-pushing cases in which arrest warrants were not executed

	Trading name	Suspect	Reasons given
1930	G Lycett & Co	RC Guest (American)	Had left country. Prosecution of other suspects but they were not the prime movers.
1930	Bank of London/Broad Street Press case	J Factor (American)	Had left country as warrants were issued. Prosecution continued against other suspects. Factor was prime mover and removed most of the gang's profit.
1933	Percy Bennett & Company	C Young, White	Could not be found.
1933	Leonard Briggs	AE Wagstaff	Absconded.
1934	Peter Gordon & Company	Cranwell	Absconded.
1934	James Stewart & Crichton	James Stewart	Absconded.

Source: Supplementary information provided to the Board of Trade by the DPP after publication of the report showed that in the cases initiated by the DPP, all of the failures to execute warrants occurred in cases investigated by the City of London Police. This was cited to support the contention that officers of the City's police force were prepared to collude with share pushers (Addendum to DPP's memorandum dated 30 September 1937, National Archives, file BT 58/302 COS 11602).

no common law equivalent so that extradition would be impermissible. This issue was to be considered by the Supreme Court of the United States, but that hearing was put off when Factor was 'kidnapped' (in a raid that he arranged) and by the time he reappeared, the arrest warrant had expired (Tuohy, 2001).

Even when suspects were apprehended successfully, as the Factor case and the record of prosecutions demonstrate, it was not always straightforward to decide which charges should be brought. As the Bodkin Committee pointed out, some of the available charges such as the charge of obtaining money with false pretences could present difficulty:

> The seller naturally praises the good he offers, and shares at one time worth little or nothing may 'jump in value' on some sudden turn in the fortunes of the company. This may well happen in regard to such fortunes as mining or oil companies, where at the time when the shares are offered the company is profitably producing neither ore nor oil and may have abandoned the working, yet after events may show that the shares, worthless when sold, become worth the price paid for them.[34]

This may explain the variety of charges that were used in cases against share promoters and hawkers, although the number of occasions on which pushers were prosecuted for immigration offences may indicate that it was easier for Home Office immigration officers to identify and apprehend offenders.

Once a charge was selected, it might prove difficult to collect the evidence necessary for a successful prosecution. Abusive promoters or pushers were well aware that a prosecution could be assisted by their records so there was an incentive either not to hold records or to destroy them when investigations began.

> where a bucketeer was seeking to bamboozle a client, there was little incentive to store evidence that might subsequently assist a prosecution.
>
> (Porter, 2006, page 105)

Notably at the end of the trial of a libel action brought by an alleged share pusher, Maurice Singer, against the *Daily Mail*, the newspaper's barrister requested that the court should retain the records adduced in court by Singer to substantiate his case:

> Mr Holmes asked that the papers in the case should be retained in the custody of the Court. The allegation was that the words complained of by the plaintiffs meant that they had been engaged in defrauding the public and in a criminal conspiracy. The defendants had pleaded justification and had succeeded. Many of the books said counsel had come from abroad.

The appropriate order was made and had the result that records which otherwise might easily have disappeared would have been available as the evidence in a subsequent prosecution of Singer.[35] The significance of the documents was described by Roderick Dew of Lewis & Lewis, the *Daily Mail*'s solicitors, in a memorandum of evidence submitted to the Bodkin Committee:

> All these companies were registered in Canada, and one of the chief difficulties with which [the Daily Mail was] faced in the course of the proceedings was to prove that Mr Singer not only had formed the companies but that he was responsible for the sale of the shares in England and elsewhere. Naturally enough the actual sales were not carried out by Mr Singer himself and the difficulty was to find the link between Canada and England, but this [the Daily Mail was] able to do by obtaining in Canada duplicates of letters written by the secretary of the various companies to Maurice Singer and/or the Bank of London sending share certificates in blank the numbers of which were afterwards found to tally with those in the possession of people who had bought shares in England.[36]

Other documents mentioned by Mr Dew included the detailed notes kept by Bank of London of salesmen's visits to potential investors who were being persuaded to buy worthless shares. Embarrassingly for Singer, it had been found necessary to keep records of which potential investors had been visited and what they had been told so that follow-up visits could be organised successfully.[37]

The contents of these records can be judged from similar documents that were disclosed in another case: the prosecution of Stanley Grove Spiro, who in 1934 had gained control of a Scottish outside broking firm, Maclean and Henderson. In that case, the salesmen's records included reports on the potential investors they had visited such as:

> Small house about six miles from Birmingham. Retired coachman. Very cautious. Has checked up on the firm. Prefers industrials to gold. Says 'yes' to everything, but then switches. Think £3,000 could be lifted.[38]

If all else failed, fraudulent promoters and pushers appear to have resorted to bribery. As the Bodkin Committee was to put it:

> It was also made plain to us that it is very desirable that the superior officers of the Police Force should keep in close touch with the action of their subordinates, especially as it is to be borne in mind that several of the recent share-pushing cases have disclosed the possession of considerable capital and the obtaining of enormous sums of money from the public, with the result that there is the possibility of police officers being tempted to act otherwise than in accordance with their duties.[39]

Other evidence suggests that some officers succumbed to the temptation. Following publication of the Bodkin report, Sir Hugh Turnbull, the Commissioner of Police for the City of London, requested the Metropolitan Police to undertake an investigation as a result of which two detective inspectors were reduced to the rank of constable and left the force while two other resignations followed.[40] Before this disciplinary action, the City of London Police appear to have been ineffective in dealing with share pushers, as an Assistant Commissioner of the Metropolitan Police explained in a letter to the Home Office:

> I think you must know that before the recent Turnbull 'purge' relations between us and the City were almost impossible. They gave us nothing about share-pushers if they could possibly help it and we dared not pass on information because we knew that it would be handed on to the share-pushers themselves.[41]

Evidence to support the Bodkin Committee's reference to this matter had come from a number of sources, including a memorandum of evidence submitted by Geoffrey Roberts, Treasury Counsel and adviser to the DPP:

> I believe that in the case of the Carlisle Investment Trust, a Bank applied in confidence to the Director of Public Prosecutions stating that they had some £70,000 standing to the credit of that customer – that they suspected a bucket shop – but that they would be forced to pay the money out in a few days unless process was obtained. Thereupon the Director of Public Prosecutions asked

for an officer from the City Police, and was allotted the Inspector who was in charge of the Murdoch & Barr case. Enquiries were made – and the statements of three victims taken. An application was then made for a warrant, but the victims were paid off, process could not be obtained, and the bank had to pay over the money. I do not know the details of this case, but it indicates that the bucket shop proprietor was receiving information from the Inspector, and so was enabled to pay off the selected victims so as to avoid arrest and a stop being put on the bank account. Two different firms of solicitors in the City have complained that they reported a share-pushing concern and that he did nothing. These reports were quite independent of each other and were separated by some months.[42]

There is later evidence that bribery may have been a common practice. At the trial of his libel action against the *Daily Mail*, Maurice Singer and the Bank of London were represented by Frederick de Verteuil, a barrister who was later to be prosecuted for conspiracy to defraud Edward Guylee, who himself had been convicted of fraudulent share pushing. In his evidence, Guylee said that de Verteuil h claimed to be able to 'arrange' matters with three gentlemen in the Public Prosecutor's office for £3,000. Guylee had given de Verteuil that sum in £1 notes. Later, after a hearing at Guildhall de Verteuil told Guylee that he could stop newspaper reports for £1,000. On February 15, 1937, Guylee had been committed for trial after which Whelan[43] told him that de Verteuil required 2,000 guineas to 'grease the wheels' in his favour, suggesting that amount was in guineas because money was to be handed to some legal people[44]

The case ended with the conviction of both de Verteuil and his instructing solicitor, Whelan. In Guylee's case, there does not seem to have been proof that the money was used to pay bribes, but Guylee accepted that the payment of bribes was normal and was prepared to make considerable sums available for the purpose. De Verteuil had defended promoters and share pushers on other occasions, and was to find himself mentioned in libel proceedings brought by one of his former clients, Martin Harman,[45] against *London Express Newspaper* in respect of an article that alleged that de Verteuil's disgrace at the bar[46] and the prosecution had been engineered by Harman who was embittered as a result of being convicted in spite of de Verteuil's defence. In evidence, it was also suggested that when de Verteuil was defending Harman, he had tried to persuade him to bribe a public official. The libel action failed.[47]

For all these reasons, in the early 1930s, company promoters and share pushers were justified in regarding prosecution as a distant and uncertain prospect: especially those such as Factor and Singer who were the ringleaders. To make their apprehension even more difficult, they were said to base themselves in Paris.[48] When there was a need to visit England, their visits were kept short and they would travel using false passports and the return halves of air tickets bought by others.

The overall implication of the experience of the early 1930s was that prosecutions were failing to deter the gangs of share pushers who had come to England from New York. In practice, the likelihood of prosecution was too remote to be taken seriously and if a suspect was prosecuted, ways could be found to limit the risk of conviction. As was said by Sir Horace Avory, the judge at Hatry's trial:

> the only real deterrent to crime is the certainty that the proper penalty will follow upon its commission.[49]

This experience was neither new nor unprecedented. To be effective as a deterrent for share pushers, it was necessary not just for the law to define appropriate offences and to provide appropriate powers for investigating alleged infractions, but for the system to be managed with determination. In the 1890s in England, the necessary determination had been provided by John Smith, the first Inspector General of Companies Liquidation (Batzel, 1987, page 364). In the 1920s in New York, it had been provided by Albert Ottinger, a newly appointed Attorney General who aimed to use his campaign against share pushers as a platform for election as Governor of New York (Ott, 2009) and in pursuing this objective, Ottinger was assisted by the grant of additional funds and the support of the legitimate market.[50] In England after 1936, the necessary determination was provided by Sir Hugh Turnbull, who as Commissioner of the City of London Police had recognised a threat to his force's existence. Between 1930 and 1936, without that determination, the criminal justice system failed to cope and, in 1936, its failure could be expected to be repeated once Sir Hugh's determination faltered.

Matters came to a head in December 1935 with the hearing of two libel actions against the *Daily Mail*. In July and August 1934, Maurice Singer and the Bank of London had both been named in a series of articles published by the *Daily Mail* that accused them of being fraudulent share pushers. 'The *Daily Mail* warned that an intensive share pushing campaign was being prepared by operators from across the Atlantic. It was suggested that Maurice Singer, a nefarious share pusher associated with Jacob Factor, had become a naturalised Canadian to obtain a Canadian passport which entitled him to travel without let or hindrance in any part of the British Empire.'[51]

Three days later, a further article stated that 'Maurice Singer, had been seen in Paris, where, 'with his trunks crammed with share boosting literature', he had taken a room at a fashionable hotel. It was pointed out that Singer's arrival coincided with the exposure in the *Daily Mail* and the *Continental Daily Mail* of plans for foisting shares of his latest creations in Canada, the Associated Gold Mining and Finance Co. and of the Plymouth Gold Mining Co. Ltd.[52]

On the next day, yet another article claimed that Singer had established a share pushing organisation in Amsterdam using the name: Bank of London. The *Daily Mail* described this organisation as a bucket-shop which should not on any account be confused with the Bank of London and South America Ltd, which was regarded as an institution of the highest repute.[53]

In suggesting a connection with Jacob Factor, the *Daily Mail* was reminding readers of earlier share-pushing scandals. In October 1930, the court had heard an action brought by Revd Arthur Travis Faber and his wife against Tyler Wilson &

Company Limited, in which the plaintiff claimed damages for loss caused in 1928 by investing in shares on the basis of fraudulent misrepresentation.[54] It was claimed that the misrepresentations were made on behalf of Tyler Wilson & Company who claimed to be stockbrokers and that the name given by the person responsible was an alias for Jacob Factor.[55] The outcome of the hearing was that damages were awarded to the plaintiffs.[56] Subsequently, the DPP issued charges against Jacob Factor which could not be served as he was found to have left the country. Attempts were made to secure his extradition from Illinois but failed[57] in part because Factor could not be found before the warrant expired.[58] The result was that the charges against Factor had not been tried in the United Kingdom.

In its defence to the allegation of libel, the Daily Mail claimed 'justification': in other words, that the articles had been correct. As the judge put it in his summing up:

> What the jury had to consider was whether Mr Singer was a swindling share-pusher and whether the Bank of London was a swindling bucket-shop. That was the real sting of the libel.[59]

In short order, the jury found that Mr Singer was a 'swindling share-pusher' and that the Bank of London was a 'swindling bucket-shop'.[60] The Daily Mail was acquitted of the alleged libel and awarded costs.

Perhaps by coincidence, the verdict in the Singer libel case was reinforced in January 1936 in the hearing of an application by the Liquidator of Broad Street Press Limited, another of Jacob Factor's companies for directions as to the disposition of a fund amounting substantially to £360,000, which had been extracted from Jacob Factor in America. In an affidavit, the Official Receiver stated that Broad Street Press Limited, had by false representations sold large numbers of shares in various companies and that the person responsible for the incorporation of Broad Street Press Limited and mainly responsible for its fraudulent activities was John (otherwise Jacob) Factor, who had left England at the beginning of October 1930 to return to Chicago. An order for his extradition not having been executed within the prescribed time, he was still in Chicago, but agreement had been reached with Factor, as a result of which the liquidator had received approximately £360,000.[61]

If the outcome of the *Daily Mail* libel action had left any doubt about Jacob Factor and his henchmen, it must have been dispelled by the fact that Factor had paid a substantial sum to the liquidator. From this point, if not before, it was evident that there had been a sustained attempt by internationally mobile fraudsters to take advantage of unsophisticated UK investors and that they had been active in several European countries.[62]

Reflections

Assessed technically, the Exchange's reforms were in large measure successful. As Chambers's work demonstrates, and the Exchange later boasted, weak issues were virtually eliminated with the result that failure rates fell and survival rates improved. This represented a success for the Exchange's efforts at self-regulation. However, any hope that success would eliminate the political criticism that the Exchange had faced in the 1920s was to prove unrealistic. Whilst some of that criticism may have been technical, some at least was based on a distrust of capitalist arrangements in principle and was unlikely to be silenced by a technical improvement in performance. What is more, concern remained about the performance of industry, so that questions about the Exchange's support for industry were still being debated. Thus, although the Exchange's reforms proved technically successful, its continued freedom to regulate its own affairs remained vulnerable and between 1930 and 1936 was confronted on two occasions.

The first confrontation occurred in 1930 when Lord Kylsant and Harold Morland stood trial for offences relating to the Royal Mail Steam Packet Company for the case challenged one of the assumptions of the Exchange's self-regulatory arrangements: that it was appropriate for the business of its marketplace to be transacted according to the private rules and practices of the market, largely untroubled by the requirements of public law (Moran, 2003, pages 53–54). Indeed, the rules of the Exchange expressly required that disputes between members should be referred not to the courts but to the committee which would resolve arguments not by adversarial confrontation but by the exercise of private pressure and internalised cultural controls.[63]

In the Royal Mail case, the general obligations of the Larceny Act were set against the commonly accepted disclosure practices which underlay companies' compliance with the company law requirement to publish audited accounts. The outcome of the trial signalled that if a significant gap were allowed between the private practices accepted within the exchange and the reasonable expectations of outsiders which in many cases would be articulated in public law, then Exchange insiders could expect to be called to account for their actions. This was troubling, partly because it carried the threat that members and others could face prosecution but also because the Exchange cannot have been confident of its power to secure changes in practice when there was no consensus within the accounting profession, the Institute of Chartered Accountants had been advised not to issue guidance on the matter[64] and opinion among quoted companies was generally not in favour of change.

The second confrontation arose in part from a perverse consequence of the Exchange's success in reforming its own processes. Although the Exchange proved successful in reducing weak issues, abusive activity was not eliminated: it moved off-market where the criminal justice system failed to cope. As this was quickly recognised as a social problem that required a resolution, the boundary between the Exchange and the government again attracted attention. As the Royal Commission of 1878 had recognised, the simplest administrative solution to this problem involved granting the London Stock Exchange a Royal Charter and a monopoly of share trading. In 1878, that solution had not been acceptable to the Exchange, partly because it would have involved accepting into membership at least some of the traders who had formerly traded off-market but also because it would have involved accepting a degree of government control. Even if a Royal Charter had granted considerable freedom to the Exchange, any proposal to change the Royal Charter would have required the approval of the Privy Council and thus of the senior politicians of the day. However firm had been the Exchange's original resolve to resist government scrutiny and oversight in 1878, it was reinforced by experience during the 1914–1918 war. Undertakings had been given to secure permission for the reopening of the Exchange in 1915 which enabled the government to delay a full return to normal trading conditions after the cessation of hostilities, frustrating members' hopes of a rapid return to business as usual.

If the Exchange's attitude had not been confirmed by the wartime experience, it would have been settled by developments in New York where the 1929 crash had led to a transformation of regulatory arrangements. Not only had the crash proved longer and deeper than the crash in London, subsequent events had destroyed the credibility of the NYSE as a regulator. Most dramatically, the 1932–1933 investigation of the causes of the 1929 crash by the Senate Committee on Banking and Currency had led, through the examination of senior bankers by its counsel, Ferdinand Pecora, to the exposure of a wide range of abusive practices by banks and their affiliates (Pecora, 1939; Seligman, 1995, pages 1–38; Perino, 2010). Legislation passed by the incoming federal administration[65] led to the creation of the Securities and Exchange Commission (SEC) against the bitter opposition of brokers and investment bankers. In addition, the imposition of severe civil liabilities in respect of misstatements in registration statements had led to a capital strike which was not to be resolved until March 1935 following the introduction of new rules by the SEC and later to the development of a working relationship between the NYSE and the SEC. These events provided ample reason for observers in London to fear and resist government intervention.

Notes

1 Wincott, 1946, pages 128–129. Wincott's view was supported by the Cohen Committee which in several places commented favourably on the Exchange's diligence (Cohen Committee report, 1945, page 14; Cheffins, 2008, page 280).

2 Labour Party (1935, pages 12–13). The pamphlet makes use of research carried out by Henry Morgan, President of the Society of Incorporated Accountants and reported at the Society's annual meeting on 26 September 1930.

3 A description of the group's structure and the network of cross-holdings of shares was published in: *The Economist*, 7 February 1931, pages 299–301.

4 The auditor had observed that the rate at which depreciation had been provided had been reduced and that the company's investments in associated companies might be overstated. *The Times*, 13 June 1929, page 22.

5 *The Times*, 17 July 1929, pages 22, 23 and 26. 23 July 1929, page 20. 30 September 1929, page 20. 7 October 1929, page 22. 18 October 1929, page 24.

6 See for example the question posed by Chuter Ede, House of Commons Hansard, 2 March 1931.

7 Until 1929, when Harold Morland retired, RMSP had appointed a single individual to serve as auditor. Morland was a partner in Price, Waterhouse and Company.

8 Annual report and accounts of The Royal Mail Steam Packet Company for the year ended 31 December 1926 (National Archives, file CRIM 1/562).

9 As *The Economist* observed of the charge against Lord Kylsant on the Royal Mail's annual accounts, 'if he was guilty then most of the chairmen of large public companies would today be in custody' (*The Economist*, 21 July 1931).

10 Having sought the advice of Jowitt, who was also a member. Jowitt advised against accepting Kylsant's resignation (Jowitt, 1954).

11 The prosecution of Kylsant and Morland was the only instance in the 1920s and 1930s of a prosecution for prospectus or accounts fraud which did not involve the illegitimate extraction of assets by the defendants. Indeed, it was accepted that Kylsant had been acting on his view of the best interests of the company and group.

12 In the case of the Royal Mail, avoidance of disputes was especially important. The group consisted of a number of companies, many of which were public companies whose shares were quoted on the Exchange. These companies were held together by an inter-locking series of cross-holdings. If individual companies failed to pay dividends on preference shares or interest on debentures, the holders would acquire voting rights in shareholders' meetings which would have undermined the Royal Mail's ability to control the group.

13 *The Times*, 5 May 1932, page 21; 14 June 1932, page 21.

14 *The Times*, 27 April 1932, page 8.

15 *The Economist*, 1 August 1931, page 212.

16 Express Dairy, Neepsend Iron and Superheater.

17 *The Times*, 25 August 1932, page 15; 1 October 1932, page 16.

18 *The Times*, 18 March 1937, page 21.

19 Rule 16 empowered the Exchange's committee to expel or suspend members who were guilty of disgraceful or dishonourable conduct.

20 Evidence of ER Dew to the Bodkin Committee, 20 January 1937, page 17 (National Archives, file BT 55/107).

21 *Money Market Review*, 1 March 1930, page 431.

22 The *Daily Mail's* circulation was under attack from the *Daily Express*. Surveys of readership in the 1930s show that the *Daily Express's* readership rose from about 1.1 million in 1930 to about 2.5 million in 1939, while the *Daily Mail's* circulation fell from about 1.8 million to about 1.5 million. The surveys also show that the Daily Mail's penetration of the more prosperous elements of the middle class was greater than the *Daily Express's*. Maintenance of the *Daily Mail's* claim to be the leading newspaper depended upon clear success among the middle classes (Jeffery and McClelland, 1987, page 27 et seq.).

23 The company which Clarence Hatry first used in company promotion activities was called Commercial Bank of London Limited. Jacob Factor's principal company was called Bank of London Limited.

24 This recommendation had proved difficult to implement partly because of the difficulty of defining and identifying companies that should legitimately be regarded as banks.

25 This was the justification for the many newspapers and circulars whose exposure was noted in Newman (1984). The offence was subject to an exemption in respect of 'persons with whom the person making the offer has been in the habit of doing regular business in the purchase or sale of shares', a phrase that was not defined (Section 356(1), Companies Act 1929).

26 Evidence of ER Dew to the Bodkin Committee, 20 January 1937, page 23 (National Archives, file BT 55/107).

27 Cases 38/30 (Cresset Trust); 7/33 (Herrick, Smithyes & White); 53/34 (Gilbert White & Company); and 268/35 (Period Investment Trust).

28 Attribution of the data to the Director's registers is suggested because the reference numbers quoted are similar to those in the Director's registers which are held in the National Archives.

29 Digital searches of *The Times, Financial Times* and *Manchester Guardian* archives.

30 *The Accountant*, 13 August 1934, page 201 et seq. The case included charges relating to an allegedly false statement in a prospectus and was presumably reported in *The Accountant* because one of the accused had been the company's auditor.

31 *Evening News*, 23 February 1937.
32 *The Times*, 19 December 1935, page 4.
33 Section 33 of the Larceny Act 1916.
34 Bodkin Committee report, 1937, pages 22–23. The shares on which the Broad Street Press case focussed all related to five gold mining companies which were registered in Canada. Each of the companies had a long history and owned a mine, although at the time of the sales was not operating. (Memorandum of ER Dew, page 2, and Evidence of ER Dew to the Bodkin Committee, 20 January 1937, page 8, National Archives, file BT 55/107).
35 *The Times*, 19 December 1935, page 4. Singer was prosecuted later on other charges.
36 National Archives, file BT 55/107.
37 National Archives, file BT 58/226, SP 25. Although the documents were made available to the DPP, no prosecution was mounted. In the libel action, evidence taken from individuals in Canada on commission was admissible but would not have been in a criminal action. It would therefore have been necessary for the witnesses in question to have been brought to London to give evidence in person at a trial and the cost of this was thought prohibitive (Evidence of ER Dew to the Bodkin Committee, 20 January 1937, National Archives, file 55/107).
38 *Manchester Guardian*, 25 March 1938, page 17 (cited in Hollow, 2015, page 81).
39 Bodkin Committee report, 1937, page 28.
40 Home Secretary's answer to a parliamentary question (*The Times*, 26 February 1938, page 7). The DPP had concluded that there was insufficient evidence to support prosecutions. Presumably, the Commissioner instigated the investigation because the Bodkin Committee's criticism had caused consternation in the City of London. Aldermen requested that the Board of Trade should provide access to the evidence on which the committee's criticisms had been based but were denied. One of the inspectors who was dismissed, Inspector Stubbings, had prepared the force's formal evidence for the Bodkin Committee and had accompanied the Commissioner and Assistant Commissioner when they gave evidence orally (National Archives, file BT 58/302 COS 11602).
41 Letter dated 13 January 1939 from Sir Norman Kendall, Assistant Commissioner of the Metropolitan Police, to AL Dixon, Assistant Secretary, Home Office. Tellingly, the DPP subsequently wrote to Kendall supporting his observations in a letter dated 27 January 1939 (National Archives, file MEPO 2/8607).
42 National Archives, file BT 58/226, SP25. Related evidence was submitted by Valentine Holmes, also barrister who had appeared for the *Daily Mail* in the Broad Street Press libel action and had conducted enquiries in Canada with Roderick Dew (National Archives, file BT 58/226, SP 22).
43 De Verteuil's co-accused, who was a solicitor.
44 *The Times*, 3 June 1938, page 4.
45 During the 1920s, Harman had become a director of Morris & Jones, a Liverpool grocery company, for the express purpose of persuading the company to buy up worthless shares in his other companies (Robb, 1992, page 131; Hollow, 2015).
46 He had been disbarred by Gray's Inn.
47 *The Times*, 28 April 1939, page 4; 29 April 1939, page 4; 2 May 1939, page 4.
48 Bank of London appears to have had three branches in Europe: at Lucerne, the Hague and Amsterdam (Evidence of ER Dew to the Bodkin Committee, 20 January 1937, page 6, National Archives, file BT 55/107).
49 Address to the Grand Jury at Exeter Assizes, May 1922 (quoted in Bell, 1939, page 237).
50 The Investment Bankers Association, the Investors Protective Association, Better Business Bureaus and the NYSE all operated in conjunction with the state authorities to gather information. Operating together, these groups sought to create an impression that the 1920s market was devoid of bucket-shop operations. The market associations and the NYSE acted in this way because they wanted to combat the threat of federal regulation by demonstrating that market forces could be effective in eliminating abuse

(Holt, 2008, page 361). There is no evidence of similar collaboration between the market and criminal justice authorities in England.

51 *Daily Mail*, 7 July 1934.
52 *Daily Mail*, 10 July 1934.
53 *Daily Mail*, 11 July 1934.
54 *The Times*, 28–31 October 1930 (McConnell, 1943).
55 Factor had been a share pusher in the United States of America after the end of the 1914–1918 war. In 1924, when action was being taken against share pushers in New York, Factor was backed by money provided by a criminal gang in New York to travel to England to make money through share pushing. Allegedly, during this first visit, Factor made a profit of US$ 1.5 million. He returned in 1925, for a second share-pushing campaign, on this occasion using the name Tyler Wilson & Company. When his operation attracted press attention in 1930, he returned to the United States, by which point his accumulated profit is said to have amounted to US$ 8 million or £1.6 million (Tuohy, 2001, page 132).
56 *The Times*, 31 October 1930, page 4.
57 Memorandum dated 23 April 1932 by Albert Robbins, an American lawyer (National Archives, files FO 115/3402, CAB 24/248/36, CAB 24/248/39).
58 It was claimed that Factor arranged to be 'kidnapped' in Chicago when the warrant was about to expire (Tuohy, 2001, page 140 et seq.).
59 *The Times*, 18 December 1935, page 4.
60 *The Times*, 19 December 1935, page 4. In the action brought by Maurice Singer, the Court found against the *Daily Mail* on minor issues relating to his alleged deportation in 1928, investigations by the Dutch police and his allegedly fraudulent application for Canadian nationality. Damages of £50 were awarded against the newspaper (but never paid). On the principal issue of whether Mr Singer was a share pusher, the court found in favour of the *Daily Mail* (Evidence of ER Dew to the Bodkin Committee, 20 January 1937, National Archives, file BT 55/107).
61 *The Times*, 25 January 1936, page 4.
62 This was subsequently confirmed in evidence presented to the Bodkin Committee (National Archives, file BT 55/104, SPC 39).
63 In 1930, the committee's dealing with members who were involved in weak underwriting demonstrates the approach. By implying to the members concerned that their membership might not be renewed if their objectionable practices continued, the committee brought an end to the practice without formal legalistic confrontations.
64 The Institute of Chartered Accountants had sought the advice of Wilfred Greene KC who had chaired the Departmental Committee which had reviewed company law in 1925–1926. He had opined that if the Institute were to publish guidance it would undermine its quasi-judicial functions, *The Times*, 12 December 1931, page 15.
65 Securities Act, 1933; Securities Exchange Act, 1934.

References

Primary works: unpublished documents

National Archives.
Warwick University Modern Records Centre, Leslie Scott Papers.

Primary works: newspapers and periodicals

The Accountant.
Daily Express.

Daily Mail.
The Economist.
Evening News.
Financial Times.
Manchester Guardian.
Money Market Review.
The Times.

Primary works: government and parliamentary reports

Board of Trade (1926), *Report of the Company Law Amendment Committee* (Cmd 2657). (HMSO, London). ('The Greene Committee Report').

Board of Trade (1937), *Share-Pushing: Report of the Departmental Committee Appointed By the Board of Trade 1936–1937* (Cmd 5539). (HMSO, London). ('The Bodkin Committee Report').

Board of Trade (1945), *Report of the Committee on Company Law Amendment* (Cmd 6659). (HMSO, London). ('The Cohen Committee Report').

HM Treasury (1931), *Report of the Committee on Finance and Industry* (Cmd 3897). (HMSO, London). ('The MacMillan Committee Report').

Primary works: contemporary books and articles

Bell, EA (1939), *These Meddlesome Attorneys* (Richards Press, London).

Brooks, C (1933), *The Royal Mail Case: Rex v Lord Kylsant, and Another* (Wm Hodges & Company, Edinburgh).

Labour Party (1935), *Labour's Call to Power* (Labour Party, London).

McConnell, TC (1943), *Luck and Witless Virtue vs Guile: In Which an English Clergyman Proves the Nemesis of John ('Jake the Barber') Factor, Alias J Wise, Alias H Guest* (Chicago Literary Club, Chicago).

Pecora, F (1939), *Wall Street Under Oath* (Simon & Schuster, New York).

Secondary works

Arnold, AJ and Collier, P (2007), *The Evolution of Reserve and Provision Accounting in the UK, 1938–1950* (ICAS, Edinburgh).

Arnold, AJ and Matthews, DR (2002), 'Corporate Financial Disclosures in the UK, 1920–1950: The Effects of Legislative Change and Managerial Discretion', *Accounting and Business Research*, volume 32, number 1, pages 3–16.

Batzel, VM (1987), 'The General Scope of the Act: A Study of Law, Moralism and Administration in England, 1844–1910', *Canadian Journal of History/Annales Canadiennes d'Histoire*, volume 22, pages 349–365.

Chambers, D (2009), 'IPO Underpricing Over the Very Long Run', *The Journal of Finance*, volume 64, number 3, pages 1407–1443.

Chambers, D (2010), 'Going Public in Interwar Britain', *Financial History Review*, volume 17, number 1, pages 51–71.

Cheffins, BR (2008), *Corporate Ownership and Control: British Business Transformed* (Oxford University Press, Oxford).

Dennett, L (1989), *Slaughter and May: A Short History* (Granta Editions, Cambridge).

Hastings, P (1949), 'The Case of the Royal Mail', in Baxter, WT and Davidson, S (editors), *Studies in Accounting*, (Third edition, ICAEW, London).

Hollow, M (2015), *Rogue Banking: A History of Financial Fraud in Interwar Britain* (Palgrave Macmillan, Basinsgtoke).

Holt, DS (2008), *Acceptable Risk: Law, Regulation, and the Politics of American Financial Markets 1878–1930*. Unpublished PhD thesis, Department of History, University of Virginia.

Jeffery, T and McClelland, K (1987), 'A World Fit to Live In: The *Daily Mail* and the Middle Classes 1918–1939', in Curran, J, Smith, A and Wingate, P (editors), *Impacts and Influences: Essays on Media Power in the Twentieth Century* (Methuen, London).

Jowitt, E (1954), *Some Were Spies* (Hodder & Stoughton, London).

Moran, M (2003), *The British Regulatory State: High Modernism and Hyper-Innovation* (Oxford University Press, Oxford).

Newman, K (1984), *Financial Marketing and Communications* (Holt, Rinehart & Winston, Eastbourne).

Ott, JC (2009), '"The Free and Open People's Market": Political Ideology and Retail Brokerage at the New York Stock Exchange, 1913–1933', *The Journal of American History*, volume 96, number 1, pages 44–71.

Perino, M (2010), *The Hellhound of Wall Street* (Penguin, New York).

Porter, D (2006), 'Speciousness is the Bucketeer's Watchword and Outrageous Effrontery His Capital: Financial Bucket Shops in the City of London c1880–1939', in Benson, J and Ugiolini, L (editors), *Cultures in Selling: Perspectives on Consumption and Society Since 1700*, pages 103–125. (Ashgate, Aldershot).

Robb, G (1992), *White-Collar Crime in Modern England: Financial Fraud and Business Morality, 1845–1929* (Cambridge University Press, Cambridge).

Seligman, J (1995), *The Transformation of Wall Street: A History of the Securities and Exchange Commission and Modern Corporate Finance* (Revised edition, Northeastern University Press, Boston).

Taylor, AJP (1965), *English History 1914–1945* (Oxford University Press, Oxford).

Tuohy, JW (2001), *When Capone's Mob Murdered Roger Tuohy: The Strange Case of Tuohy, Jake the Barber, and the Kidnapping that Never Happened* (Barricade Books, Fort Lee, NJ).

Wincott, H (1946), *The Stock Exchange* (Sampson Low Marston & Company, London).

11 Negotiating a new partnership 1936–1939

Introduction

The outcome of the Broad Street Press libel trial proved significant because it confirmed that there were financial interests which sought to take advantage of unsuspecting investors, and because, in proving its case, the *Daily Mail* had substantiated its descriptions of how share pushers went about their predatory activities. This served as a demonstration that the criminal justice system had failed to deter abusive traders and appeared to validate the long-established critique of capitalist institutions that were seen to be failing to achieve post-war aspirations for a fairer, prosperous society.[1]

The critique of capitalism

In 1936, there were many groups who shared a common concern that capitalism had failed to realise the hopes for post-war reconstruction which had originally been articulated among others by Addison, the Minister of Reconstruction:

> reconstruction is not . . . a question of rebuilding society as it was before the war, but of moulding a better world out of the social and economic conditions which have come into being during the war.
>
> (cited in Johnson, 1998, page 7)

When the ecstatic post-war boom was brought to an early close on the government's realisation that public spending at wartime levels would not be sustainable in peacetime, there had been a sudden depression that brought with it the despair captured by TS Eliot (1922) in *The Waste Land* and described later by CM Bowra (1949, page 161). More prosaically, the despair had led a number of authors to attribute the dashing of deeply cherished hopes to a failure of capitalism and its institutions. In 1923, Sidney and Beatrice Webb argued that capitalism had proved that it was inimical to civilisation itself and proposed fundamental institutional reform (Webb and Webb, 1923, page 6). A year later, Keynes, in a series of articles in the *New Statesman* and a subsequent lecture, argued that more limited institutional reform was necessary to achieve the practical changes in behaviour that were necessary:

> I believe that some co-ordinated act of intelligent judgement is required as to the scale on which it is desirable that the community as a whole should save, the scale on which these savings should go abroad in the form of foreign investments, and whether the present organisation of the investment market distributes savings along the most these matters should be left entirely to the chances of private judgements and private profits, as they are at present.
>
> (Keynes, 1924, page 320)

As the 1920s proceeded, these different approaches were reflected in the policies of the principal political parties. Keynes's ideas strongly influenced the Liberal Industrial Inquiry, whose report was published in 1928 and accepted that the system for promoting new issues of shares was deficient and proposed the creation of a Board of National Investment which would be able to:

> direct investment into profitable fields of investment at home at present uncared for and incompletely explored in which the national savings can be employed to the fullest economic and social advantage.
>
> (Liberal Party, 1928, pages 113–114)

In the same year, the Labour Party Conference adopted a policy statement which had been prepared at its request by RH Tawney and built on the Webbs's more dismissive account of capitalist institutions. Suggesting that the Liberal Industrial Inquiry report was hesitant partly to accommodate the 'propertied interests' which supported the Liberal Party (Labour Party, 1928, page 13), the statement proposed that the Bank of England should be nationalised and commented that the existing system for capital issues achieved the:

> diversion of a considerable proportion of the national credit and national savings into enterprises which, from a public point of view, are at best useless, and at worst, mischievous. It holds that any sane method of allocating them among different undertakings should be based on qualitative, as well as quantitative, considerations, and that services of national importance must be adequately financed before resources are placed at the disposal of enterprises concerned with luxuries or amusements.
>
> (Labour Party, 1928, pages 13, 26)

Formally, the Conservative Party did not support this type of thinking, but in 1927, a small group of young Conservative MPs published an analysis of the relationship between industry and the state which accepted that the capitalist system had to some extent proved dysfunctional and that it would be desirable for government to create new structures to avoid repeated disputes between labour representatives and employers (Boothby et al., 1927).

Election of a Labour government in 1929 on a manifesto based on the 1928 policy statement brought an expectation that institutional reform would follow. In the event, although the Labour government commissioned the first step towards reform as presaged in the 1928 statement (Labour Party, 1928, page 26) by appointing the Macmillan Committee, the political difficulties surrounding the economic recession that followed the 1929 crash and the further crisis of 1931 supervened and no institutional changes were implemented. However, the 1931 crisis seemed to confirm the suggestion that existing laws and structures were no longer appropriate to deal with changed conditions and re-fuelled interest in how the institutions of capitalism might be improved (Macmillan, 1938, pages 7–8; Marwick, 1964, page 286).

Indeed, for many, the Hatry crash and other scandals justified the cause of reform. In his preface to Tom Johnston's book, *The Financiers and the Nation*, Sydney Webb suggested that the egregious swindles of such as Hatry, Bottomley and Kreuger were inseparable incidents of the capitalist system and complained of the honest bankers and respectable stockbrokers who, whenever the question of reform arose, claimed that such 'accidents' were 'inseparable' from their essential freedom to make profits.(Webb, 1934, pages vii–viii)

Tom Johnston was a former Cabinet minister who had resisted proposals in 1931 to reduce unemployment benefit and accused City of London financiers of wasting the country's resources (Walker, 1988, page 114). Although Johnston's book did not propose replacement of the Stock Exchange, it supported radical institutional reform whose introduction would in his view require extra-parliamentary action, as he doubted whether gradual evolutionary progress was possible.[2]

Within Labour circles, the failure of the Labour government to implement institutional reform and its subsequent collapse had led to much soul-searching and the creation of new groups such as the New Fabian Research Bureau formed in March 1931 under the leadership of GDH Cole, Clement Attlee and Christopher Addison (Durbin, 1985, page 80). In 1935, the Bureau published a collection of essays which opened with an essay by HD Dickinson, a professor at Bristol University, arguing that economic individualism had failed and that the financial system needed radical reform (Cole, 1935, pages 11–40). A later essay by a 'group of Cambridge economists' reviewed recent new issues of capital and argued for a central planning agency that would direct capital and into which insurance companies and investment trusts would be absorbed (Cole, 1935, pages 11–40).

Books such as these were significant because related ideas had appeared in the publications and manifestos of political parties[3] and in the thinking of many who did not necessarily support the market socialism of Professor Dickinson (Currie, 1979, page 104 et seq.; Middlemas, 1979, page 214 et seq.; Smith, 1979, page 28 et seq.; Newton and Porter, 1979, page 65 et seq.; Clift, 1999). Groups such as Political and Economic Planning, which had also been formed early in 1931, published reports on the organisation of industry and reform of the capital market.[4] For other groups and commentators, company law reform offered an opportunity:to enable what Laski called 'public regulation of the company'. This was a staging post on the way to public ownership. Both Tawney and Laski recognised the desirability of minimising private ownership, but also the need for governance arrangements which would increase public accountability over the transitional period (Maltby, 2007, page 42; Clift, 1999; Tawney, 1921, page 96; Laski, 1925, page 113).

In 1933, Horace Samuel, a solicitor who specialised in company law matters, published *Shareholders' Money*, in which he argued for a thoroughgoing reform of company and securities law:

> So far as the author is aware, the present impetus of Company Law Reform tends mainly to be confined to the question of company accounts. Without in any way detracting from the importance of this question . . . the author puts forward the view that in . . . wide and important matters . . . the law, as it now stands, is also riddled with loopholes.
>
> (Samuel, 1933, page viii)

The title of Samuel's book was, like the title of Garvin's editorial in *The Observer* in 1929, a reference to Louis Brandeis's book *Other People's Money*. In that book, Brandeis had argued vehemently for an end to abusive share-selling practices to be achieved by reforms partly based on the mandatory disclosure requirements of English law. Brandeis's advocacy had encouraged the movement towards securities law reform state by state (Loss and Cowett, 1958) underlay the Securities Act introduced by President Roosevelt in 1933, in response to the 1929 Wall Street Crash. Samuel analysed the reforms introduced by Roosevelt and proposed equivalent reforms for Great Britain.[5] Samuel's approach was supplemented a year later by a pamphlet published by PE Gourju and the journalist Hargreaves Parkinson, calling not only for reform of securities law but also for reform of the Stock Exchange itself.[6]

In short, by the end of 1935 when the Broad Street Press libel trial took place, there were many groups sharing a sense that the organs of capitalism were in some way dysfunctional and that some intervention would be necessary to improve economic performance. What they did not share, however, was a view of what that intervention should be and how it might best be achieved. Some favoured extensive institutional reform; others did not.

1936

Support for reform to eliminate share pushing was growing and was further encouraged when the liquidator of Broad Street Press Limited sought the court's direction on how he should apply funds to the sum of £360,000 which had been received from Jacob Factor himself:

> That such a sum should have been received from Factor, whom it had proved impossible to extradite from Chicago, dispelled any doubt there may have been about the outcome of the libel action.

As trials and hearings were taking place in one part of London, in Westminster MPs were asking questions of ministers: seeking a review of company law.

Whenever this happened, ministers were advised to resist requests for a review on the ground that the recommendations of the last review had only been brought into force in 1929 and that there had not yet been time to understand the full effect of the changes that had been made. These occasional exchanges were enlivened in June when Tom Johnston created an opportunity for a debate on the subject. The government had been embarrassed by a leak of budget secrets to the extent that it had been obliged to appoint a tribunal chaired by a High Court judge to investigate and, on publication of the report, two members who had been involved in the leak had resigned.[7] In the ensuing debate, Tom Johnston used the fact that the budget leaks had been used to make profit by taking out insurance policies to justify an amendment to the government's motion calling upon the government to take appropriate action in the light of the gambling practices in the City of London.

In speaking for his amendment, Johnston suggested thatthere had been a stream of Factors, Hooleys,[8] Hatrys and Bevans.[9] He suggested that year after year, there was always some larger vulture than the others who succeeded in skimming off the savings of hundreds of thousands of poor people. The City of London, the centre of the Empire, had found a system of gambling on policies which were not enforceable at law on contingencies on which the gambler had no insurable limit.

In the government response to the amendment, Johnston may have received more than he expected. For the most part, the Chancellor of the Exchequer, Neville Chamberlain, rebutted the call for a review of company in the usual way but added:

> Personally – and he was careful to say that this was only his personal opinion – (laughter) – he thought there was some need for the amendment of the present company law[10]

This was the first occasion on which any government minister had acknowledged that there was a case for further amendment of company law, and it gave a further impetus to the calls to review company law and to outlaw share pushing. Thus encouraged, MPs continued to ask questions. In July, a month later, the Parliamentary Secretary to the Board of Trade responded to further questions about share pushing by saying that the possibility of registration and the amendment of company law was under review.[11]

Appointment of the Bodkin Committee

With the coming of autumn, the calls for reform became more troubling.

On 4 October 1936, the British Union of Fascists (BUF) attempted to hold a march through East London. By the time the [British Union] ranks were massed outside the Royal Mint, a sizeable anti-fascist presence of tens of thousands was in East London ready to ensure that the [British Union] would not pass. Such had been their conviction that in Cable Street a lorry had been overturned and incorporated into a barricade. Fearing a melée, Sir Philip Game[12] changed the path of the march away from East London.

The event is remembered partly for the defeat of a fascist demonstration and partly for the swift action taken to prevent public disorder.[13] It is less well remembered for its relationship to the BUF's criticisms of financial institutions. The BUF's general programme envisaged that the country's economic problems had arisen because of the baleful effects of the financial system which, according to the BUF's Director of Policy, A Raven-Thomson, had fallen under the control of Jewish interests:

> The hidden dictatorship of finance operating from the City of London had been one of the major causes of the economic decline of this country. The great financial houses of the city, controlled as they are by alien forces, have entirely failed to realise their responsibilities towards the British people, and have directed their immense resources into foreign investment.
>
> (Thomson, 1935, page 19)

The BUF's programme envisaged that these problems could be resolved by removing the influence of financial and particularly Jewish interests and reorganisation of the government along corporatist lines.[14] In short, the BUF's programme represented an extreme attempt to reform the constitutional framework as a precondition of dealing with the problems which many others had identified and had proposed to resolve by other less dramatic means.

By chance, on the day after the Cable Street disturbances, another group began a protest demonstration although in an intentionally orderly and disciplined manner as a contrast to the style adopted by the BUF. The Jarrow marchers set out to march to the Houses of Parliament in Westminster. They were protesting about the high rate of unemployment in Jarrow which had been caused by the closure of Palmer's Shipbuilding Yard. Ellen Wilkinson, the MP for Jarrow and one of the leaders who organised the march, blamed the yard's closure on City financial interests which, she alleged, not only decided that Jarrow's yard should be sacrificed to safeguard interests in other yards but also had prevented the development of a new steelworks in Jarrow to replace the jobs which had been lost (Wilkinson, 1939).[15]

That reform of the financial system had become the subject of street protests and disorder echoed Tom Johnston's hint in 1931 of extra-parliamentary action.

Against this background, the Board of Trade, in the person of Edwin Marker,[16] Comptroller of Companies, turned again to consider again whether a review of company law should be commissioned. He prepared a memorandum examining the possibilities that had been raised in the debate on 15 July and concluded that the suggestion that company law should be reviewed as a whole was the least attractive,

The memorandum admitted that the case for action on share pushing was much stronger; but Marker suggested that the real difficulty lay in knowing what to do. Questions in the House of Commons had focussed on four possible lines of action, each of which had drawbacks. Some had suggested that dealing in shares should be restricted to the Stock Exchange which should be granted a Royal Charter.

This was subject to the drawback that the Exchange did not want to take on this responsibility. Alternatively, it had been suggested that all outside brokers should be registered. Marker's memorandum contended that registration would be useless unless there was also control. As a variant, it had been suggested that outside brokers should be obliged to register with some recognised association (other than the Exchange). Finally, others had suggested that no person should be allowed to deal in shares unless a deposit had first been made, although, as Marker commented, the value of this proposal on its own was doubtful.

A way out of this impasse had recently been suggested by Roderick Dew, a solicitor who had acted for the *Daily Mail* in the Broad Street press case. In an address to the provincial meeting of the Law Society in September, which was subsequently published, he explored means by which it might be possible to control share pushing and suggested that the registration of share traders should be explored.[17]

Dew's suggestion offered the Board of Trade a way of moving forward and, on this basis, Marker's memorandum suggested that appointment of a committee of inquiry should be considered.[18]

Until this moment, there had been no urgency about the Board of Trade's reaction to calls for a review and reform. But matters were now to proceed at almost indecent haste. By the end of October, having prepared his memorandum, Marker had gone on to consult the Treasury and the Home Office on the suggestion that a committee should be appointed to review share pushing. In turn, they had consulted the Bank of England, the Stock Exchange and the DPP, E Tindall Atkinson. All were in favour and apparently were agreed that Sir Archibald Bodkin should chair the committee.[19] On 4 November 1936,[20] Marker discussed the subject with Sir Horace Hamilton, the Permanent Secretary of the Board of Trade, who agreed that a committee should be appointed.

Two weeks later, the intention to appoint the committee was announced by the President of the Board of Trade on 17 November 1936 to be greeted by a riposte by Sir Michael Samuel that on previous occasions it has taken five years for any changes to be implemented, a precedent that he hoped would not be followed.[21]

On 18 November 1936, Edwin Marker prepared a further version of his memorandum setting out draft terms of reference and suggesting how the committee might be composed. Apart from Sir Archibald, the only other candidate named was Roderick Dew, a solicitor who had acted for the Daily Mail in the Broad Street Press libel action and had presented a paper suggesting the registration of share pushers.[22] Presumably to forestall further delays, only a week later, the President of the Board of Trade announced the terms of reference and membership of the committee.[23] Formal appointment followed a few days later on 2 December 1936 (Bodkin Committee report, 1937, page 2).

Appointment of the committee had eventually received wide departmental support. For the Board of Trade, the committee offered a way of dealing with a problem which had caused public concern and which threatened to encourage those who were campaigning for widespread reform of company law. Since the Board had appointed other committees to examine areas of company law (e.g., fixed trusts and motor insurance), it was more difficult to resist examination of share pushing. What is more, the Fixed Trusts Committee had referred to the problems of share pushing so that implementation of that report, which was presaged in the King's Speech, would have drawn attention to any failure to deal with share pushing. For the Treasury and the Bank of England, the new committee offered a way of dealing with concerns about distraction of investment by untrammelled speculation and roguery. For the Home Office and the Stock Exchange, wider considerations must have been involved.

Quite apart from issues relating to public order, the Home Office was aware that the DPP strongly favoured action to deal with share pushing presumably because he shared his predecessor's unease about the inability of the criminal justice system to cope. There was one more factor. At this time, Clarence Hatry was residing in Maidenhead Prison. By all accounts he had proved an untroublesome prisoner, save in one respect. Throughout the early years of Hatry's sentence, the Governor of the prison received a series of requests seeking Hatry's assistance with litigation arising from the crash of Hatry's companies in 1929. In dealing with these requests, the Governor, the Prisons Commission and the Home Office were concerned not to accord Hatry privileges that would not be permitted to any other prisoner and that by permitting such visits, they should not find that they had inadvertently permitted Hatry to continue with his business activities whilst still in prison.[24] In late 1935, Clarence Hatry's son, Cecil, recommenced the campaign[25] to seek an early release for Hatry by publishing a pamphlet reviewing the story of Hatry's collapse. Although there was wide support for the application for early release,[26] the Home Office was concerned that as there were no powers to prevent anyone from acting as a share trader, on release, Hatry would have been able to return immediately to his previous activities. Thus the call for Hatry's release provided a clear demonstration to the Home Office of the weakness in regulation of share speculation that might be resolved by registration of share traders.[27]

For the Stock Exchange, appointment of a committee of inquiry was more challenging. On the one hand, elimination of abusive share dealing would help to avoid involving the exchange in the sort of criticism voiced by Tom Johnston in the debate in June 1936. On the other hand, the prospect of the introduction of a licensing system for share traders could potentially threaten the independence of the Stock Exchange by, for example, recommending that registration should apply to all and might also reduce the distinctiveness of members of the Exchange by requiring that all share dealers should be licensed in the same way. That the Exchange welcomed the committee's appointment suggests that the Exchange trusted that appointment of its Deputy Chairman to the committee would provide a means of securing a congenial outcome.

What had changed is the political environment, which in 1936 was febrile:

> The crises seemed to grow like a geometrical progression.
>
> (Middlemass and Barnes, 1969, page 926)

Any thoroughgoing attempt to review company law and the raising of finance in particular would have been bound to take into account a wide range of proposals for institutional reform with an outcome that might not have been predictable or manageable. In the political atmosphere of 1936, the desire to avoid a broad spectrum review of company law was understandable.

Any risk that the committee might recommend a form of regulation inimical to the interests of the City was guarded against by careful selection of the members, who included Charles Vickers VC, a partner in Slaughter & May, the eminent firm of City solicitors;[28] RP Wilkinson, the Deputy Chairman of the London Stock Exchange; CL Dalziel, a partner in Higginson & Company; JH McEwen, Chairman of the Associated Provincial Stock Exchanges; and Sir Malcolm Hogg, the Deputy Chairman of the Westminster Bank. Whatever such a group might recommend, it was likely to be well aware of and to take account of the City's interests.

The Bodkin report

Almost all witnesses before the committee urged that share dealing should be restricted to properly registered persons. By 16 March 1937, barely two months after the committee had commenced its work, the chairman was able to circulate a memorandum entitled 'Points for Consideration' which suggested what the eventual report might say:

> The majority of suggestions made by witnesses before the Committee indicate that there should be some kind of machinery for insisting on Registration of all stockbrokers and dealers in stocks and shares, who are not already members of the London Stock Exchange, or of one of the recognised Stock Exchanges . . . Registration involves some general legislative provisions prohibiting any form of dealing in stocks and shares by unregistered persons and any form of approach to the public by offers to deal in or to dispose of securities, by advertisement or circularisation, except as permitted by the rules of membership of any such organisation.[29]

That was to be the approach adopted in the final report which recommended that no person should be permitted to transact business in shares with any member of the public or to describe himself in a way that indicated that he transacted such business unless he were registered or were an exempt person. Members of the London Stock Exchange and certain other exchanges should be exempt for this purpose.[30] It was envisaged that the Board of Trade should appoint a Registrar to maintain a register for this purpose and to define the conditions of registration. Those conditions should include the provision of appropriate references by a bank, a member of a recognised stock exchange and a solicitor, barrister or Justice of the Peace. An applicant would be required to give undertakings about the way in which he proposed to conduct his business. The Board of Trade was to be empowered to recognise additional stock exchanges and other associations whose persons would be exempted from the requirement for registration, and to make such changes in the list of recognised stock exchanges as seemed from time to time to be appropriate. As far as share pushing was concerned, the committee proposed that it should be unlawful for anyone who purported to be a dealer in shares during any call (including a telephone call) made by him upon any other person to offer any shares for subscription or to negotiate the purchase of shares by that other person (Bodkin Committee report, 1937, pages 67–70).

From the point of view of the Stock Exchange, these proposals may not have appeared too troubling. Whilst a licensing scheme had been recommended, the Exchange's position had been protected as it was suggested that the implementing statute should recognise the Exchange's members as exempted persons. The practical effect of this would have been that the Exchange would have been given statutory recognition without being subjected to oversight by the Board of Trade. Moreover, recognition in primary legislation would have been likely to be long-lived as pressure on parliamentary time discouraged amendment. In other words, such recognition would have provided some safeguard of the Exchange's position without the disadvantages that had led the Exchange to resist proposals that it should become a chartered body.

Satisfaction at this position was to be short-lived.

The Board of Trade's reaction

The Board consulted interested parties on the committee's recommendations and found that there was general support for them, subject to a small number of reservations. These concerned the definition of 'share hawking', or the offering of shares made in any call on a member of the public;[31] the requirement for a dealer to produce a reference from a member of a recognised stock exchange as it was thought this would give such exchanges an unjustified veto on recognition;[32] the absence of a disciplinary power to remove names from the register except after a court judgment; and the form of the register, which some argued should include all of those recognised.[33]

After reflection, the Board of Trade therefore proposed that the Bodkin Committee's recommendations should be implemented by creating a register to include the names of all people entitled to deal in shares (whether members of a recognised exchange or not). In recognition of the standing of the London Stock Exchange and certain provincial stock exchanges, the Board of Trade would have the power to recognise them so that their members would automatically be included in the register. Inclusion in the register would be open to other dealers, subject to their satisfying conditions to be specified by the board; and subsequent exclusion from the register would follow decisions of the court.

The effect of these proposals would have been that the Board of Trade would not only have been empowered to recognise exchanges, but would also have been left to monitor the way in which exchanges discharged their responsibilities. This would have created the possibility that an exchange's recognition could be withdrawn if it fell short of the Board's expectations. Unsurprisingly, this approach was unacceptable to the Exchange.

In discussion with the Exchange on Trafalgar Day 1937, the Board disclaimed any intention of undermining the privileges of the Exchange. However, it was suggested that when debated in parliament there would be opposition to discrimination in favour of members of a club which might refuse membership on other than objective grounds. In other words, the Board of Trade had accepted that regulation could not be left to a private body such as the Stock Exchange.

As the minister's brief for the meeting had observed:

> To have a register which omits by far the most important would be like Hamlet without the Prince of Denmark or a medical register which omitted from it Fellows and Licentiates of the Royal College of Surgeons and the Royal College of Physicians.

At the same meeting, the Exchange's Chairman responded:

> members of the Stock Exchange would resent the new proposals mainly on the ground that they would alter the status of members of the Stock Exchange who would be placed on a level with outside brokers and for the first time in history a measure of governmental control over them would be introduced.[34]

No conclusion was reached immediately, and, as the Exchange remained obdurate, the argument continued for some months. In the end, the Board of Trade was encouraged by the Treasury to give way and did so:

> The reason for exempting the London Stock Exchange by Statute is that we know we shall, in any case, have to give an exemption and that, so far as it is possible to foresee, there is no possibility of the exemption being withdrawn. This is not the case with the Provincial stock exchanges taken as a body. The order exempting the London Stock Exchange would, therefore, to that extent be farcical.
>
> If it should be decided that the London Stock Exchange should be exempted by Statute, then it may be suggested that it should be impressed upon them that they should do what they profess to do and that is act in the public interest in connection with share-pushing legislation and not merely in what they conceive to be the narrow interests of the London Stock Exchange. This came out forcibly recently in connection with their refusal to extend commission terms to persons who should join the proposed Association of Outside Dealers . . . It is suggested that a body that takes so narrow a view of its public duties cannot properly be placed in the special position in which it desires to be placed.[35]

The Board's irritation at the Exchange's lack of co-operation over the proposed Association of Outside Dealers is understandable. It had no wish to become heavily involved in regulating individual dealers and to this end was attempting to arrange that associations existed that every dealer could be encouraged to join rather than seeking approval from the department itself. An agreement with the Exchange over commission rates would have provided an incentive for dealers to join the proposed association but had been refused by the Exchange, which maintained its customary resistance to providing special access rights for brokers who were not members.

In this respect, the Board of Trade was adopting a similar approach to that adopted by the Securities and Exchange Commission (SEC) in the United States which promoted 'over the counter' (OTC) organisations to deal with the difficulty for the commission of regulating so decentralised an activity[36]

Officials did not expect the Exchange's negative response. At root, the Exchange still saw itself as no more than an association of people who agreed to undertake a particular business in a common market place and subject to common rules. The members had attempted to create an orderly place in which share dealing could be undertaken at a time when no public agency considered that it was a public responsibility to arrange this. For all members, their continued membership depended on the sustained demonstration that the benefits of membership outweighed the costs of membership: not simply the direct financial cost of membership but also the costs which flowed from subjection to the common rules of the Exchange and the constraints that they placed on the conduct of members' business.

Since 1919, the members had gradually become more defensive about their business interests and their control over the rules was becoming more important. Any suggestion that their control of the rules would be subject to oversight from some external agency was bound to attract suspicion and opposition, as was any suggestion of external interference with the committee's freedom to deal with applications for membership.

Moreover, as concern was growing that the Exchange was being bypassed, suggestions such as the preparation of a common register that appeared to diminish the differences between Exchange and outside brokers were inevitably contentious. That this appears to have caught officials by surprise suggests that they had forgotten Roderick Dew's paper which attempted to explain his understanding of the reasons for the Exchange's opposition becoming a chartered body: that it would involve equal recognition of outside brokers and that it would lead to their inclusion in the Exchange's membership. It appeared a first step to government control and eventually nationalisation.[37]

In its battle with the Board, the Exchange was assisted by the fact that the pre-eminent issuing houses in the City were no more enthusiastic about joining any form of register that included the outside dealers. Indeed, in discussions with the Board of Trade, they made it clear that they simply would not register.[38] Yet the Board of Trade could not afford to exclude them from share dealing and new issues in particular and needed to find a way of exempting them from the registration requirements. In other words, the Board was fighting on two fronts and the Exchange had powerful allies.

In the end, a resolution was found for most of these difficulties. The Prevention of Fraud (Investments) Act 1939 (PF(I)) was passed and provided that a licence would be required by anyone carrying on business as a share dealer.[39] Members of stock exchanges and of associations of dealers recognised by the Board of Trade were to be exempted from this requirement,[40] as were persons carrying on banking activities who were recognised for this purpose by the Board of Trade.[41]

In effect, the Stock Exchange had won the battle, with the support of HM Treasury.[42] The Act defined 'recognised stock exchange' as:

> the Stock Exchange, London, or a body of persons declared by an order of the Board of Trade for the time being in force to be a recognised stock exchange for the purposes of this Act.[43]

Some minor arguments were also won. For example, the Board of Trade was required to publish only the names of people who were granted licences to deal (i.e. there was no requirement to publish a register naming all those permitted to deal whether licensed or in some way exempted from licensing),[44] although the Stock Exchange had undertaken privately that it would provide to the Board of Trade a copy of its register of members which the Board agreed not to publish.

In Parliament, the bill's passage was not without incident. Although the bill was generally welcomed by the Opposition, which did not formally oppose it, questions were raised over the powers being granted to stock exchanges without effective oversight:

> nowhere in this Bill is there anything to prevent stock exchanges from continuing to be what they are now, private unregulated bodies. A stock exchange can refuse any application for membership and give no reasons. It can and does from time to time act unreasonably . . . At present any stock exchange can refuse membership on any ground it pleases, or on no grounds at all. Such arrogant power is bad enough at present, but when this Bill passes into law it will be much worse.[45]

In effect, this was the point that the Board of Trade had put to the Exchange in negotiating the way in which the Bodkin Committee's recommendations should be implemented. For the Opposition, it was suggested that certain stock exchanges (including London) used their power to exclude women from membership and that the passage of the bill would seriously disadvantage women who were trading as share dealers independently unless they were able to secure individual licences from the Board of Trade. One of the few amendments proposed by the Opposition which would have empowered the Board of Trade to oversee all exchanges, including the London Stock Exchange, was lost on a division after a junior minister had argued that oversight of such matters as admission to membership, 'a minor matter', was not necessary to prevent fraud among their members.[46]

Whilst it may have seemed a minor matter to the minister, for the Exchange the amendment was aimed at a key freedom: the freedom to control the composition of the membership.

The Act was passed on 28 April 1939,[47] and the Board of Trade intended that it should be implemented forthwith. To this end, preparatory work had been undertaken so that a consultation on drafts of the enabling regulations could begin almost immediately. The regulations themselves were promulgated in July 1939.[48] Although the Board of Trade did not immediately announce the date on which the requirement for registration would come into force, applications were invited by 15 September 1939 by those intending to register as dealers. In the event, the declaration of war intervened and the deadline for applications was put off, in the first instance until 15 March 1940.

Reflections

Throughout the deliberations of the Bodkin Committee and the subsequent negotiations over its recommendations, there was tension between the position adopted by the London Stock Exchange and that of the Board of Trade.

The Board of Trade, in response to the Committee's report, adopted a position that was consistent with the government's general approach to industrial organisation. The National government which had won the General Election in 1931 on a 'Doctor's Mandate' to deal with the economic crisis had adopted industrial planning together with tariff protection as the two guiding principles of its strategy for recovery. In a series of industrial schemes, moves had been made to control production and encourage rationalisation. Yet the government was usually reluctant to force rationalisation upon industry. Rather than intervening directly, the government preferred to encourage planning initiatives from industries themselves, applying pressure and influence through third parties. This general approach was also adopted by the Conservative government which succeeded the National government after the General Election of 1935:

> Intervention could only extend to state assistance to industry in its independent search for a more effective form of organisation; it could not involve the government 'in any continuous connection with the subsequent running of the industry within the new framework' . . . moreover, such assistance could not take the form of either compulsion or a sweeping devolution of statutory powers. Compulsion would only antagonize the business community. Devolution of state authority, on the other hand, would 'introduce political ends into the conduct of business and to make the Government a conferrer of favours instead of what it should be, a guarantor of freedom' . . . the proper Conservative approach should be to foster the new collective outlook in industry by encouraging existing trade associations to develop their own structures of 'voluntary' authority.[49]

This approach had the disadvantage that without direct state intervention the strength or reaction against change might slow down rationalisation but also had the advantage of avoiding the charge of collusion with radical or politically extreme ideas (Ritschel, 1997, page 58).

Within this framework, professional organisations would be expected to display a number of characteristics. First, they would generally achieve a monopolistic position having the right to exercise particular skills on the basis of a body of specialist knowledge. Second, members of the organisations would be licensed by their professional associations which would in some way be recognised as such by the state. Third, the organisations would defend their positions in part by maintaining a necessary discipline over their members. Finally, the associations would act and would claim to be acting in a public-regarding manner in exchange for the state's recognition of their monopolistic status (Noguchi and Edwards, 2004, pages 61–62).

In contrast, the London Stock Exchange still saw itself as a private club serving only the interests of its members. To the extent necessary to defend those interests, the Exchange would consider adopting policies that would defend the interests of others, as it did in 1929 and 1930 in responding to the Hatry crisis, creating a compensation fund to meet public investors' losses caused by the crisis. However, that action would be taken not principally to defend the interests of outside parties but to defend the interests of members from the possible consequences of any failure to respect others' interests.

Obviously, these two positions were in conflict. The precise nature of that conflict and the way in which it was resolved in the PF(I) Act can be analysed using the corporatist conception of the characteristics of professional associations.

Plainly, the most straightforward approach to organising the regulation of share trading would have been to grant monopolistic status to the London Stock Exchange as had been recommended by the 1879 Royal Commission and was mentioned in Edwin Marker's October 1936 memorandum, leaving the Exchange to license all share dealers.

The formal recognition of monopolistic status was not acceptable to the Exchange, but perhaps the Exchange did not see such status was necessary. After all, by 1914, the Exchange had established and maintained its pre-eminence. It was the only stock exchange in the country where the largest transactions could be handled without a serious risk of affecting market prices and listed the broadest range of securities. All this had been achieved without formal recognition of its status. Thus, it was not clear what in practice would be gained by accepting formal public recognition, whilst there would be a cost of recognition in the form of acceptance of government oversight and the dilution of responsibility to members by acceptance of responsibility for outside parties' interests.

Members would also have expected there to be a cost for public recognition of monopolistic status. To avoid claims that formal recognition had unreasonably deprived respectable traders of their livelihood, it would have been necessary to offer membership of the Exchange to at least some if not all the members of the provincial exchanges and perhaps others. In other words, it would have been necessary for the Exchange to accept into membership people with whom its members had been competing and from whom it had traditionally held itself aloof.

This would not have been an attractive prospect. Many members had been disappointed by their incomes since the 1914–1918 war, and had been wary of the challenge to the more traditional personal broking business by new, more corporate business. They had responded by using the rules to defend the old ways and had come to rely on their control of the committee. The possibility that formal recognition of the Exchange's monopolistic status would involve recognition of the status of provincial brokers, perhaps even restricting the ability of London members to control the committee, was unwelcome.

The Exchange was, however, concerned that attractive business was bypassing the House, deterred among other factors by the fixed scale of commissions and the denial of direct access to the market. Bypassing was gradually to erode the Exchange's pre-eminence and denied members the chance of benefiting from business which might otherwise have directed to the House. Many debates on this subject are recorded in the Exchange's minute books from the 1930s. Throughout, there was no recognition of the risk that the defensiveness of a majority of members would prove inimical to the factors to the creation of the pre-eminence of the House: its reputation for risk-taking and its ability to reflect changing circumstances.

By passing the PF(I) Act, the government achieved an arrangement by which all share traders were licensed, largely either by the Exchange or other associations. Applicants not thought acceptable could be excluded. Although only those associations recognised by the Board of Trade had to demonstrate that they complied with the government's regulations about the minimum conditions that applicants had to satisfy, and the Exchange was not strictly bound by these conditions; in practice, it could not afford to ignore the regulations. Its own rules were more restrictive and, if it were to maintain its exclusiveness, it would have to ensure that its rules remained more restrictive.

Similarly, the government had achieved an arrangement by which all share traders were subject to some degree of oversight by their associations. Although the Exchange remained subject to the will of its members, and would quickly have been made aware of members' displeasure at disciplinary measures they thought inappropriate, in practice, the Exchange could not afford to appear less stern than the exchanges and associations directly recognised by the Board of Trade for that would undermine its reputation.

In 1939, the London Stock Exchange could not be described as altruistic or public-regarding. It was a private club interested in fostering the interests of its members. This position was embedded in its constitution for all of the members of the Exchange's committee served for only one year and were obliged to stand for re-election annually. Members who were disenchanted with the committee's decisions were thus able to express their displeasure immediately.

For its part, the compromise underlying the PF(I) Act met the Exchange's concerns. It gave the Exchange formal recognition without formal oversight by the Board of Trade. It thus offered the prospect of cleaning up the off-market abuse without formally constraining the Exchange's ability to defend its members' perception of their own interests. However, the absence of formal constraints did not mean there were no constraints. In practice, Exchange found that it would have at least to match the performance of the directly recognised associations to maintain its own reputation.

In parallel, the government may not have achieved everything that Edwin Marker's memorandum might have sought but it achieved a measure of regulation of off-market share trading without the unpleasantness of a public dispute with the Exchange, avoided pressure for more radical institutional reform and created an arrangement that offered to put pressure on the Exchange at least to match the practice of other exchanges and associations.

Notes

1 As a sign of the failure of the criminal justice system, at the end of the trial of the Broad Street Press action, the judge ordered that the documentary evidence adduced by the *Daily Mail* should be preserved and made available to the police investigation.
2 Speech in the debate on the National Economy Bill, 11 September 1931 (Bassett, 1958, page 233).
3 For example, in 1935, the Labour Party published *Labour's Financial Policy* proposing nationalisation of the bank of England, creation of a National Banking Corporation to control the clearing banks and of a National Investment Board 'to control the flow of investment in the national market' (Labour Party, 1935, page 15).
4 Marwick (1964, page 288). PEP was led by Sir Basil Blackett, a director of the Bank of England and Marcus Sieff of Marks and Spencer.
5 Samuel was not the only voice pointing to the significance of the reforms of securities laws being implemented in the United States. Felix Frankfurter, who had supervised the development of the new law at the request of President Roosevelt, spent 1934 in Oxford as a visiting professor.
6 Parkinson called for reforms of the minimum scale of commissions, raising the bar on advertising by members of the Exchange, the creation of a Mutual Guarantee Fund, modifying the system of dual capacity by allowing representatives of buyers and sellers to meet without recourse to intermediaries, and permitting members' firms to admit 'limited' or 'sleeping' partners who in bankruptcy proceedings would only be liable for the amount of capital they had introduced (Gourju and Parkinson, 1934, pages 20–2).
7 The tribunal's chairman was Mr Justice Porter; the two members who resigned were JH Thomas (a government minister) and Sir Alfred Butt. The budget secret leaked concerned proposals to increase the standard rate of income tax and the tea duty. Making use of this information, certain individuals had sold securities and insured against an increase in income tax (*The Times*, 3 June 1936, page 14).
8 Ernest Terah Hooley was the fraudulent promoter of Jubilee Cotton Mills and for his involvement was prosecuted and convicted in 1921.
9 Gerard Lee Bevan was senior partner of Ellis & Company, stockbrokers and chairman of City Equitable Fire Insurance Limited. Both companies failed in 1922. Bevan was subsequently convicted of fraud by extracting the funds of the insurance company.
10 *The Times*, 12 June 1936, page 8.
11 *The Accountant*, 4 July 1936, pages 4–5.
12 Commissioner of the Metropolitan Police.
13 On 16 November 1936, the Public Order Bill passed through the House of Commons and became law on 1 January 1937. It prohibited the wearing of a political uniform in public and gave discretionary powers to police commissioners to ban marches in defined areas for period up to three months. The police were also empowered to respond to breaches of the peace in all public areas, not merely outdoor venues as previously.

14 It was envisaged that on attaining power, the BUF would establish central authority by an enabling bill so that the government could rule by order in council. Decisions would be taken by a small executive, with a new form of House of Commons acting as a sounding board for the executive. The House of Lords would be replaced by a national corporation made up of representatives from a number of self-governing industrial corporations. The government would plan both production and distribution.

15 Apart from Ellen Wilkinson's assertion, there is no evidence that abusive company promotion or share pushing had contributed to the failure of Palmer's Yard. There had been an issue of debentures which exceptionally was sponsored by a clearing bank; the funds raised had been used to develop the Yard's facilities but these had never been fully used because of the slump in world demand for ships. The Yard's last ship was launched in 1930. After that, some jobs had been created through the intervention of John Jarvis who had been a company promoter in 1919 as a partner in Clare and Company. Raising funds in Surrey, where he was by the 1930s an MP, be bought redundant liners which were taken to Jarrow to be broken up.

16 An exact contemporary of Clarence Hatry at St Paul's School.

17 *The Accountant*, 24 October 1929, pages 359–363.

18 National Archives, file BT 58/226, COS 6734, SP17. That Roderick Dew's suggestion was instrumental in leading to the appointment of the Bodkin Committee was recognised by Sir Archibald at the end of Dew's evidence to the committee: 'we are most grateful to you, and the public should be most grateful to you, because this paper of yours, no doubt, was the cause of this inquiry' (National Archives, file BT 55/107, page 49).

19 Sir Archibald had been DPP before E Tindall Atkinson and in that capacity had given evidence in 1925 to the Greene Committee on amendment of company law on the prosecution of offences related to share dealing.

20 On that day, a new session of Parliament opened with the King's Speech which included a reference to the Public Order Bill, and the Jarrow marchers' petition was presented in the House of Commons.

21 *The Times*, 18 November 1936, page 8. The Greene Committee had begun its work in 1925. Its recommendations were not implemented until 1929.

22 National Archives, file BT 58/226, COS 6734. Roderick Dew's paper, 'Share Pushers and the Law', had been presented to the provincial meeting of the Law Society in September and was published in October (*The Accountant*, 24 October 1936, pages 559–563). Marker recorded that the DPP spoke highly of Dew.

23 *The Times*, 27 November 1936, page 7.

24 They were unable to prevent this. Through his solicitor, Atherton Powys, and his son, Cecil Hatry, Clarence Hatry appears to have been able to pass instructions for investment of his wife's funds. During Hatry's incarceration, Atherton Powys acted in respect of Hatry's personal affairs, whilst Sir John Crisp of Ashurst Morris Crisp continued to act in respect of Hatry's corporate matters and as a leading light in the campaign to free Hatry. Powys had first encountered Hatry in 1915–1916 when he acted as solicitor for the Earl of March who served as a director of various companies promoted by Hatry (National Archives, file HO 144/21218).

25 It seems probable that the recommencement of the campaign occurred then because the judge at Hatry's trial, Sir Horace Avory, died on 13 June 1935. It was known to be the normal practice of the Home Secretary to consult the trial judge on any application for early release from a prison sentence and it was assumed that Sir Horace would not have approved an early release in Hatry's case. In due course, the Home Secretary was to consult the Lord Chief Justice, Lord Hewart (National Archives, file HO 144/21218).

26 Applications for early release were supported by Sir William Jowitt, who as Attorney General conducted Hatry's prosecution, and GB McClure who had assisted Jowitt. The campaign was also supported by other MPs (AP Herbert, Harold Nicolson and George

Lansbury), Henry Newnham (the editor of *Truth* which campaigned against promoters and share pushers) and Ben Tillett (the dockworkers' union leader) (Anonymous, 1937, pages 3–5).

27 As matters developed, a decision to release Hatry was delayed by the Home Secretary personally by six months until mid-1938. His release was finally approved by the Home Secretary in July 1938, two days after the Cabinet had approved the draft legislation that would introduce registration of share traders and the date chosen for his release was just before Parliament's approval of the bill that became the Prevention of Fraud (Investments) Act 1939. The decision to release Hatry early was not made known in a formal statement but 'leaked' on a date chosen by the Home Secretary immediately before the Prime Minister visited Munich to meet the German Chancellor, Adolf Hitler, and immediately after a Cabinet group (including the Home Secretary) had met throughout the weekend to consider the diplomatic crisis created by Hitler's speeches. As the newspapers' attention concentrated on foreign affairs, the decision to release Hatry received little attention. In modern parlance, it was a 'bad news day'. No formal statement was ever made. The manner of the announcement was chosen on the basis of advice from officials (National Archives, file HO 144/21218).

28 Whose name had been preferred to that of Roderick Dew.

29 National Archives, file BT58/226, SP 22.

30 The other exchanges listed by the committee were the 'Associated Stock Exchanges', the Provincial Brokers' Stock Exchange, the Mincing Lane Tea and Rubber Share Brokers' Association Limited (Bodkin Committee report, 1937, page 67).

31 Responding to complaints of the ineffectiveness of the new offence of door-to-door selling of shares recommended by the Greene Committee, the Bodkin Committee had suggested that it should be an offence to offer shares in the context of any call. Objection was made to the proposal on the ground that it was too broad and would constrain legitimate business.

32 There was some resentment over the possibility of the London Exchange gaining influence over registrations.

33 Board of Trade memorandum on criticisms of the committee's report (National Archives, file BT 58/226, SP3).

34 Notes of a meeting between the Board of Trade and representatives of the Stock Exchange on Trafalgar Day 1937 (National Archives, file BT 58/226, SP4).

35 Memorandum, undated, probably spring 1938 (National Archives; file BT 58/226, SP 4).

36 Eisner (2000, page 110). Adoption of this approach became possible for the SEC after amendment of the Exchange Act in 1938: the year in which the Board of Trade was negotiating implementation of the Bodkin Committee's recommendations. In the event, the amended US legislation led to the creation of only one body: the National Association of Securities Dealers which registered in 1939, the year in which the PF(I) Act was promulgated (Macey and Novogrod, 2011–2012, page 968).

37 'Share-pushers and the Law', *The Accountant*, 24 October 1936, pages 559–563.

38 The principal houses concerned were Baring Brothers and Company Limited, NM Rothschild and Sons, Morgan Grenfell and Company Limited, Lazard Brothers and Company Limited and J Henry Schroder and Company. The Board of Trade considered that if these houses were to be granted some form of exemption it would in practice also be necessary to exempt Higginson and Company, Helbert Wagg and Company Limited, Erlangers Limited and S Japhet and Company Limited (undated memorandum, National Archives, file BT 58/226, SP5).

39 Section 1.

40 Sections 12 and 1. The power to recognise associations of dealers was introduced as the Board wished to encourage the formation of new associations that would take responsibility for monitoring their members and thus relieve the Board of Trade.

41 The terms of the power of recognition were drafted with assistance of lawyers acting for a number of issuing houses to exclude them from the requirement to register (Sections 13 and 1).
42 Board of Trade files (National Archives, file BT 58/215, SP4).
43 Section 26(1).
44 Section 7.
45 Speech by William Leech, MP for Bradford Central (House of Commons Hansard, 14 February 1939, column 1627]). The issue of membership had attracted some public attention in May – July 1936 when a woman, Mrs M Gosnell, had applied for membership but been refused by the Exchange's committee on the ground that she was not eligible (Michie, 1999, page 203).
46 Ronald Cross, Parliamentary Secretary to the Board of Trade (House of Commons Hansard, 14 February 1939, column 1633).
47 House of Lords Hansard, 28 April 1939, column 793,
48 Licensing Regulations were issued on 26 July 1939 (SR&O 1939 Number 794). Conduct of Business of Licensed Dealers were also issued on 26 July 1939 (SR&O 1939 Number 787). The Conduct of Business Rules did not prohibit advertising by Licensed Dealers.
49 Ritschel (1997, pages 60–61), citing a Conservative Research Department memorandum written by Henry Brooke.

References

Primary works: unpublished documents

National Archives.
Stock Exchange Archive, Guildhall Library.

Primary works: newspapers and periodicals

The Accountant.
The Times.

Primary works: government and parliamentary reports

Board of Trade (1937), *Share-Pushing: Report of the Departmental Committee Appointed By the Board of Trade 1936–1937* (Cmd 5539). (HMSO, London). ('The Bodkin Committee Report').

Primary works: contemporary books and articles

Anonymous (1937), *The Hatry Case: Eight Current Misconceptions* (Privately Published, London).
Boothby, R, Macmillan, H, Loder, J and Stanley, O (1927), *Industry and the State: A Conservative View* (Macmillan, London).
Bowra, CM (1949), *The Creative Experiment* (Macmillan, London).
Cole, GDH (1935), *Studies in Capital & Investment: Being a Volume of New Fabian Research Bureau Studies in Socialist Problems* (Victor Gollancz, London).

Eliot, TS (1922), *The Waste Land*. Reprinted in Eliot, TS (1962), *Collected Poems 1909–1962* (Faber and Faber, London).

Keynes, JM (1924), *The End of Laissez-Faire*, the Sidney Ball Lecture published separately as a pamphlet in 1926. Reprinted in Keynes, JM (1965), *Essays in Persuasion* (WW Norton Company, New York).

Labour Party (1928), *Labour and the Nation* (Labour Party, London).

Labour Party (1935), *The Labour Party's Call to Power* (Labour Party, London).

Laski, H (1925), *The Grammar of Politics* (George Allen & Unwin, London).

Liberal Party (1928), *Britain's Industrial Future: Being the Report of the Liberal Industrial Inquiry* (Ernest Benn, London).

Macmillan, H (1938), *The Middle Way* (Macmillan, London).

Raven-Thomson, A (1935, reprinted 2017), *The Coming Corporate State* (Black House Publishing, London).

Samuel, HB (1933), *Shareholders' Money* (Heinemann, London).

Tawney, RH (1921), *The Acquisitive Society* (G Bell & Sons, London).

Webb, S (1934), 'Preface', in Johnston, T (editor), *The Financiers and the Nation* (Methuen, London).

Webb, S and Webb, B (1923), *The Decay of Capitalist Civilisation* (Fabian Society, London).

Wilkinson, E (1939), *The Town that Was Murdered* (Victor Gollancz, London).

Secondary works

Clift, B (1999), 'The Labour Movement and Company Law Reform 1918–1945', *Political Economy Research Centre, University of Sheffield*, Working Paper 1.

Currie, R (1979), *Industrial Politics* (Oxford University Press, Oxford).

Durbin, E (1985), *New Jerusalems: The Labour Party and the Economics of Democratic Socialism* (Routledge and Kegan Paul, London).

Eisner, MA (2000), *Regulatory Politics in Transition* (Second edition, Johns Hopkins University Press, Baltimore).

Johnson, PB (1998), *Land Fit For Heroes: The Planning of British Reconstruction 1916–1919* (University of Chicago Press, Chicago).

Loss, L and Cowett, EM (1958), *Blue Sky Law* (Little Brown & Company, Boston).

Macey, JR and Novogrod, C (2011–2012), 'Enforcing Self-Regulatory Organizations' Penalties and the Nature of Self-Regulation', *Hofstra Law Review*, volume 40, pages 963–1003.

Maltby, J (2007), 'Was the Companies Act 1947 a Response to a National Crisis?', *Accounting History*, volume 5, number 2, pages 31–60.

Marwick, A (1964), 'Middle Opinion in the Thirties: Planning, Progress and Political "Agreement"', *English Historical Review*, volume 79, number 311, pages 285–298.

Michie, RC (1999), *The London Stock Exchange: A History* (Oxford University Press, Oxford).

Middlemass, K (1979), *Politics in Industrial Society: The Experience of the British System Since 1911* (André Deutsch, London).

Middlemass, K and Barnes, J (1969), *Baldwin: A Biography* (Weidenfeld and Nicolson, London).

Newton, S and Porter, D (1979), *Modernization Frustrated: The Politics of Industrial Decline in Britain Since 1900* (Unwin Hyman, London).

Noguchi, M and Edwards, JR (2004), 'Corporatism and Unavoidable Imperatives: Recommendations on Accounting Principles and the ICAEW Memorandum to the Cohen Committee', *Accounting Historians Journal*, volume 31, pages 53–95.

Ritschel, D (1997), *Politics of Planning: The Debate on Planning in Britain in the 1930s* (Clarendon Press, Oxford).

Smith, T (1979), *The Politics of the Corporate Economy* (Martin Robertson & Company, London).

Walker, G (1988), *Thomas Johnston* (Manchester University Press, Manchester).

12 Surviving another war 1939–1945

Introduction

When war came on 3 September 1939, it had long been expected. Remembering the experience of the 1914–1918 war, preparations had been made. The hard-learned lesson that success might depend on which countries could best harness their economies to the overwhelming national objective did not have to be re-learned, and senior officials who had begun their careers in the earlier war found that they could build upon their experience. Members of the public knew what they could expect to happen. In the City, the markets understood what their role would be and that business as usual could not be expected (Kynaston, 2001, pages 460–461; Michie, 1999, pages 287–288). As a result, the onset of war was accompanied by the introduction of capital issue controls which largely avoided the difficulties experienced in 1915.

Inception of capital issue controls

Consequently, the transition to a wartime economy began smoothly. Accomplishing the transition in terms of financial policy had been considered by the Committee on Economic Information[1] immediately before the war. In a report entitled 'Defence Expenditure and the economic and financial problems connected therewith', the committee recommended that:

> the investment expenditure which firms and individuals in this country are permitted to incur should be rationed, to maintain investment available for defence production and for exports.
>
> (Sayers, 1956, page 163)[2]

In the committee's view, financial control was not as important as control of materials. Indeed, Keynes argued that control of new issues would have such slight effect that it would be immaterial to control of materials and not worth introducing at a preparatory stage. This view did not convince the committee, partly because of the administrative simplicity of a control of new issues, and Keynes's view was not supported. The desirability of a new issues control was also urged by others, including the Committee on Control of Savings and Investment, which reported in August 1939, suggesting the peacetime Foreign Transactions Advisory Committee, chaired by Lord Kennet, should extend its work to cover 'domestic and imperial; as well as "foreign"' issues. It was envisaged that as far as foreign issues were concerned, the criteria which the committee had been using to assess applications would continue to be appropriate and that for domestic issues the prime consideration would be rearmament finance.(Sayers, 1956, page 164)

These recommendations were incorporated in the Treasury's War Book which made detailed plans for the transformation of Lord Kennet's committee. On 25 August 1939, Lord Kennet returned to London on being advised by the Treasury that his committee might be required to act rapidly. His committee met on 1 September 1939 to consider the implications. The necessary regulations were issued by the Treasury on 3 September 1939, and announced in a press release on Monday 4 September 1939 which indicated the broad principles on which the various classes of issues would be considered. On the same day, the Treasury sent Lord Kennet a memorandum of guidance that elaborated the information provided in the press release and specified the way the committee should consult with interested parties. *The Times* commented that two principles underlay the new regulations for controlling capital issues. Whilst no issue could be made without the prior consent of the Treasury, permission will be given when the operation does not involve the subscription of new money or where it is shown to be in the natural interest. Moreover, permission would not be withheld for transactions renewing bills of bills or other short-dated maturities. *The Times* concluded that the measures were prudent and that, although they entailed a restriction of individual enterprise, the change was not as radical as that entailed at the outset of the 1914–1918 war.[3]

The Treasury had learned a lesson from the 1914–1918 war: the control of capital issues was implemented by government regulation[4] that thus applied to outside as well as Exchange issues, rather than by a temporary regulation of the Exchange that could only apply to members. Other lessons had been learned. Rather than establish a new committee to apply the new controls, it was decided to adapt an existing committee: the Foreign Transactions Advisory Committee. That committee had been established in April 1936 under the chairmanship of Lord Kennet to advise the Chancellor of the Exchequer on application of the restrictions on borrowing for the purpose of foreign lending or the purchase of foreign securities.[5] Although the committee's work had not been completely uncontroversial, under the chairmanship of Lord Kennet, a stockbroker, it had a reputation for beneficence and a manner of working that was well understood.[6] Moreover, the committee included people with experience of the Exchange[7] and was to work with a certain elasticity[8] that ensured that there were few complaints about its operations: indeed, the earliest public complaint to be reported came in March 1945 from the Chairman of the Premier Investment Company Limited who complained of a slow response to application to raise new capital.[9] Most comments were positive; for example, the comment by Philip Hill of Philip Hill & Partners, whose new issue business had been decimated by the regulations, that no sane mane could find fault with the regulations.[10]

Relationship with the Stock Exchange

This benign state of affairs owed much to the constructive relationship between the committee and the Stock Exchange. From the beginning, there were clear divisions of responsibility between Lord Kennet's committee and the Exchange. Whilst Lord Kennet's committee dealt with the approval of new issues within the terms of the government's regulations, the Exchange dealt with questions relating to trading within the Exchange and the grant of permission to deal in a newly issued security. To this end, in parallel with the issue of the Defence (Finance) Regulations in September 1939, the Exchange issued its own Temporary Regulations which provided that if the Treasury's committee objected to an issue it would not be listed or traded and, as in 1915, required that all trading was to be for cash and for immediate delivery (i.e. fortnightly settlement was suspended). Continuations and options were banned. Minimum prices were set for all government debt and associated securities (Stock Exchange, 1945, pages 74–77). By these means, it was hoped to avoid speculation particularly in relation to news of military successes or failures.

There was thus an active co-operation between the Exchange and the Treasury in which the Exchange readily accepted its junior role. As the Exchange's committee was to suggest in its Annual Report for the year ended 24 March 1942:

> The Stock Exchange has settled down to a wartime routine which not only affords all essential facilities to the investing public but at the same time provides means for carrying out the policy of the Government in various important directions such as the control of new capital issues.[11]

There were, of course, occasional difficulties in the relationship as practical problems in applying the government's controls arose and were resolved. Although the legal framework established in September 1939 was to remain largely unchanged throughout the war, there was continual agitation for changes to be made, even though the committee was 'comparatively inactive' (Sayers, 1956, page 167). Although most cases went smoothly, there was a minority of cases in which irritation and misunderstanding were serious. Sayers attributes this 'paradoxical contrast' between the stability of the framework and the agitation for change to confusion over the purposes for which the control had been introduced. He suggests that public opinion accepted that its principal purpose had been to check the use of real resources for inessential purposes, although a control of new issues was of little use for this. In practice, the Treasury and the Bank of England turned it to quite different service as an instrument to 'groom the market' in gilt-edged securities. He therefore suggests that the control became devoted to questions not of whether an issue should be permitted but of what should be the terms of the issue. If so, it would help to explain why market reaction to the operation of the control during the 1939–1945 war was so much less negative than reaction during the 1914–1918 war (Sayers, 1956, page 167).

Agitation was incited in May 1940 when the Chancellor of the Exchequer introduced a Limitation of Dividends Bill which aimed to set a maximum level for dividend declarations but, inter alia, provided that no securities should be issued by way of capitalisation of profits or reserves.[12] It was proposed that the maximum amount should be determined by reference to dividends declared by a company between 1936 and 1939 irrespective of subsequent changes such as the issue of additional capital. Thus, even if the issue of additional capital had been sanctioned by Lord Kennet's committee, it would not have been permissible to increase proportionately the total amount paid by way of dividend. After consultation, and protests, the bill was withdrawn.[13]

Similarly, a practical solution was found by agreement in 1942 when experience showed that companies had been taking advantage of an exemption from the ban on new issues that had been granted to facilitate mergers and amalgamations. A holding company would be formed to acquire the capital of another, usually in the same trade, by the allotment of shares that would then be sold to stockbrokers for introduction to the market. This was thought to be contrary to the spirit of the regulations and was dealt with by an agreement that permission to deal on the London Stock Exchange (or the provincial exchanges) would not be granted except with the consent of the Treasury. As *The Times* observed the changes involved little change from existing practice.[14]

The position of members

The fact that the Exchange could work harmoniously with the Capital Issues Committee did not mean that wartime conditions were proving benign for members. In the years immediately before the onset of war, members' incomes had proved disappointing. No member can have expected that incomes would be improved by wartime conditions, but the experience may have been worse than expected. After all, the Exchange's position had deteriorated since 1919. There had been a gradual development of the volume of business handled by provincial exchanges partly because of the London Stock Exchange's policy on rates of commissions and its attitude towards the provincial exchanges. Although an attempt had been made in 1939 to reach an accommodation with the provincial exchanges in the hope that the activities of country jobbers might be restrained, the attempt had been undermined by the London Stock Exchange's refusal to grant provincial brokers direct access to the London market. Even the limited compromises that were reached faded away following the onset of war.[15] At the same time, overseas brokers remained active competitors through their offices in London. In September 1939, there had been 15 offices, all of which became members of the newly formed Association of New York Stock Exchange Member Firms having representation in the United Kingdom.[16]

Above all, although there had been a considerable increase in public interest in investment and shareholding, the London Stock Exchange had done little either to attract this new business or to encourage the lower-cost investment media that were being developed to meet the demand.

There was yet one other factor. The government's need to borrow to finance the war might have led to an increase in business for members. Yet among the lessons that the Treasury and the Bank of England had learned from the 1914–1918 war was that there were ways of raising loans that did not involve the Exchange or the cost of that involvement. In other words, the government tended to design its securities so that they appealed directly to institutions and to members of the public.

Large sums were raised in the form of securities not quoted on the Stock Exchange; Treasury Bills, Treasury Deposit Receipts, Tax Reserve Certificates, Savings Certificates, Defence Bonds and annuities issued to the savings bank. At the end of the financial year 1945–6, the total internal national debt was £23,373 million, but only £12,268 million was in Stock Exchange securities. Individuals seem to have done their saving largely through the institutions and the National Savings Movement, and their holdings of Stock Exchange securities increased by much less than they had done in the First World War. (Morgan and Thomas, 1961, page 196)

These factors cohered to undermine the volume of business transacted on the Exchange and thus the incomes of members. The initial decline in the volume of business is reflected in Paukert's statistics, based on Stamp Duty data which suggested that transactions amounted to £348 million in 1939–1940, fell to £233 million in 1940–1941 and then rose gradually to £553 million in 1944–1945 (Paukert, 1961, page 304).

As a comparison, Paukert's data suggest that the highest annual volume reached during the 1930s was £1,034,000,000 in the year 1936–1937, a level that was not reached again until the year 1946–1947. Although matching data for members' incomes do not exist for these years, they must have been proportionately lower than in the pre-war years as without fees from new issues and without income from 'own account' speculation, which was discouraged by the requirement of cash trading, income was bound to be almost wholly commission-based.

Consistent with this conclusion, the numbers of members fell between 1939 and 1945. In 1938–1939, the total number of partners and clerks in broking firms had been 4,212 and in jobbing firms 2,419. By 1945–1946, these totals had fallen to 3,618 and 1,914 (Stock Exchange Annual Reports, Stock Exchange Archive, Guildhall Library).

These data demonstrate that there was an absolute decline in the numbers of firms between 1938 and 1946 and that this decline affected jobbers more than brokers. Moreover, among jobbing firms, the decline in profit-sharing participants was greater than the decline in participants remunerated largely by salary. This is consistent with pressure on the profitability of jobbing firms reflecting the increased cost of maintaining trading liquidity against a background of declining trading volume. As further confirmation of the pressure on incomes, the cost of a nomination remained low throughout the war (Michie, 1999, page 302).

There were other signs that members were under pressure. The increased cost of maintaining trading liquidity led jobbers to try to increase the margin between quoted buying and selling prices.[17]

For brokers, as there was no possibility of increasing trading volumes, the obvious response was to re-examine commission rates and rebates although this option was not without risk. Both increases in commission rates and reductions in rebates payable to introducers threatened to increase the incentive for counterparties to bypass the Exchange. The campaign on these issues began soon after the beginning of the war, for in February 1940 JB Braithwaite of Foster & Braithwaite was suggesting that there was both an opportunity and need to reduce rebate costs:

> war conditions present us with a unique opportunity . . . We cannot raise our charges to the public to meet these conditions, as is being done on every hand by other businesses and industries, but we can, and I think that in the interests of members we must, achieve a similar end by the internal economy of reducing our rebates to agents.[18]

Discussions led to a proposal in May 1940 that the rebate payable to all agents should be reduced from 50% to 33%, a proposal that encountered opposition from banks. It was eventually agreed that, with effect from June 1941, the rebate payable to banks would be reduced to 33% and that, at the banks' insistence, the rebate payable to all other agents would be reduced to 25%.[19]

There always was a possibility that reductions in rebates would encourage introducers to direct their business away from the Exchange, either managing transactions through their own private networks in the case of issuing houses and institutional investors or directing business to provincial or overseas brokers. To mitigate this possibility, the Exchange was prepared to recognise all members of certain overseas exchanges as eligible to be agents who would qualify for the higher level of rebates of commission.[20] Members of the New York Stock Exchange were not included in this arrangement as the London offices of New York brokerage houses presented direct competition for London brokers.

Sources of competition

Provincial brokers were regarded as a greater and more dangerous form of competition, however. Indeed, in May 1940, when commissions and rebates were being re-examined, there was support for a suggestion that provincial brokers should not be eligible for any rebate at all.[21] The result was that the Exchange looked again at its relationship with provincial exchanges and at the threat posed by provincial jobbers which had dominated attention at a conference with provincial exchanges in June 1939, before the war. The outcome of the Exchange's re-consideration was to attempt to deny access to non-members who were involved in jobbing and thus involved in closing deals that otherwise might have been directed through London. To this end, as was to be done for members of overseas exchanges, the London Stock Exchange offered the higher rate of rebate to provincial stock exchanges, thus treating them in the same way as banks. The offer was, however, conditional on provincial exchanges outlawing double capacity.[22] Although this change was implemented, it proved unsuccessful because provincial brokers who had combined broking business with jobbing easily evaded its effect by dividing their businesses between broking and jobbing activities. The divided firms that were the result thus formally complied with the London Exchange's requirement for eligibility for rebates although they continued to operate in practice as joint businesses. Time was to show that the provincial exchanges remained disinclined to assist in eliminating this practice unless the Exchange permitted direct access for provincial brokers to the London market, a negotiating position that had long been held by the provincial exchanges. This the London Exchange would not grant, as it threatened the income earned by London brokers by handling business on behalf of provincial brokers.

Frustration over the difficulty of finding a way of mitigating the competition from provincial brokers was joined by frustration over the tendency for issuing houses and institutional investors to close deals in larger blocks of shares outside the Exchange. Although the regulations introduced in September 1939 regulated new issues, they did not apply to private placements of shares. It was thus possible for blocks of existing shares to be placed with purchasers acting privately outside any organised exchange. Such sales were not illegal since the regulations on new issues did not apply to existing shares. If the transaction was to be unaccompanied by any request for permission to deal in the shares on the Stock Exchange, such a placing would escape all independent scrutiny on grounds of investment merit or public interest. This single route to realisation of an equity interest appears to have been used by business owners for whom the attractions of continuing to own a business were undermined by the introduction in 1939 of an Excess Profits Tax levied at a rate of 100% on excess profits calculated by reference to pre-war profits and subject only to a credit of 20% payable after the end of the war (Sayers, 1956, pages 88–89).

Of course, this was a problem that had arisen during the 1914–1918 war, although in that war, the problem was even more extensive, as in regulating the new issue, market reliance was placed upon the Stock Exchange's own regulations, which did not apply to non-members. By September 1942, the problem was causing such concern to members that the Exchange was obliged to complain to the Treasury:

> For the placing of issues of the highest class, the Stock Exchange has developed a system which works satisfactorily as an alternative to an offer through the press. The brokers who handle such issues have learnt by experience the type of investor with whom the stock can best be placed; the amount of stock which it is wise to offer to each, and the extent to which the market can best be used for the transaction of the business . . .
>
> If brokers are to be debarred from the exercise of their knowledge and experience in the placing of securities for the companies for whom they act the gradual development of an outside and uncontrolled market both for the original placing and subsequent transactions in securities is a danger which cannot be ignored . . .

The issue is confined to a very small circle of large institutional investors, and the price received by the Company may be, through lack of competition, thereby depressed. The public can only participate later at an advanced price.[23]

This complaint did not bring forth a response from the Treasury, perhaps understandably, since extending the existing regulations to cover private transactions of the sort that had led to the complaint would have involved a serious interference with private dealing. Thus, the Exchange returned to its complaint in December 1943:

The capital market is controlled by the Treasury through its Advisory Committee and by agreement gives to the Treasury complete control over all Stock Exchange markets, but it leaves wholly uncontrolled the very large and powerful, but mainly non-professional markets that are outside the Stock Exchange jurisdiction. The principal constituents of those markets are the Banks, the Insurance Companies, the Investment Trust Companies, the Acceptance Houses, the Finance and Issuing Houses, the Association of Stock and Share Dealers, the Mincing Lane Tea and Rubber Brokers' Association, and the large number of 'Somerset House' and other outside stock and sharebrokers up and down the country . . .

The effect of leaving this large outside market uncontrolled is naturally to drive into it that very business that the Treasury thinks it is against the national interest to permit.[24]

The combination of pressure on members' incomes and the inability of the Exchange to secure any significant improvement in their circumstances either by reaching agreement with provincial exchanges or by lobbying the Treasury led the Exchange to take a number of new directions.

New directions

In June 1942, a committee was created jointly with the provincial exchanges to discuss matters of common interest on a regular basis for although the interests of the various exchanges were not completely aligned, there were points on which they were in agreement.[25]

Also in spring 1942, informal discussions began between members and the proprietors of the London Stock Exchange with a view to unification of control: discussions that were to lead in July 1942 to the formation of a joint committee to develop proposals and in May 1943 to an agreement to the formation of the Council of the London Stock Exchange to replace both the Committee for General Purposes and the Committee of Trustees and Managers.[26] In part, this constitutional innovation resulted from the parlous financial condition of the Exchange which, as between 1914 and 1918, had resulted from the reduction in activity and active membership brought about by the war.

But at this time, thoughts were beginning to turn to post-war conditions and their implications for the Exchange. In July 1943, Nuffield College, Oxford, published a report entitled 'Employment Policy and Organization of Industry after the War', which was based on private conferences during the previous 12 months that had involved representatives of many interests. The report envisaged that after the war there would be a continuing need for some form of control of investment, both domestic and overseas because the likelihood of a high post-war demand for capital goods would make it necessary to see that priority was given to forms of investment most serviceable to the community.[27]

These objectives implied that there would be support for continuation of capital issue controls after the end of the war. In other words, the Stock Exchange must have been contemplating a future in which members would be permanently disadvantaged by a permanent system of new issue controls that allowed certain types of unregulated trading to continue outside the Exchange. Added to this prospect would have been the realisation that however harmoniously the exchange had been able to work with the Capital Issues Committee, it had not been able to capitalise upon this relationship when lobbying the Treasury to seek relief for members from outside trading. The Exchange needed to become more effective in lobbying on behalf of members' interests and to find a way in which outside trading could be regulated.

The formation of a joint committee with provincial exchanges was one element of a response, for chances of success in lobbying were bound to be maximised by campaigning together. Moreover, the innovation in London of a council replacing the two former committees was intended to create a single unified voice that could speak authoritatively for the London Stock Exchange.

It was against the background of these developments that in December 1943 the Exchange had renewed its request that the government should discourage the outside trading in blocks of shares. To this request was added a request that the PF(I) Act 1939 should be brought into force:

> If the Prevention of Fraud Act had been brought into force, the Treasury would have had ready to its hand an easy means of exercising its control over the outside market, because all dealers in stocks and shares outside the recognised Stock Exchanges would have had to become either licensed or exempted dealers and so would have been known and controllable.[28]

Although the proposed legislation had caused the Exchange some difficulty in 1937, these difficulties had subsequently been resolved and the Board of Trade's draft regulations had found general approval in the City[29]

Moreover, in 1939, it had seemed that implementation of the Act would have the desired effect on outside activity[30]

Although the onset of war had prevented full implementation in the autumn of 1939, in formal terms, it had only been postponed by six months, a postponement that had subsequently been repeated at six-monthly intervals. The Stock Exchange's request in December 1943, doubtless supported by the provincial stock exchanges, found a receptive audience in the Board of Trade, a rumour that implementation was about to be ordered appearing in the newspapers as early as 1 January 1944.[31] A month later, on 1 February 1944, it was formally announced that applications for licences should be submitted by 15 April 1944 in preparation for implementation in mid-July 1944.[32]

The 'grey' market

Although the Board of Trade had responded positively to the Exchange's request for the 1939 Act to be brought into force, it did not agree that the Act could or should be used as a form of protection against the circumvention of its controls and thus against the grey market; although it was accepted that there was a problem that required some action. Instead, the Bank of England was invited to open negotiations with issuing houses and institutional investors which led to a 'gentleman's agreement' in June 1944. It was agreed that shares involved in a placing would only be sold to institutions on an approved list. In turn, those institutions undertook that they would not re-sell the securities at a discount within six months and that they would not buy new unquoted securities unless the proposed placing had first been approved by the Treasury, approval that would be given on the basis of voluntary disclosure as the regulations were not amended to require prior disclosure of proposed placings. This approach was adopted because of nervousness over the extent of interference that would be involved to regulate private transactions of this sort (i.e. transactions that did not take place through a recognised exchange). This agreement appears to have reduced the incentive to bypass the recognised exchanges but did not eliminate it since houses that were not parties to the agreement were not to be bound by it. In the end, the agreement collapsed.[33]

In December 1944, matters came to a head when the Stock Exchange refused an application for permission to deal in the two million new 4¼% 'C' preference shares of General Electric Company Limited which had been issued to repay a loan from an insurance company. In accordance with the informal agreement with the Bank of England, although it was not intended that the shares would be offered to the public or to the existing shareholders, the Capital Issues Committee's approval was sought, and obtained, before the shares were placed with a syndicate of finance houses. Subsequently, the shares were placed with institutions on the approved list, including an allotment of £150,000 to three firms of jobbers. A delay had occurred between approval of the transaction and its completion, during which time prices rose on news that the German offensive in the Ardennes had been defeated with the result that the allottees of the shares benefitted from a substantial unforeseen profit. This caused some resentment as the financial institutions involved in this transaction appeared to have benefitted from a private arrangement: especially since an opportunity to subscribe for the shares would normally have been a right of the existing shareholders. Whatever the merits of the the Stock Exchange's decision may have been, it exposed the unattractiveness of reliance upon an informal agreement, leading *The Times* to adopt a parsonical tone that whilst there was general agreement that further regulation should be avoided, the efficacy of a gentleman's agreement depends on the willingness of all people to be gentlemen' (*The Times*, 21 December 1944. Cited in Morgan and Thomas, 1961, page 230).[34]

In response to these events, in February 1945, the Bank of England proposed with Treasury support that those to whom securities were allotted in similar circumstances should not be permitted to dispose of them for six months: a proposal that the Exchange opposed on the grounds that it would discourage anyone from investing in new securities. Whilst this suggestion was withdrawn, the penalty for the Exchange was an agreement by which issues would continue to be cleared with the Bank which would also be entitled to declare that the new issue market was closed. By this point, the timing and amount of new issues could be determined by the government acting through the Capital Issues Committee and the Bank of England whilst the Exchange was left considering applications for permission to deal and thus determine whether the securities were acceptable.

Reflections

By the end of the 1939–1945 war, there was no questioning that statutory regulation would continue in the form of the PF(I) Act 1939 under the umbrella of the Board of Trade. In parallel, the Capital Issues Committee would continue and was soon afterwards to be given formal statutory authority, working under the guidance of the Treasury.[35]

In response, the Exchange had continued to move away from its traditional positions and attitudes. Formally it had not itself become a monopoly, and the continued bypassing of the London market had eaten into its position of pre-eminence. However, by making common cause with the provincial stock exchanges through a grouping that could negotiate with government, the Exchange had established its leadership of a grouping that represented a substantial proportion of the market. This did not remove all tensions between the London Stock Exchange and the provincial exchanges, since arguments about direct access to London and bypassing were to continue, but it was a further step away from the distant relationship of the past.

Moreover, the Exchange was taking steps to distance itself from the control that its members had exerted over its policies. Previously, that control had been exercised through the requirement for annual election of all members of the Committee for General Purposes. On 12 May 1943, control was unified by the creation of the Council of the London Stock Exchange which replaced both the Committee for General Purposes and the Committee of Trustees and Managers, a move justified at the time not in terms of administrative convenience but by the need to present a unified position in discussions with government:

> Conditions after the war will be subject to rapid political and financial changes, and the problems which will arise will be far-reaching, and your Board feel that a single body composed of the Board of the Trustees and Managers and Members of the Committee for General Purposes will, in the

interest of the Stock Exchange, be better able to overcome the many difficulties which will be present.[36]

At the time, it was acknowledged that unification of control involved risks:

> Under the dual structure there was a distinction between the activities of the members and the activities of the Stock Exchange as an institution. If the members became solely responsible for running the Stock Exchange they could be asked, collectively, to accept responsibility for the actions of the membership.[37]

Acceptance of this risk was significant in the development of the Exchange's role and carried with it an implication that the Exchange must become a little more distant from its members, as it could not convincingly discharge a responsibility for members if it were so closely controlled by members as it had been in the past.

The formal reflection of this unification in the constitution of the Exchange had to wait for some time, not least until a solution could be found to the transfer of ownership of the Stock Exchange as a business. When it was agreed that this would be achieved by substituting annuities for the proprietors' shares, a new constitution could be approved, and the Committee for General Purposes and the Committee of Trustees and Managers were finally wound up on 8 March 1948.[38] The new constitution did not repeat the previous arrangements for elections of members of the Committee for General Purposes. Instead, members of the Council were to serve for three-year terms, a third of its membership being elected each year. The practical effect was that members were no longer afforded the opportunity to remove in its entirety a committee whose decisions had aroused their displeasure.

This was important when, after the war, the Exchange was trying to persuade the government that trading conditions should be normalised quickly through, for example, the reversion to fortnightly settlement and the re-introduction of contangoes and options. It was helpful to demonstrate that the Exchange was doing its best to ensure that members were trading responsibly.

The change in election mechanism reflected a change in attitude. Whereas in the 1930s the Stock Exchange had been prepared to defend the interests of outside parties but with the intention of avoiding further damage to members' interests, by 1945, the Exchange's Council had accepted that it was a part of its purpose to defend the interests of the public.in 1948, FW Hirst observed thatmaxim of *caveat emptor* had gradually been watered down since 1929. Although the buyer was still expected to beware, the Committee had continually tightened up the rules to protect the public from errors of judgement and the depredations of financial sharks (Hirst, 1948, page 212).

In 1905, competition between brokers had been nearly as absolute as it could be. Between 1905 and 1909, however, as a result of continuous pressure, the committee had been persuaded to introduce the scales of minimum commissions, which remained in force in 1945. To a large extent, the committee's reforms had substituted competition in service for competition in price. All these changes had fostered an altered attitude among brokers: an attitude whichpreferred reasonable, but secure, profits to the alternatives of brilliant success or equally striking failure. *The Economist* summed up these changes by saying that:

> the business of stock broking is becoming a service industry, and the members are behaving in a way which tends to limit the possibilities of speculation both for themselves and for the public.[39]

This change in attitude lies behind the case of St Helena Gold Mines quoted in Chapter 1 and took place against the wishes of a notable group of members whose views were to be articulated by a leading broker, Graham Greenwell, who complained that there would be no free market unless the Exchange returned to its laissez-faire roots. He believed that the Exchange should be a free market, with the Council holding the ring; it should be the function of the Council to guard its members from the public, not the reverse.The Council should support free trade in securities and permit every device for that trade, whether contangoes, options or dealings for the Account. It would be a mistake for the Council to see itself as a 'court of morals' for it would stultify the market if the Council tried to become one.[40]

Greenwell was inveighing against the Faustian pact that had been struck between the Exchange and the government. The Exchange had wanted to preserve its control of the conduct of business rules so that it could continue to use those rules to defend the position of the more traditional personal broking members. Whilst this had been achieved, the condition imposed by the Exchange's Faustian pact with the government was that it should more closely satisfy corporatist expectations of professional associations. It had become more public-regarding and had accepted responsibility for policing the behaviour of members towards outsiders and not simply the behaviour of members towards each other. Government had acceded to the appearance of independence, but at the expense for the Exchange of privately consulting on government's views and abiding by them.

Notes

1 Originally set up in 1931 as a standing committee of the Economic Advisory Council, this committee was charged with making regular reports on the economic situation. It was chaired by Lord Stamp, and in 1939 the other members were GDH Cole, HD Henderson, JM Keynes, Sir Alfred Lewis, Professor DH Robertson, Sir Arthur Salter, Sir Frederick Leith-Ross and Sir Frederick Phillips.
2 Sayers, 1956, page 163.
3 *The Times*, 4 September 1939, page 14.
4 Defence (Finance) Regulation Number 6 under the Emergency Powers (Defence) Act 1939.
5 House of Commons Hansard, 7 April 1936. Sayers (1976, Volume II, page 582). For the terms of reference and initial membership of the committee see Sayers (1976, Volume III, Appendix 30, page 299). Apart from Lord Kennet, the members included the Deputy Governor of the Bank of England and the Chairman of the Stock Exchange (Peden, 2000, page 314).

6 *The Times*, 15 September 1939, page 13. Remarkably, Lord Kennet was to remain as Chairman of this committee until March 1959: almost to the end of the committee's life (*The Times*, 23 March 1959, page 10).

7 The wartime membership included the Deputy Chairman of the London Stock Exchange (Sayers, 1956, page 164).

8 'The war-time Treasury control of capital issues has always, and rightly, been characterised by a certain degree of elasticity . . . .' (*Financial Times*, 24 November 1942, page 2).

9 *Financial Times*, 9 March 1945, page 1.

10 *The Times*, 7 June 1940, page 11.

11 *Financial Times*, 2 October 1942, page 3.

12 Bill 1940/46, 9 May 1940, BPP; *Financial Times*, 17 May 1940, page 2.

13 'Exit Dividend Limitation', *Financial Times*, 5 June 1940, page 2. The bill was dropped in part because Excess Profits Tax was raised to 100%, but also because it was believed that the bill's objects could be achieved through the existing controls on capital issues.

14 *The Times*, 23 May, page 7; *Financial Times*, 22 May 1942, pages 1 and 2.

15 Conference between the London Stock Exchange and the Associated Stock Exchanges, June 1939 (Stock Exchange Archive, Guildhall Library; Michie, 1999, page 239).

16 *Financial Times*, 16 September 1939, page 3.

17 Stock Exchange Committee minutes, 16 October 1939 (Stock Exchange Archive, Guildhall Library).

18 Stock Exchange Country Jobbing Sub-Committee, 27 February 1940 (Stock Exchange Archive, Guildhall Library).

19 Stock Exchange Committee minutes, 28 January 1941 (Stock Exchange Archive, Guildhall Library).

20 Stock Exchange Committee minutes, 5 August 1941; 8 September 1941 (Stock Exchange Archive, Guildhall Library).

21 Stock Exchange Committee minutes, 6 May 1940 (Stock Exchange Archive; Guildhall Library).

22 Stock Exchange Country Jobbing Sub-Committee, March 1940 (Stock Exchange Archive, Guildhall Library).

23 Stock Exchange Committee minutes, 21 September 1942 (Stock Exchange Archive, Guildhall Library).

24 Stock Exchange Committee minutes, 6 December 1943 (Stock Exchange Archive, Guildhall Library).

25 The committee consisted of four delegates from the London Stock Exchange, four from the Council of Associated Stock Exchanges and two from the Provincial Brokers Stock Exchange (*Financial Times*, 2 October 1942, page 3).

26 Morgan and Thomas (1961, page 232). The council was to consist of nine Trustees and Managers *ex officio* as foundation members and 30 ordinary members elected by ballot. The constitution therefore recognised the supremacy of the membership in all matters. In 1920 negotiations about mutualisation had foundered on the issue of acquisition of the proprietors' shares. In 1943, this issue was deferred and finally resolved in 1948 when redeemable annuities were substituted for the shares.

27 Nuffield College (1943); *The Times*, 1 July 1943, page 5. The survey had begun work in 1941 (Nuffield College Library, MSS NCSRS).

28 Stock Exchange Committee minutes, 6 December 1943 (Stock Exchange Archive, Guildhall Library).

29 *Financial Times*, 2 June 1939, page 5.

30 *Financial Times*, 10 August 1939, page 4.

31 *Financial Times*, 1 January 1944, page 1.

32 *Financial Times*, 2 February 1944, page 3; 6 March 1944, page 2.

33 *The Times*, 5 June 1944, page 4; 6 June 1944, page 7; 23 June 1944, page 9; 21 December 1944, page 9; Morgan and Thomas (1961, page 230); Michie (1999).
34 *The Times*, 21 December 1944, pages 4 and 9; Morgan and Thomas (1961), page 230.
35 Borrowing (Controls and Guarantees) Act 1946. A draft memorandum of guidance to the committee was then published by the Treasury as a White Paper (Cmd 6726; Peden, 2000, page 376).
36 Trustees and Managers report, 20 April 1944 (Stock Exchange Archive, Guildhall Library; Michie, 1999, page 297).
37 Stock Exchange Trustees and Managers minutes, 28 May, 1940; 24 April 1945 (Stock Exchange Archive, Guildhall Library).
38 Stock Exchange Council minutes, 8 March 1948 (Stock Exchange Archive, Guildhall Library).
39 'Responsible Stockbroking' (*The Economist*, 23 June 1945, pages 858–859).
40 *Banker*, April 1949, pages 29–33 (cited in Kynaston, 2001, pages 30–31).

References

Primary works: unpublished documents

Nuffield College Library.
Stock Exchange Archive, Guildhall Library.

Primary works: newspapers and periodicals

Banker.
The Economist.
Financial Times.
The Times.

Primary works: contemporary books and articles

Nuffield College (1943), *Employment Policy and Organization of Industry After the War: A Statement* (Oxford University Press, London).
Stock Exchange (1945), *The Stock Exchange Since 1939: An Outline of the Main Alterations to the Rules and Practices of the Stock Exchange Since the Outbreak of War* (E Couchman & Company, London).

Secondary works

Hirst, FW (1948), *The Stock Exchange: A Short Study of Investment and Speculation* (Fourth edition, Oxford University Press, Oxford).
Kynaston, D (2001), *The City of London: A Club No More 1945–2000*, volume 4 (Chatto & Windus, London).
Michie, RC (1999), *The London Stock Exchange: A History* (Oxford University Press, Oxford).
Morgan, EV and Thomas, WA (1961), *The Stock Exchange: Its History and Functions* (Elek Books, London).

Paukert, F (1961), 'The Value of Stock Exchange Transactions in Non-Governmental Securities, 1911–1959', *Economica*, volume 28, number 111, pages 303–309.

Peden, GC (2000), *The Treasury and British Public Policy, 1906–1959* (Oxford University Press, Oxford).

Sayers, RS (1956), *Financial Policy 1939–1945* (HMSO and Longmans Green & Company, London).

Sayers, RS (1976), *The Bank of England 1891–1944* (Cambridge University Press, Cambridge).

13   Reflections

At the close of business on 14 May 1945, a week after VE Day, members gathered around the South African War Memorial on the trading floor for a service of thanksgiving to mark the end of the war. In the presence of the Lord Mayor and a Sheriff,[1] the Doxology was sung in hearty voice:[2]

> *Praise God from whom all blessings flow.*

The thanksgiving in May 1945 followed the examples of earlier years: a similar gathering had given thanks for an end to war in November 1918.[3] Appearances had not changed. Similar people, with similar functions sang the same words to the same tunes as if to convince themselves that they and their institution, the Exchange, had emerged unchanged from the tribulations they and their countrymen had endured.

Appearances belied the truth. The Exchange of 1945 was no longer the Exchange of 1914. The intervening years had seen a series of commercial, social and political challenges. New actors had become involved in investment and old actors had declined. As each group's economic and political influence changed, so members had been forced to re-consider how best to foster their own interests: which aspects of the pre-1914 Exchange should be defended and which should be ceded.

Two relationships were central to the Exchange's navigation of this process of institutional adjustment: its relationship with government and its relationship with the Bank of England. In 1914, both the Exchange and the government had preferred to maintain a distance from each other. By 1945, they had formed a marriage of convenience as the best means of securing each other's objectives. Guided by Montagu Norman, who for most of the period was Governor of the Bank of England, the Exchange had endured a series of experiments in the search for a lasting accommodation. During the 1914–1918 war, the Exchange had endured the imposition of controls which members believed did not respect their understanding of the special circumstances of the market. Chastened by that experience, in the decade following the war, the Exchange was left to its own devices. When those years ended in crisis, the Exchange reformed its own practices for fear of government intervention. When forcibly reminded that its freedoms still depended upon government's forbearance, the Exchange opted for willing co-operation with government only to object strenuously when the government appeared to insist nonetheless on the right to oversee the Exchange's use of its freedoms. On this occasion, the Treasury, with the encouragement of the Bank of England, persuaded the Board of Trade to back down and accept recognition of the Exchange's special status in the PF(I) Act. By 1943, the Exchange had accepted that government control would persist after the 1939–1945 war and that willing compromise was preferable. In response, the PF(I) Act was implemented, recognising the independence of the Exchange but accompanied by an understanding that the Exchange would co-operate by supporting government's objectives.

As a result of this process, the Exchange had preserved its independence including vitally its control over access to membership and over the conduct of business rules. In parallel, the government had achieved the substance of its main objectives: mitigation of the social distress caused by abusive speculation and support for its economic policies.

In 1914, the Exchange had been a private community where doing business, deciding policy and maintaining social contacts were all intermingled. People joined the community by being granted membership in a process that valued and respected personal qualities more highly than formal qualifications. It was a community in which the spoken word mattered more than a formal agreement. Trading took place under rules prescribed by the committee, rather than by public law. Behaviour was monitored by the committee in a process that was seen more as an exchange between partners than as an exercise of authority. Information tendered to the committee by members was taken on trust in processes that were informal, anti-bureaucratic and untroubled by the intervention of lawyers.

In these respects, the Exchange's position was neither accidental nor unique. At various moments, the Exchange had been obliged to defend its autonomy and had done so vigorously: perhaps most notably when a Royal Commission was appointed in 1877. The complaints which led to the appointment of a Commission arose from a Select Committee report on foreign loans which suggested that the Exchange did not appreciate the dangers which attached to the markets' manipulation of loans and had not demonstrated an interest in dealing with them (Kynaston, 1994, pages 275–286). It was a matter for self-congratulation by the Exchange that the Commission's report had supported the Exchange's conduct:

> The existing body or rules and regulations have been formed with much care, and are the result of long experience and the vigilant attention of a body of persons intimately acquainted with the needs and exigencies of the community for whom they have legislated. Any attempt to reduce these rules to the limits of the ordinary law of the land, or to abolish all checks and safeguards not found in that law, would in our opinion be detrimental to the honest and efficient conduct of business.
>
> (Royal Commission report, 1878)

With this endorsement, the Exchange was able to brush off the Commission's recommendation that the London Stock Exchange should be granted a Royal

Charter with authority over all share trading whether within or outside its market. Resistance to the proposal was guaranteed by the promise it carried of political oversight of changes to the rules and the constitution. However exiguous that oversight might prove to be,[4] members regarded it as a threat to their autonomy.

The Exchange was not alone in its autonomy. Throughout the nineteenth century, a series of professional institutions had either been re-organised or, in the case of new occupations, created. They were all characterised by a concentration on three principles: a limited resort to law as a form of validation of and support for the powers of a professional organisation, control of entry to membership by way of qualification, and the development of codes as a guide to conduct as a means of encouraging trust among potential consumers and delineating legitimate competition between members. The legal context for some professional associations was provided by an Act of Parliament.[5] In other cases, a royal charter was granted.[6] In the Exchange's case, a legal context was provided by contract law as it applied to the agreements between members and the Exchange. In each case, whatever the legal context, the purpose was to manage relationships between the community of members and to preserve its solidarity. Regulation depended upon co-operative relations.

More narrowly, the London Stock Exchange was not unique among City institutions, for the retail banking, merchant banking and insurance markets were all organised in a similar manner. Wider City interests were increasingly monitored by the Bank of England, which became the City's principal interlocutor with government, providing some insulation for individual institutions from immediate pressures and interpreting for government the intentions and fears of the City.

In the decades before 1914, these arrangements had been challenged by repeated crises and challenges from new actors. Judicious reforms aimed at diverting criticism had ensured that the institutional culture survived.

Increasingly, management of the market came to be a key concern for government. To an extent that was not appreciated at the beginning of the 1914–1919 war, the existence of a functioning stock market was to be critical to government's ability to finance the war, and afterwards to finance its peace-time expenditure. To this interest was added concern over managing foreign exchange requirements through issues of foreign loans and concern over the market's growing role in financing industry.

In parallel, operation of the market became a concern for a growing number of investors who had not previously regarded themselves as potential investors. A growing number of professional and managerial workers were enabled to save for longer-term contingencies by increasing incomes and attracted to the stock market by the promise of rates of return that could not easily be matched by other investment media. In this they were encouraged by the tax system which maintained reliefs which channelled savings into life insurance and pensions policies. The risk appetites of these investors and the insurance companies as their agents were radically different from the risk profiles of typical nineteenth century investors. Investors were placing savings which they needed to protect and grow rather than marginal cash to whose loss they could afford to be indifferent. Institutional investors were seeking longer-term sustainable returns to support their marketing propositions to savers. Neither individual nor institutional investors could tolerate a marketplace that maximised rather than minimised the risks inherent in investing in the undeniably uncertain commercial prospects of a business.

Equally, to meet the demands of investors for investment opportunities, British businesses were coming to see the stock market as a continuing source of finance rather than simply as a means by which ownership could be transferred. They too expected that the market would support sustained relationships and that exchanges between shareholders and directors would not be bedevilled by exploitative speculation.

Finally, public dismay at the economic failure to realise post-war promises coupled with extension of the right to vote rendered damaging any perception that the Exchange had failed to support economic development and, even worse, any perception that the Exchange had contributed to economic failure.

Changing expectations of this sort brought with them changes in members' sources of income. Before 1914, members had been able to augment their commission income earned from transacting clients' bargains by offering to finance clients' speculation and speculating themselves. As the antipathy of investors and vendors to speculative activity grew, this became more difficult and, with the decline in the London market's international position which had occurred during the war, members' income was undermined. The effect on members was not consistent, however, for members with a more corporate style of business, servicing institutional investors and industrial and commercial companies achieved higher profits whereas the smaller firms with a more traditional style of business were especially vulnerable to disappointing incomes.

For the Exchange, this was to be a significant weakness in dealing with external developments. As the smaller firms commanded a majority of the membership, and the constitution ensured that the committee was constrained by members' expectations, the Exchange favoured the interests of the smaller firms at the expense of larger broking firms, jobbers and entrepreneurial members who wished to develop new lines of business. Challenged by disappointing incomes, the Exchange tended to resist all change unless circumstances arose in which members accepted that change had to be embraced to protect the culture of their community.

This occurred on three principal occasions between 1914 and 1945.

At the end of 1914, members knew that they had no choice but to accept government controls of trading and of new issues if their hopes of a resumption of trading were to be realised. For its part, the government was obliged to accept, doubtless with encouragement from the Bank of England, that re-opening the Exchange was necessary to the financing of the war effort. It did not, however, trust the market sufficiently to be candid. Whilst the market was encouraged to believe that the Capital Issues Committee would permit some degree of normal trading to continue, the Chancellor was privately advising the committee's chairman to resist all new issues that were not directly related to the war effort. When this lack of candour became evident, not least in the way in which the committee conducted its business, it was interpreted as a lack of respect for the market. The appearance of high-handedness was re-affirmed by the Treasury's attempt to impose a regulation prolonging the controls after the war by the use of public law. Inevitably, the market had reacted with such dismay that the Treasury had been forced into an ignominious retreat.

The experience confirmed prejudices. Members were confirmed in their prejudice that outsiders could not understand the market and should not be allowed to interfere. However necessary government control had been to the war effort, it had been a mistake to allow that control to be implemented by a committee of outsiders who, however eminent, had acted arrogantly in reaching decisions that appeared capricious and unjustifiable. In contrast, government was confirmed in its belief that the markets tended to unruliness by the tendency for agents to seek and find ways around the controls.

In place of the unwilling war-time partnership the Exchange was largely left to its own devices with the result that it reverted to the pre-war pattern and concentrated on policing relationships between members rather than responding to the concerns of others. In responding to internal considerations, it tried to remain aloof from external problems such as the growth in abusive off-market trading.

The outcome was an existential crisis in 1929 when a series of trading failures and mistakes coincided with the advent of a Labour government which was believed to regard the Exchange, together with other City institutions, as a target for reform. The need for private reform to demonstrate an ability to control excesses within the market and thus prevent government action was evident not only to the Exchange but also to other City institutions that would have expected to be the subject of government action. In retrospect, people might doubt the power of the minority Labour government to carry through a programme of reform. At the time, the risk of government intervention did not seem worthwhile so the Exchange, with the Governor's encouragement, carried through a reform programme. It was provided with the opportunity to do this by the smokescreen of the Hatry prosecution which was used to imply that the problems had been caused not by systemic failings but by an exceptional 'rogue trader'.

The reform programme demonstrates the value which members and the City generally placed on elements of the culture that they were trying to protect. *Caveat emptor* and an unquestioning trust in members' honesty were abrogated to preserve the autonomy of the Exchange, including its freedom to set its own conduct of business rules and to oversee members' conduct beyond the tentacles of public law. Under the guidance and leadership of the Governor, the Exchange was successful in preserving these freedoms. Remarkably, since the problems which occurred in 1929 had grown despite the Exchange's oversight, the Macmillan Committee was to reach a conclusion that, in affirming that insiders knew best, mirrored the Royal Commission's conclusion in 1878:

> An important thing to bear in mind is that financial policy can only be carried into effect by those whose business it is. We have in this country a great financial and banking organization with great experience and traditions. It is through and with that organization that we have to work, for they alone are the

repositories of the skill and knowledge and they alone possess the equipment
necessary for the management of our financial affairs.

(Report of the Macmillan Committee, 1931, page 6)

In short, the Macmillan Committee's conclusion implicitly accepted the Exchange's
success in safeguarding its independence.

Any temptation to feel complacent was soon to be dispelled by three interventions by government.

The first of the three interventions, the prosecution of Lord Kylsant and Harold
Morland, signalled that the public law was to be taken seriously as a constraint on
the Exchange's freedoms. Superficially, the outcome of the trial seemed to confirm the Exchange's privileged position. After all, both defendants were acquitted
of the charges which related to annual accounts published by the Royal Mail Steam
Packet Company on the footing that they had followed normal practice and had
not intended to mislead. Furthermore, although Lord Kylsant was convicted of the
charge arising from a misleading prospectus, he had acted without professional
advice. Subsequently, company law had changed to require the auditor's involvement and it seemed certain that the auditor's advice would have been followed (as
it had been in drawing up annual accounts) so that the conviction would have been
avoided. Yet the superficial impression was wrong. From the explanations given
during the trial, there was little doubt that even an informed reader of Royal Mail's
accounts could not have understood the trend of the group's trading performance.
So, it was not a surprise that the judge, in summing up, made clear his view that
the accounts were misleading and questioned why it should be thought acceptable
for current practice to permit this. A gap had opened between what the Exchange
regarded as proper practice and the standard of disclosure which, under public law,
outsiders had a right to expect. Such a gap was unjustifiable and unsustainable.

Technically, it would have been possible for the Exchange to close this gap by
imposing its own requirements on quoted companies. But, in practice, it had only
rarely done this, preferring to leave accounting and disclosure requirements to be
prescribed by company law for fear that the imposition of additional requirements
would encourage companies to seek quotations elsewhere. It was well known that
additional disclosure requirements would not be welcomed by quoted companies,
many of which continued to use the practices employed by the Royal Mail in spite
of the judge's observations. They were valuable because they enabled companies
to mitigate one of the risks of raising money by way of a quotation, by facilitating
the declaration of consistent dividends and avoiding disputes with shareholders.

It was not until 1939 that the Exchange grasped this nettle by requiring that
companies seeking to be quoted should publish consolidated accounts. Although
most companies continued to resist change, the committee had been convinced
that publication of consolidated accounts was a necessary reform but had been
asking companies seeking a quotation to publish voluntarily. The committee
decided to impose a requirement when companies refused to oblige voluntarily.
Even then, the new requirement only applied to newly quoted companies and in
its annual report, the committee disclaimed any intention of arrogating to itself

the right of Parliament to legislate on such matters. This signalled that the self-regulatory Exchange was nervous about its ability to command the compliance of non-members.

From this point, the Exchange's interaction with government was accompanied by a willingness to co-operate in achieving the government's objectives as was demonstrated in connection with the conversion of War Loan in 1932. To ease the process of conversion, the government requested a pause in new issues. Initially no mechanism was proposed for imposing or policing the pause, which was implemented on a purely voluntary basis and proved successful. The pause in domestic issues proved short-lived although the restraint on foreign issues continued for some time on a voluntary basis. After some time, an advisory committee consisting of people with impeccable market experience was appointed to consider proposed foreign issues: a device that worked to the reasonable satisfaction of all parties. Both the government and the Exchange had learned the advantages of willing co-operation.

The third intervention occurred in 1936 on the appointment of the Bodkin Committee to consider the introduction of a scheme of registration for all share traders, an intervention made with the support of the Exchange. This was yet another threat to the Exchange's autonomy, for it carried the risk that the reputation of outside traders whose status might be enhanced by being licensed. It was feared that this might ill serve members by diminishing the distinctions between them and outside traders. It also carried the risk that the Exchange itself would find its freedoms constrained.

The government sought to make the enquiry palatable by ensuring that the Bodkin Committee comprised members who were sympathetic towards the Exchange's concerns, as they demonstrated by making recommendations that proposed a favoured position for the Exchange, which would not have been subject to governmental oversight but whose members would have been licensed automatically. The spirit of willing co-operation with the Exchange was to be threatened when the Board of Trade questioned the committee's recommendations and proposed that the Exchange should be subject to oversight. In the face of determined opposition by the Exchange, the Treasury with the support of the Bank of England persuaded the Board of Trade to back down and revert to the committee's proposal as a better basis for legislation.

The law which resulted, the PF(I) Act, was to be the basis for the lasting accommodation between the government and the Exchange which was implemented in 1944. Recognising that the PF(I) Act provided a means of limiting off-market competition for members, and that government's interest in the market would continue long after the war, the Exchange decided that requesting that the Act should be implemented before the end of the war would be advantageous. In return for the government's agreement to the privilege of avoiding explicit oversight, there was tacit acceptance that the Exchange would willingly co-operate with the government's policy objectives. In contrast to the distance that characterised the relationship before 1914, there was a recognition that the two parties would have to work together.

As the experiments in regulation succeeded each other, the members were constantly striving to protect their commercial interests. The loss of international pre-eminence, hastened by the 1914–1918 war and not subsequently recovered, coupled with the changing risk appetites of investors and vendors combined to depress members' incomes. Attempts to reduce costs proved unavailing. Moreover, there were few avenues for the development of new lines of business, not least because some possible avenues would have involved competing with other City institutions for their members' business. Perhaps it was inevitable that members increasingly looked to the rule book for protection of their livelihood. This tendency towards defensiveness was not unopposed for there were members whose livelihood depended upon a less traditional style of business and resented the restrictions represented, for example, by minimum rates of commission and the ban on direct access. But a majority of members, largely in small firms, depended upon a traditional personal style of business and were able to insist upon maintaining the rules which had protected that business: rules barring practising through companies, restricting sources of capital, limiting the number of clerks, banning advertising, imposing minimum rates of commission and banning direct access to jobbers. As time went by, members' dependence on these rules grew in spite of the increasing evidence that they led to business bypassing the Exchange. As dependence grew, so did the importance of maintaining members' control of the rules and the freedom from oversight. Members will have shuddered when the Labour Party's only point of objection to the PF(I) bill was that it gave formal recognition to a private club which could use its power quixotically to exclude women from membership. Irrespective of the position of women, control of access to the membership was crucial to control of pressure on members' incomes. No wonder that in 1944 members did not want to risk leaving the PF(I) Act to be re-considered by a new government after the end of the 1939–1945 war.

That the Exchange survived these years was not inevitable. There were moments when politicians might have taken advantage of the Exchange's embarrassment to abolish or limit its freedom. But the Exchange which survived was a somewhat shrunken, less self-assured and more defensive institution which knew that its privileged position was conditional upon external tolerance. Celebration and thanksgiving were justified in May 1945. The tribulations had been great and survival had been hard-won. But in the hearts of the most thoughtful, thanksgiving would have been accompanied by a nervousness about what lay ahead.

Notes

1 The Sheriff in question was also a member: the senior partner of Charles Stanley & Company, one of the firms involved in weak underwriting in 1929.

2 *Financial Times*, 15 May 1945.

3 On that occasion in the presence of the Lord Mayor and the Governor of the Bank of England. (*The Times*, 12 November 1918, page 13).

4 Oversight for chartered bodies was (and still is) exercised by the Privy Council, in effect a grouping of the most senior government politicians of the day. A chartered body wishing to change its constitution (i.e. its charter) or its regulations needed to seek the

approval of the Privy Council. In practice, this requirement need not be onerous, but it provided a mechanism by which the government might object to changes of which it did not approve or might seek change which it wished to encourage.

5 Such as the Apothecaries Act.
6 Such as Accountants in 1880, Surveyors in 1881 and Actuaries in 1884.

References

Primary works: newspapers and periodicals

The Times.

Primary works: government and parliamentary reports

HM Treasury (1931), *Report of the Committee on Finance and Industry* (Cmd 38987). (HMSO, London). ('The Macmillan Committee Report').
London Stock Exchange Commission (1878), *Report of the Commissioners* (Cd 2157). (HMSO, London). ('The Royal Commission Report').

Secondary works

Kynaston, D (1994), *The City of London: A World of Its own 1815–1890*, volume 1 (Chatto & Windus, London).

Index

Note: Italicized page numbers indicate a figure on the corresponding page. Page numbers in bold indicate a table on the corresponding page.

Milton Keynes UK
Ingram Content Group UK Ltd.
UKHW011417020224
437133UK00004B/24